An Introduction to **Early Childhood Studies**

An Introduction to **Early Childhood Studies**

edited by **Trisha Maynard**
Nigel Thomas

⑤SAGE Publications
London • Thousand Oaks • New Delhi

Editorial arrangement, introduction and part introductions © Trisha Maynard and Nigel Thomas 2004
Chapter 1 © Ruth M. Ford
Chapter 2 © Tricia David
Chapter 3 © Stephanie James
Chapter 4 © Trisha Maynard
Chapters 5, 12, 14 and 16 © Bob Sanders

Chapter 6 © Roy Lowe
Chapters 7 and 9 © Nigel Thomas
Chapter 8 © Sonia Jackson
Chapter 10 and 15 © Branwen Llewelyn Jones
Chapter 11 © Kate Wall
Chapter 13 © Anne Kelly
Chapter 17 © Sharon Airey

First Published 2004

 SAGE Publications Ltd
1 Oliver's Yard
55 City Road
London EC1Y 1SP

SAGE Publications Inc.
2455 Teller Road
Thousand Oaks, California 91320

SAGE Publications India Pvt Ltd
B-42, Panchsheel Enclave
Post Box 4109
New Delhi 110 017

British Library Cataloguing in Publication data

A catalogue record for this book is available from the British Library

ISBN 0 7619 7073 8
ISBN 0 7619 7074 6 (pbk)

Library of Congress Control Number available

Typeset by C&M Digitals (P) Ltd., Chennai, India
Printed in Great Britain by TJ International Ltd, Padstow, Cornwall

To our children and grandchildren

Contents

List of Tables and Illustrations

Tables

Figures

Notes on the Contributors

Sharon Airey is Lecturer in Early Childhood Studies at the University of Wales Swansea. A qualified primary school teacher, she worked as a research associate and fellow at Heriot-Watt University and Stirling University, investigating various aspects of primary education including children's use of interactive technology and the effects of noise on learning. Sharon's PhD thesis is focused on inclusion in primary schools, with particular emphasis on classroom acoustics and the detrimental effects on hearing-impaired children.

Tricia David has officially retired, after some twenty years as a teacher, headteacher, and community educator, and twenty years of research and lecturing in higher education. She has been awarded the title Emeritus Professor by Canterbury Christ Church University College, where she continues to supervise doctoral students. Tricia is widely known for her publications (over seventy articles and eighteen books), the latest being the research review for the Birth to Three Matters project published by the Department for Education and Skills.

Ruth Ford is a lecturer in developmental psychology at the University of Wales Swansea. She joined the Department of Psychology in 1995 and her research focuses on aspects of memory and cognitive development in young children. Ruth is interested in the applications of developmental psychology to everyday life, and currently is carrying out studies of 'good practice' in the forensic interrogation of young children and, as part of the Sure Start initiative, the efficacy of involving parents in children's early education.

Sonia Jackson is a Professorial Fellow at the Thomas Coram Research Unit, Institute of Education, University of London, and was previously Head of Social Policy and Applied Studies at the University of Wales Swansea. She started her career as a clinical child psychologist, and later worked as an education adviser, primary school teacher and local authority social worker, before becoming a university lecturer. She has directed many research projects on children's issues, including childminding, early years education, day care, child protection, the health of looked after children, resilience and quality of life, and most recently a five-year study of care leavers in higher education. She is a Trustee of the Who Cares? Trust and a number of other children's charities, and has published many books and articles including *People Under Three: young children in day care* (2nd edition 2004). She is an Academician of Social Sciences, and in 2003 was awarded the OBE for services to children and young people in public care.

Stephanie James is a tutor in Early Childhood Studies at the University of Wales Swansea and a primary school inspector in England and Wales. She taught in junior and infant schools in London for a number of years, including a two year secondment as an Advisory Teacher for Reading. She was a lecturer in the First Years of Schooling at Roehampton Institute before joining the Department of Education at Swansea in 1989. Here she worked on the Primary PGCE, specialising in English. She first became interested in children's language development in the early 1980s, when studying for her MA in English in Education and has maintained her interest in this aspect of children's development ever since.

Anne Kelly is a lecturer in Public Health and Primary Health Care at the University of Wales Swansea. She specialises in aspects of health policy related to the improvement of preventive health and social services and collaborative community care, and has a particular interest in the implementation of policy at the operational level of services. Research interests are currently focused on evaluation of family support programmes and child care provision. Publications include *The Social Construction of Community Nursing* (with Anthea Symonds, Palgrave 2003).

Branwen Llewelyn Jones has been an early years teacher, deputy, headteacher and lecturer. She was a member of the working party that produced 'Quality and Diversity in Early Learning: A Framework for Early Years Practitioners'. A member of the Children in Wales Early Childhood Advisory Panel, she was also a senior lecturer in early years education before taking up the headship of an infant school which under her leadership experienced considerable success, especially in teaching through the arts. The school's success was featured in newspapers, on television and in the TES. She is now a co-director of PACE, Consultants in Early Years Education, and a schools inspector.

Roy Lowe is Visiting Professor at the Institute of Education, University of London and Research Professor of Education at the University of Wales Swansea. He has published widely on aspects of the history of education in Britain and North America. His books include *Education in Post-War Years* (Routledge 1988) and *Schooling and Social Change* (Routledge 1997). He is currently working on a history of progressive education since 1945. He recently stepped down as President of the History of Education Society of the United Kingdom and was awarded an OBE in the 2002 New Years Honours for services to education.

Trisha Maynard is Head of Early Childhood Studies at the University of Wales Swansea. Trisha taught in an infant school before joining the Department of Education at Swansea in 1991, where she worked on the Primary PGCE and undertook research on student teachers' school-based learning and the role of the mentor. In 1997 Trisha took on the role of Course Director of Early Childhood Studies: this is currently being established as a university department. Trisha has recently returned to her original research interests of young children's learning and gender development. Her recent publications include *Boys and Literacy: Exploring the Issues* (2002).

Bob Sanders is Lecturer in Applied Social Studies at the University of Wales Swansea. He worked in social work in urban and rural areas before becoming a trainer and then lecturer in 1992. He specialised in work with children and families from the mid-1970s, and has maintained that interest in his teaching and research activities. His current research is focused on the effectiveness of family support, and the impact of family adversity and stress on sibling relationships. His publications include *The Management of Child Protection* (Ashgate 1999), and *Sibling Relationships: Theory and Issues for Practice* (Palgrave 2004).

Nigel Thomas is Senior Lecturer in Childhood Studies at the University of Wales Swansea. He was for many years a social work practitioner and manager, before becoming a lecturer in social work in 1992. He has been responsible for postgraduate teaching programmes both in social work and in childhood studies. Nigel's research interests are principally in child welfare, children's rights and participation. His publications include *Children, Family and the State* (Policy Press 2002) and a forthcoming book on children and young people in care.

Kate Wall is Programme Director of the Early Childhood Studies degree programme at Canterbury Christ Church University College. Prior to becoming a Senior Lecturer in 1999 she worked in early years settings (mainstream and special) for many years, latterly as the Head of a pre-school special needs unit. Kate has published *Special Needs and Early Years: A practitioner's guide* and *Autism and Early Years Practice: A guide for Early Years Professionals, Teachers and Parents*. She has also written a range of articles for early years practitioner journals. Kate's interests and research lie in the areas of special needs provision, the affective needs of children and autism.

Introduction
Trisha Maynard and Nigel Thomas

In recent times, early childhood appears to have become a much higher priority on the agenda of politicians and policy makers in the United Kingdom. To some extent this has been part of a closer focus on children and young people in general, reflected in the pledge to eliminate child poverty, in the appointment of independent Children's Commissioners (first, we are proud to say, in Wales, but now being followed by similar appointments in Scotland and Northern Ireland, and at the time of writing finally proposed for England) but also in increasingly strident campaigns against youth crime and 'antisocial behaviour'. Children are in the news and in the minds of policy makers, to an extent that they have not been for some time, if ever.

Within this general concern with children and young people, the specific interests and needs of young children and their families have attracted particular kinds of attention. This is reflected in the introduction of major initiatives such as 'Sure Start', in the more intensive promotion of inter-agency and multidisciplinary working, and in attempts to address the inconsistencies that exist in the training, education, status and pay of early years practitioners. It is also reflected in arguments over the content and form of the early years curriculum, in which there are embedded assumptions about the relationship between what happens in early childhood and what happens in later life.

On a practical level, this growing recognition of the importance and significance of early childhood has resulted in many additional employment opportunities for those wishing to work with young children and their families. It has also, unsurprisingly, resulted in a proliferation of undergraduate degrees which have children and childhood as a key area of study. The primary purpose of this book is to provide a core introductory text for the many undergraduate students who are now studying early childhood.

The idea for such a text emerged soon after the establishment of the BSc (Econ) degree in Early Childhood Studies (ECS) at the University of Wales Swansea. The ECS scheme at Swansea is genuinely interdisciplinary, with 'strands' focusing on children's care and welfare, health and education, as well as those which explore the child and childhood from historical and sociological perspectives.

We noticed that there were many excellent books that focus on a particular aspect of the study of young children and childhood – for example, education or welfare, sociology or psychology. What seemed to be needed, however, was one text that would introduce students to the significant ideas in each of the key areas of study, and so provide them with a sound basis for further reading, thinking and research. Of equal importance, we reasoned, was the need for a text that would introduce students to a number of *themes* within the general field of early childhood studies, and would help to show how these themes are reflected and played out in different areas. This seemed to be of particular importance given that most under-graduate courses are now modular; it can be hard for students to make the links between the various topics or modules studied.

It should be noted, however, that as well as being of use to undergraduate students, we hope that this text will also be of interest to those already working with young children. We believe that all practitioners need to have a sound knowledge of different theoretical perspectives if they are to evaluate and attempt to improve their own practice. That is not to suggest that the theory–practice relationship is straightforward; indeed, the characteristics of the 'reflective practitioner' (Schön, 1983) have been debated for many years. There does appear to be a consensus, however, that practical experience, while essential in developing expertise, is not in itself sufficient.

For a busy practitioner it is easy to view a setting through the 'frame' of a partic-ular set of experiences, knowledge, values, attitudes and beliefs. This frame will have an impact on what the individual pays attention to, how he or she interprets children's behaviour, and so on. When practitioners are aware that there are differ-ent perspectives that can be brought to bear upon a situation and have knowledge and understanding of these, they have at their disposal different 'frames' which can be used to gain more insight into their own ways of working and the possibilities and limitations of approaches suggested by other theorists.

Key themes of this book

Four key themes are emphasised throughout this book. The first is the *social con-struction* of childhood. This is the idea that childhood is not a naturally given phe-nomenon, but the result of social processes of discourse, definition and interaction. As a result, the characteristics of children and childhood are not the same in differ-ent times and places. One implication for policy is that the way in which childhood is perceived, and the social space which children occupy, can be challenged and changed.

The second theme is the interaction of *nature and nurture*. Arguments about whether 'nature' or 'nurture' – the child's biological inheritance and her/his social and cultural environment – is more important obscure the fact that it is often the relationship between the two influences which is most significant, and that this relationship is extremely complex.

Our third theme is *working with the whole child*. By this, we mean that children's development and needs do not easily separate into discrete categories labelled, for example, 'education', 'health', 'welfare' or 'play'. It is vitally important that service providers recognise this, and that when making policy and delivering services a coherent and integrated inter-agency approach is adopted.

The fourth theme is the importance of seeing *children as subjects*. This again can be interpreted in two ways: 'scientifically', by recognising children as active in their own development and learning; and 'politically', by accepting them as young citizens with rights to autonomy and to participation in decision making.

Organisation of the book

The seventeen chapters in this book between them cover a very extensive territory, ranging from the history of childhood to the place of play in the early years curriculum. In order to make the text more manageable and accessible we have organised the book into four parts: I The Developing Child, II Perspectives on Childhood III Policy and Provision for Young Children, IV Developing Effective Practice. We do not suggest that these four dimensions are in any significant way independent of each other. Readers will find that the relationships between child development, historical and cultural perspectives on childhood, local and national policy and the nature and quality of provision, and the implications of all this for professional practice, are emphasised throughout the text.

Part I includes chapters on cognitive, emotional and social development, on language and learning and on the development of a gender identity. Part II considers how childhood differs culturally and historically, and introduces sociological approaches to the study of childhood. Part III is the most substantial part of the book: the Swansea programme includes a strong emphasis on *policy* – on how ideas about the needs of young children and their families are turned into reality – and we have deliberately emphasised this aspect. Part III therefore includes an overview of early years services, as well as specific chapters on law, education, special needs, social welfare and health care. Finally, Part IV focuses on some particular aspects of practice – inter-agency work, the use of play, child observation and inclusive practice. Each part of the book begins with a brief editorial introduction that explains what is in the chapters that follow and which draws attention to some common themes and to differences of emphasis.

Each individual chapter aims to introduce its subject to an intelligent reader with limited previous knowledge, and also to indicate some of the important areas of debate within the field. Some chapters include case examples or practical exercises. Each chapter concludes with some questions or ideas for further work, and with suggestions for further reading. The full list of all sources referred to is at the end of the book.

Each of the contributors is an expert in her or his own field, and – reflecting the multidisciplinary nature of the subject as well as the strong interchange between theory and practice – their professional backgrounds are very different. Most of them teach their particular subjects on the Swansea degree course, although we have also enlisted the support of colleagues from elsewhere. Readers will note that individual contributors do not necessarily see everything the same way. This is intentional: one of the key purposes of the book (and of our degree scheme) is to expose students to a range of ideas and perspectives.

Although there are differences of emphasis in the chapters that follow, one perspective we hope runs throughout the book. This is our theoretical and practical commitment to respecting the rights of children and seeing children as active participants in all matters relating to their health, care, welfare and education. Children, we are convinced, should be seen *and* heard!

Part I
The Developing Child

This part of the book focuses on children's cognitive, social, personal and emotional development as well as the acquisition of language and of a gender identity.

A consideration of the developing child necessarily encompasses an exploration of many different theories. Initially, some of these theories may appear contradictory. We need to recognise that theories may emerge from or reflect the particular interests of the theorist: consider for example the relationship between Piaget's theory and his early grounding in biology, or between Vygotsky's theory and Marxism. In addition, the promotion or acceptance of theories at particular times in history can reflect the interests of dominant groups in society. However, the approach taken in this text is, in so far as it is possible, to consider and use different theoretical models in a complementary way, taking what each can offer to help build a holistic understanding of children's development.

One key theme underlying all the chapters in this part of the book is 'nature versus nurture'. In other words, how far is children's development related to their biological inheritance and how far is it related to the environment in which they live? While this argument has in the past been polarised, there now appears to be a general consensus that development is best understood in terms of a complex interaction between biological inheritance and environmental experiences: it is this process of interaction that now demands to be explored in more detail.

A second theme in this part of the book is the role of children in their learning and development. Children are no longer viewed as passive beings who are moulded and shaped by those around them, but are seen as being active in this process: rather than being passively 'socialised', they are actively 'self-socialising'. Thus the young child appears driven to learn the rules relating to particular cultural/social categories or groups and, at least initially, to fit in with those around her or him.

In Chapter 1 Ruth Ford develops these themes in her review of theories of cognitive development, asking questions such as: does children's cognitive development proceed gradually and incrementally or more abruptly through a series of stages? Do children learn independently or do they require assistance from others? Are improvements in children's thinking generic or 'domain-specific'?

In Chapter 2 Tricia David turns to children's social, personal and emotional development, making it clear that understandings about oneself and others are dependent on cognitive processes as well as social and emotional interactions. She shows the importance of 'attachment' and relationship not only in the development of identity, self-concept and resilience, but also in a 'theory of mind'.

In Chapter 3 Stephanie James also sees children as active participants in their learning and development – this time, in relation to the acquisition of language. James shows how children's urge to make sense of the world leads them not only respond to the communication of others but, even at a few weeks old, to initiate communication for themselves.

Finally, in Chapter 4 Trisha Maynard explores gender development in the young child. Through a consideration of numerous theoretical perspectives, Maynard again emphasises that children are now considered to be active in constructing their own gender identity and that cognitive processes as well as the social/cultural context are considered to be significant factors in this development.

Together these four chapters give us a picture of young children striving to make sense of the world around them, in particular the world of social interaction, and quickly becoming a part of it – influenced profoundly by their surroundings and by what happens to them, but also exerting their own influence on the world from their earliest days.

1
Thinking and Cognitive Development in Young Children
Ruth M. Ford

Contents

- Issues in cognitive development
- Theories of cognitive development
- Applied issues and future research directions
- Conclusion

The term *cognition* encompasses a range of mental processes, including perception, attention, language, reasoning, and memory. The term *cognitive development* thus refers broadly to the growth of children's cognition between birth and adolescence (Bjorklund, 2000; Siegler et al., 2003). Because cognitive development has such diverse aspects, it has not yet been explained fully by any single theory. This chapter provides an overview of some of the foremost accounts of cognitive development, highlighting similarities and differences in their key assumptions. The chapter begins by outlining some contentious issues in cognitive development. It concludes by drawing attention to practical applications of cognitive developmental research and possible directions for future study.

Issues in cognitive development

Theories of cognitive development differ on a number of significant issues (Bjorklund, 2000; Siegler et al., 2003; Slee and Shute, 2003). One area of contention has been the role of nature versus nurture, in other words, heredity versus the environment. The question of nature versus nurture asks whether children's development depends on innate (i.e. genetically determined) ability or environmental factors such as family background and schooling. A second issue is continuity versus discontinuity. This issue concerns whether cognitive development occurs smoothly and incrementally or, alternatively, in the form of abrupt transformations from one level of functioning to another. Third, the issue of active versus passive development asks to what extent children themselves initiate their learning. The idea of active development holds that children actively seek and construct knowledge as they attempt to make sense of their world. The idea of passive development suggests that children are inertly moulded by their experiences and heredity. Fourth, arguments about domain-general versus domain-specific development relate to the scope of cognitive growth. Domain-general theories assume that developments in children's thinking occur broadly across many areas of cognition whereas domain-specific theories assume that progress in one domain is largely dissociated from progress in others. Fifth, theories differ in their claims regarding the impact of the socio-cultural context. Whereas some accounts view the child as being an independent learner, others postulate that cognitive development requires input from other people in the course of everyday social interactions. Finally, there is the problem of how change occurs. Rather than merely charting typical developmental progress and milestones, recent approaches to cognitive development seek to understand the precise mechanisms by which children attain successively higher levels of cognitive functioning.

Theories of cognitive development

Piaget's theory: the child as scientist

The study of cognitive development was initiated in the 1920s by Jean Piaget, a Swiss psychologist who carried out both large-scale studies of children's thinking and detailed examinations of the development of his own three children. Piaget's theory has been hugely influential, not only owing to its pioneering nature but because it provided so many thought-provoking ideas that have continued to stim-ulate research programmes to the present day. In terms of central developmental issues, Piaget's theory acknowledges a contribution of nurture as well as nature to intellectual ability, describes both continuity and discontinuity in development, and stresses the active contribution of the child to its intellectual growth (e.g. Piaget, 1952; Piaget and Inhelder, 1969). Piaget originally trained in biology and philoso-phy, and these orientations informed his approach to the study of psychology. His background in biology led to an interest in the relations between evolution and human cognitive development, prompting him to speculate that children are moti-vated to acquire knowledge because such behaviour is adaptive. His background in philosophy, particularly in logic, inspired him to search for internal consistency underlying children's errors in problem solving. Piaget's theory is described as *con-structivist* in the sense that it depicts the child as actively constructing knowledge in reaction to experiences (Slee and Shute, 2003). When Piaget's work began gaining attention during the 1960s, its impact was so great partly because it rejected ideas about passive, associative forms of learning (i.e. mechanistic or behaviourist models of learning) that had dominated psychology for the past thirty years. The essence of Piaget's theory is the notion of the 'child as scientist', carrying out simple tests to discover how the world works.

According to Piaget, continuity in development arises from three processes: assimilation, accommodation, and equilibration. *Assimilation* occurs when new experiences are integrated into existing knowledge, *accommodation* occurs when children modify their knowledge in response to new experiences that cannot be assimilated, and *equilibration* reflects the child's attempts to balance assimilation and accommodation to create stable understanding. Siegler et al. (2003) provide the hypothetical example of a pre-school child who believes that only animals are living things because only animals move in ways compatible with preserving their life. This child's ideas about life develop as she encounters new animals and assimilates these examples into her schema for living things. However, when she discovers that plants similarly move in ways that promote their survival, namely towards sunlight, she experiences a state of disequilibrium in which she is unsure about how living and non-living things differ. After accommodating her knowledge structures to the new information about plants, she decides that since adaptive movement signifies life, plants as well as animals must be living things.

In Piaget's theory, cognitive development is additionally viewed as discontinuous such that children proceed through four discrete stages of ability. His theory assumes *epigenesis* in that later stages of development build on earlier achievements, furthermore the stages are argued to be universal (i.e. true for all human cultures) and age-invariant (i.e. passed through in the same order by all children irrespective of their rate of progress). Crucially, the theory claims that patterns of thinking are qualitatively distinct at different stages and that development entails making an intellectual leap from one way of thinking about the world to a new, more advanced level of thinking. Thus, development does not merely involve an accumulation of skills and knowledge; a twelve-year-old differs from a four-year-old not only quantitatively in terms of experience but also qualitatively in terms of thinking patterns.

The first stage of development is the *sensorimotor* stage, which lasts from birth to approximately two years of age. During this stage, infants are largely reflexive creatures whose thinking is dominated by immediate perceptual input. Through the mechanisms of assimilation, accommodation, and equilibration, infants construct progressively more sophisticated sensorimotor schemas (i.e. links between sensation and motor activity) that allow them to develop their notions of time, space, and causality. As they grow older, infants integrate simple reflexes such as gazing and grasping to achieve more advanced behaviours such as visually guided reaching, they attain an understanding that objects continue to exist even when they cannot be seen (i.e. the concept of object permanence), and they test ideas about cause and effect, for example shaking and biting a rattle to discover how to produce a noise.

By the time of their second birthday, most infants have entered the *pre-operational* stage of development. During this stage, which lasts until approximately age seven years, children are capable of representing their experiences mentally using imagery and language. Their thinking is therefore described as reflective rather than merely reflexive. Piaget referred to children's newly developed representational capacity as the *symbolic function* and argued that it could be observed both in their deferred imitation and their frequent engagement in make-believe play. An example of make-believe play would be a three-year-old girl holding a banana to her ear and speaking into it as if it was a telephone. According to Piaget, such behaviour indicates that the child is capable of mentally representing the banana as something other than it really is. She thus understands and manipulates symbols of reality and not just reality itself. Once the symbolic function is in place, Piaget's theory suggests that subsequent cognitive development involves the acquisition of new modes of thinking, known as mental operations. Pre-operational children are misled by superficial appearances during problem solving because they lack important mental operations necessary for logical reasoning. For example, until they acquire 'reversibility', namely the ability to mentally undo an action, children are unable to understand that the amount of liquid in a container does not change when it is poured into a container of a different shape (i.e. a failure of *conservation*). Three other important features of the pre-operational stage are *egocentricism*, the inability to take another person's point of view, *centration*, the tendency to focus attention on a single aspect of a problem at a time, and *animism*, the tendency to attribute lifelike qualities and intentions to non-living things.

In the *concrete operational* stage, which typically lasts from ages seven to twelve years, children demonstrate the use of logic when dealing with problems involving concrete objects and events. Because they have acquired an understanding of reversibility, they succeed in solving conservation problems for number, volume, mass, and area. Children are also able for the first time to pass tests requiring *seriation* (i.e. the understanding of spatial and temporal sequences), *transitive inferences* (i.e. the mental rearrangement of a set of objects along a quantifiable dimension), and *class inclusion* (i.e. the manipulation of hierarchical part-whole relations). However, they do not yet show evidence of thinking in abstract or hypothetical terms and they cannot easily combine information systematically to solve a problem.

Finally, children enter the *formal operational* stage of development at approximately age twelve years. They can now consider abstract situations, formulate hypotheses, and test hypotheses in a scientific manner. For example, if given a pendulum with varying weights and lengths of string then formal operational children systematically manipulate the problem parameters to deduce what determines the rate of oscillation. Their ability to conceive of several possible realities also leads them to query the way society is structured and to ponder philosophical questions about truth, justice, and morality (Inhelder and Piaget, 1958).

Over the years, Piaget's theory has stimulated an enormous number of research studies. Many of these studies have concluded that Piaget underestimated young children's capabilities because he failed to take into account their memory and language limitations (reviews by Flavell, 1996; Schaffer, 2004). Whereas Piaget's basic findings in relation to the *sequence* of development have been extensively replicated, other research has challenged the fundamental assumptions of his theory on several grounds. The most contentious issues have been Piaget's notion of stages of development, his emphasis on domain-general reasoning abilities, and his neglect of the contribution of social interactions to children's thinking (Berk, 2003). These points have been addressed in turn by information-processing approaches, core-knowledge approaches, and socio-cultural approaches to cognitive development.

Information-processing approaches: the child as a computational system

Information-processing theories reject Piaget's ideas about abrupt transformations in cognitive development and instead posit the gradual improvement of basic cognitive processes and memory capacities, an increase in knowledge, and the emergence of new learning strategies. In terms of core issues, information-processing approaches assume that development reflects both nature and nurture, is continuous rather than discontinuous, involves active planning and problem solving by the child, and that the mechanisms of change can be precisely specified.

Research within the information-processing framework has revealed both wide-ranging developments across the entire cognitive system and narrow forms of domain-specific learning (McShane, 1991). As children grow older they become more efficient at encoding information from the environment (Siegler, 1976), faster in their speed of mental processing (Kail, 1997), better able to use learning and memory strategies (Bjorklund et al., 1997), and more knowledgeable (Schneider and Pressley, 1997). From the information-processing perspective, such changes are sufficient to explain children's growing competence on Piagetian tests without recourse to ideas about the acquisition of mental operations.

Developmental improvements in information processing are likely to reflect both maturation and experience. Thus, superior learning and problem solving in older children relative to younger ones could be attributed either to the more efficient functioning of the brain's neurons with increasing age or to increments in relevant knowledge (Siegler et al., 2003). Certainly, knowledge acquisition is implicated in significant gains in memory capabilities during childhood. Both for children and adults, memory for new material is greatly enhanced when it can be related to what is already known (Chi, 1978). For example, young children become better at remembering novel events as they develop *scripts*, that is, mental representations of the usual sequence of activities for commonly experienced routines such as eating at a restaurant, attending a birthday party, or visiting the doctor (Fivush et al., 1992).

Recent years have seen a proliferation of information-processing theories of cognitive development. Whereas many such theories assume sequential processing of information, connectionist or neural-network models posit parallel processing in which different kinds of cognitive activity occur simultaneously. Connectionist models claim to mimic the physiological workings of the human brain, which are known to involve dense interconnected parallel-processing units (Elman et al., 1996). Another influential approach comes in the form of neo-Piagetian information-processing views, which attempt to account for evidence of stage-like development in terms of age-related improvements in processing capacity (Case, 1985). Finally, dynamic systems theories reject ideas about linear causality (i.e. x causes y) and, instead, view development as a move towards greater complexity as mutually inter-dependent parts of the cognitive system co-operate in a non-linear fashion to produce new, emergent properties (Lewis, 2000; Thelen and Smith, 1994).

Core-knowledge theories: the child as a product of human evolution

Similar to both Piaget's and information-processing theories, core-knowledge theories assume that the child is an active agent in their own development who strives to learn. Uniquely, however, such approaches argue that children are born with learning abilities already in place that are specialised for particular domains of thought.

That is, they emphasise the contribution to cognitive development of innate forms of knowledge that have arisen in response to human evolutionary history, without which it is presumed infants would have difficulty in beginning to make sense of the world. Innate knowledge is thought to be crucial to the development of such skills as face recognition, semantic categorisation, language, and the understanding of people's minds. Importantly, core knowledge theorists assume that innate knowledge is domain-specific rather than domain-general, that is, restricted to particular, narrow areas of cognition (Carey and Spelke, 1994).

Core-knowledge theories are sometimes called *theory theories* because they argue that children's innate understanding in particular areas is organised in terms of naive or informal theories (Wellman and Gelman, 1998). Naive theories have been postulated to operate in the domains of physics, psychology, and biology (commonly known as *core domains*). For example, there is evidence that from a very early age children understand that the world contains physical objects that occupy space, move in response to external forces, and move continuously rather than discontinuously (Spelke, 1994), that people's behaviour is driven by their goals and desires (Wellman and Gelman, 1998), and that there are important differences between animals and inanimate objects (Springer and Keil, 1991). Evidence that young children have surprising competence in particular aspects of their cognitive development would not be predicted by a domain-general theory of cognitive development such as Piaget's.

According to theory approaches, cognitive development proceeds as the acquisition of new knowledge enables children to refine and extend their rudimentary theories to create better ones (Hatano and Inagaki, 1996). Notably, another suggestion is that learning can occur even in the absence of exposure to new information. Karmiloff-Smith (1992) posited a process of *representational redescription* by which existing knowledge is spontaneously converted to new and superior forms of knowledge (see also Mandler, 1992). According to her theory, knowledge is represented at both implicit (i.e. unaware) and explicit (i.e. aware) levels. Implicit knowledge is specific to particular parts of the cognitive system and is inaccessible to consciousness (for example, neonates' knowledge about physical objects). This knowledge is subsequently redescribed and made available to other parts of the cognitive system; eventually it reaches consciousness such that it can be verbalised and shared with others.

Core-knowledge theories form part of a larger class of theories in the rapidly growing field of evolutionary developmental psychology. As a whole, this approach seeks to explain how genes and the environment interact to produce development and the way in which specific cognitive skills have developed in response to environmental pressures (Geary and Bjorklund, 2000). Evolutionary developmental psychology distinguishes between biologically primary abilities (i.e. cognitive skills determined by evolution, such as language) and biologically secondary abilities (i.e. cognitive skills determined by culture, such as reading). It is assumed that whereas the development of primary abilities requires little nurture from the environment, the development of secondary abilities draws on cognitive skills that evolved for other purposes and thus requires a higher level of external support (Bjorklund, 2000). Finally, the sub-domain of developmental cognitive neuroscience attempts to understand cognitive development in terms of brain structures and functions. For example, research in this tradition has implicated the maturation of the frontal lobes of the brain as underpinning age-related improvements in children's ability to curb their impulses (Dempster, 1993).

Socio-cultural theories: the child as a social being

The theories reviewed so far have uniformly stressed children's active role in their own development as they identify problems and attempt to solve them independently. In contrast, socio-cultural theories view development as taking place in a social context such that young children learn primarily through their communicative interactions with other people (Bornstein and Bruner, 1989). Socio-cultural perspectives have in common the notions of *guided participation*, referring to the way that adults assist children to achieve higher levels of skills than they would be capable of attaining on their own, and *cultural tools*, referring to language, other symbol systems, artefacts, skills and values that are important to a particular culture (Rogoff, 1990).

The socio-cultural approach to understanding cognitive development was initiated by the Russian psychologist Lev Vygotsky. Although Vygotsky was a contemporary of Piaget, his work received little attention in the Western world until it was translated into English as *Mind in Society* (Vygotsky, 1978a). Vygotsky was intrigued by the idea that young children are born into a social world in which adults are motivated to help them learn. Whereas Piaget claimed that a child constructs knowledge by actively engaging with the environment, Vygotsky suggested that development arises from social interchanges and is thus a joint endeavour between the child and its care takers. Moreover, whereas Piaget postulated the existence of qualitative stages in cognitive development, Vygotsky argued that social interactions produce continuous rather than discontinuous growth. Vygotsky's theory acknowledges the contribution of nature to development in the sense that infants are thought to enter the world equipped with basic cognitive functions such as the ability to attend and remember. Vygotsky argued that these basic abilities are transformed into higher mental functions by nurture in the form of social interactions and dialogues between a child and its parents, teachers, and other representatives of culture. He suggested that, through these interactions, children internalise increasingly mature and effective ways of thinking and problem solving (Vygotsky, 1978a, 1981).

Vygotsky (1986) reasoned that social interactions benefit children's thinking owing to the input of language. He argued that language makes thought possible and that progress in thinking is mediated by language. Vygotsky described three stages of language–thought development. In the first stage, called *external speech*, thinking comes from a source outside the child. For example, a father who is watching his young son scribbling might introduce the idea of representational drawing by asking, 'What are you drawing? Is it a dog?' In the second stage, called *private speech*, children talk to themselves as a way of directing their own thinking. Thus, while drawing the boy might verbally describe his progress by saying, 'This is my dog. Now I'm drawing his tail'. In the final stage, called *internal speech*, children have internalised their thought processes. At this stage of development the boy might think to himself, 'What will I draw? I know. I'll draw a picture of my dog'. Consistent with Vygotsky's views about the pivotal role of language in thinking, research has indicated that children who engage in private speech during problem solving achieve better results than children who are silent (Berk, 1992).

Vygotsky also introduced the idea of the *zone of proximal development*. This refers to an area of functioning just beyond the child's current level to which they are capable of progressing given appropriate assistance from other people with greater knowledge. Vygotsky defined it as 'the distance between actual developmental level as determined by independent problem solving and the level of potential development through problem solving under adult guidance or in collaboration with more capable peers' (1978a: 86). Vygotsky thus assumed that in most instances children's potential level of functioning exceeds their actual level of functioning.

Subsequent work in the Vygotskian tradition drew attention to the role of *intersubjectivity* in social interactions, that is, mutual understanding arising from joint attention to the same topic as well as sensitivity to the other person's point of view (Gauvain, 2001; Rogoff, 1990). It additionally described *social scaffolding*, that is, the process by which adults provide a temporary framework to support a child's thinking at a higher level than they can yet reach on their own (Wood et al., 1976). As an analogy, the child can be viewed as a building under construction. Scaffolding takes the form of explaining the goal of the task, demonstrating how the task should be done, and carrying out the more difficult aspects of the task. At first, children require extensive support to attain a higher level of thinking about a particular problem but, over time, they come to require less assistance until eventually they can complete the task on their own. Importantly, children who receive appropriate scaffolding show faster acquisition of new skills than children who learn independently. Successful teachers are those who pitch their instructions and demonstrations at the right level to suit the child's current expertise. That is, they discover and operate in the child's zone of proximal development (Wood, 1998). The following example from Berk (2003) illustrates a social interchange between a mother and her three-year-old son as she attempts to help him solve a jigsaw puzzle while keeping her suggestions and prompts at an appropriate level of difficulty (p. 258):

> *Sammy*: I can't get this one in. [*Tries to insert a piece in the wrong place.*]
> *Mother*: Which piece might go down here? [*Points to the bottom of the puzzle.*]
> *Sammy*: His shoes. [*Looks for a piece resembling the shoes but tries the wrong one.*]
> *Mother*: Well, what piece looks like this shape? [*Pointing again.*]
> *Sammy*: The brown one. [*Fits it in; attempts another piece and looks at mother.*]
> *Mother*: Try turning it just a little. [*Gestures to show him.*]
> *Sammy*: There! [*He puts in several more pieces while his mother watches.*]

Vygotsky's theory is an example of a *dialectical theory*; it emphasises the development of cognition under social influence. Other socio-cultural approaches can be described as *contextualist*; they stress the wider influence of environmental contexts on development. Interest in contextualism was prompted by the publication of *The Ecology of Human Development*, by Urie Bronfenbrenner, in 1979. Bronfenbrenner suggested that 'the ecology of human development involves the scientific study of the progressive mutual accommodation between an active, growing human being and the changing properties of the immediate settings in which the developing person lives, as this process is affected by relations between these settings, and by the larger contexts in which the settings are embedded' (1979: 21). His approach therefore views cognitive development as proceeding within a nested series of contexts.

Bronfenbrenner (1979) distinguished between three main levels of the environment. First, the *microsystem* comprises the various settings in which the child directly participates, such as home, school, and neighbourhood. Second, the *exosystem* comprises systems that affect the child indirectly by virtue of their influence on microsystems. Such settings include the extended social network of the family and the media. Finally, the *macrosystem* comprises the cultural environment of the child, for example, characteristic of a particular socio-economic or ethnic background. More recently, Bronfenbrenner (1986) incorporated the notion of the *chronosystem*. The chronosystem refers to influences on development that are specific to a particular historical period. For example, children growing up today differ from previous generations in their extensive exposure to television and home computers. Importantly, Bronfenbrenner advocated a transactional view of development in that he believed children, care givers, and the environment are mutually influential (Bronfenbrenner and Morris, 1998; Sameroff et al., 1993). In this sense, the child is not a passive recipient of environmental forces but to some extent selects their experiences. For example, a child who is raised in a home where reading is encouraged might develop an enjoyment of literature that later leads them to seek out friends with similar interests.

Applied issues and future research directions

It is clear that theories of cognitive development have profound implications for the education of young children. Approaches to formal schooling have been heavily influenced by Piaget's theory, with its suggestion that allowing children to interact with the environment will facilitate their learning, its notion of cognitive *readiness* for determining when and what children should be taught, and its detailed analysis of children's emerging concepts about number and physical causality (Piaget, 1965a, 1969). More recently, information-processing theories have contributed to educational research by introducing microgenetic methods of exploring learning (Siegler, 2000), studies of core knowledge have provided important information regarding young children's ability to reason about unobservable causes of events (for example, the role of germs in producing illness and the role of genes in biological inheritance; Solomon and Johnson, 2000), and discoveries within developmental cognitive neuroscience have indicated ways that stimulating specific brain regions by appropriate experiences during early childhood can improve aspects of academic learning (for example, using music and arts training to enhance young children's performance in mathematics; Gardiner et al., 1996). Finally, socio-cultural theories of cognitive development can be credited with drawing educators' attention to the importance of make-believe and socio-dramatic play in children's learning (Fromberg and Bergen, 1998) as well as prompting moves to encourage co-operative learning and peer tutoring in schools (Palincsar and Herrenkohl, 1999). Similarly, growing awareness of the ecological context of development has led to efforts to involve members of the wider community in the educational system with the aim of developing a culture of learning both within and beyond the classroom (Brown, 1997).

Theories of cognitive development are relevant to the education of young children even before they start school. All contemporary theories are agreed that the environment, both physical and social, plays an important role in children's learning. They therefore imply that children's cognitive growth can be enhanced by enriching their pre-school experiences, for example, by increasing their access to books and toys, their opportunities for play, and their exposure to social interactions with more capable others. For example, studies in the socio-cultural tradition have revealed that instructing parents in the use of specific conversational techniques with their young children can enhance pre-schoolers' language (Whitehurst et al., 1988), event memory (Boland et al., 2003), and problem-solving capabilities (Tzuriel, 1999). Such findings have implications for early intervention programmes targeting low-income families, many of which have highlighted deficient verbal mediation within the parent-child dyad as a prime factor in children's poor school achievement (Duncan and Brooks-Gunn, 2000; NICHD Early Child Care Research Network, 2002).

In conclusion, the study of children's thinking and learning is a dynamic and evolving field that covers a diversity of topics. Not surprisingly, recent writings have emphasised the need for synthesis (Parent et al., 2000; Richardson, 1998). Bjorklund (2000) identified a growing recognition of the *joint* role of biological factors and the social/cultural context in children's development. These perspectives are no longer seen as mutually exclusive and attention has shifted towards the reciprocal transaction of a child's biological constitution and their environment, both physical and social (Lerner, 1998; Siegler, 2000). The challenge for future research is therefore to work within a theoretical framework that integrates these different perspectives on cognitive development.

Conclusion

In summary, theories of cognitive development grapple with issues of nature versus nurture, continuity versus discontinuity, active versus passive development, domain-general versus domain-specific learning, the role of the socio-cultural context, and how change occurs. Pioneering studies by Piaget led him to propose that there are four distinct stages of cognitive development, with progress marked by the emergence of more advanced modes of thinking in each successive stage. Piaget viewed young children as amateur scientists who carry out simple experiments on their world to discover how it works. Subsequent investigation in the information-processing tradition suggested that development is continuous rather than stage-like and that it can be understood in terms of age-related improvements in processing mechanisms, memory capacity, and knowledge. Additionally, research into innate competences has indicated that infants are born already possessing certain kinds of knowledge that facilitate their learning in particular core domains. Finally, the work of Vygotsky has implicated a contribution of social and cultural factors to children's learning. Vygotsky argued that cognitive development occurs within social interactions such that children are guided into increasingly mature ways of thinking by communicating with more capable others. All accounts have important insights to offer, and recent writings have emphasised the need for theoretical integration, particularly with the aim of explicating the reciprocal relations between biological and social influences on children's development.

Questions and exercises

1 Evaluate Piaget's contribution to contemporary theories of cognitive development.
2 Why do information-processing theorists claim that cognitive development is continuous rather than stage-like?
3 What are core domains of thought? Explain how core knowledge is thought to support children's early learning.
4 What are the key assumptions of the transactional approach to understanding the contributions of nature and nurture to cognitive development?
5 Give examples of ways in which parents can use guided participation and social scaffolding to facilitate their children's learning.

Reading

Berk, *Child Development* (2003) is a comprehensive text about child development that relates theory to practice. Bjorklund, *Children's Thinking* (2000), reviews competing theories about cognitive development in relation to children's thinking, perception, language, and intelligence. Gauvain, *The Social Context of Cognitive Development* (2001), extends Vygotsky's ideas about the role of the socio-cultural context in cognitive development by examining recent research into children's problem solving, attention, and memory. Miller, *Theories of Developmental Psychology* (2002), contains chapters summarising the developmental theories of Piaget and Vygotsky and their impact on current thinking about cognitive development. Schaffer, *Introducing Child Psychology* (2004), is an accessible introduction to the field of child psychology that is designed for readers with little background knowledge and charts both cognitive and social/emotional development. Siegler, DeLoache and Eisenberg, *How Children Develop* (2003), is an introductory textbook about child psychology aimed at undergraduate students, including chapters on cognitive development that provide a good description of information-processing and core-knowledge approaches.

2
Young Children's Social and Emotional Development
Tricia David

> **Contents**
>
> - Born to be social
> - So what is attachment?
> - The bedrock of emotional development
> - A growing sense of self: personal development
> - Children with special needs
> - Mind reading experts
> - 'Belonging'
> - Conclusion

This chapter explains how emotional and social development form the bedrock of all areas of a child's development. It uses research evidence to highlight the crucial nature of close and loving relationships, as well as discussing the ways in which young children learn about themselves and how their social worlds 'work'. The importance of the relationships between children and their parents, with siblings and with friends is also covered.

Born to be social

From the moment of birth, babies are intensely interested in other people. In the first months of life they are trying to form close relationships and they are beginning to develop an individual sense of self. At the same time they are coming to know if those individual selves have any agency, or power, over their own lives. Babies' *attachments* at four months old are said to be good predictors of their attachments and their ability to regulate their emotions at a year old (Braungart-Rieker et al., 2001).

> In social interactions, the infant whose behavior succeeds in eliciting a positive and sensitive response from the parent feels encouraged to continue the behavior. During the first year, interaction patterns, coping experiences, and resulting views of self are the building blocks of the child's working models of self and relationships.

(Davies, 1999: 147)

Understanding about oneself and others is dependent on social and emotional interactions in which cognitive processes come into play. This interweaving of all areas of development is now recognised. As Judy Dunn (1999) points out, in the past psychologists studied children's development in prescribed compartments but they are now aware of the need to explore the influence different areas have on each other. Human beings seem to be born to be social and human emotions are the most basic building blocks of their entire, holistic development, including the personal and social aspects.

Even in the first months of life, babies make distinctions between people/objects, self/other (Stern, 1985; Rosser, 1994). They appear to need to form *attachments* to the people who are familiar and significant to them (usually a parent or other relative at first). It is in the everyday interactions of being sensitively cared for that they begin to be aware of themselves and despite the fact that researchers a quarter of a century ago argued that children do not develop a sense of self (i.e. recognise themselves as separate people with an individual identity) until the second year, more recent research indicates that this amazing feat begins soon after birth (Bretherton et al., 1981; Odofsky, 1987). These first attachments provide a 'model' which will be drawn upon later in life. When adults – and older children – adjust their behaviour sensitively to what they perceive as the baby's needs and wishes, we say they are behaving *contingently*.

So what is attachment?

John Bowlby formulated the theory of attachment (Bowlby 1951, 1953, 1969, 1973, 1980) and his ideas were supported and developed by his colleagues (for example, see Ainsworth, 1967; Robertson and Robertson, 1989). He proposed that attachment is an innate device intended to protect the immature offspring of a species by attracting adults who will ensure their survival. This idea fits with the observation that a newborn can be comforted by anyone but a slightly older baby prefers his/her primary attachment figure/s. Some researchers suggest attachment is universal, but others argue that it is expressed differently in different cultures (LeVine and Miller, 1990). One important 'message' from recent research is the fact that babies can have a network of attachments made up of different members of 'the family' – all the familiar people with whom the baby has attachments (Forrest, 1997). It is when they reach three to six months of age that babies start making preferential attachments. They behave in ways that are designed to attract the person's attention – smiling, cooing, trying to make eye contact – when that person is near and they will be pacified by that person's voice, a look from them or the presentation of a toy, for example. Some of these preferred attachment figures will be the older children in a household. Different attachment figures will elicit different responses from a baby, for example it may be that a young child starts to cry when collected from an early childhood education and care (ECEC) setting and this can be disconcerting to a 'new' parent. In fact the tears do not mean the baby is rejecting the parent, or that they do not feel contented at the setting. Passionate crying in such a circumstance can mean that this is the baby's preferred attachment figure and it may indicate the strength of the attachment (Davies, 1999; Watson, 1994).

Murray and Trevarthen (1985) showed that from two months of age, around the time they also engage in social smiling, infants are sensitive to *social contingency* (the mother's responsiveness to the infant's signals), especially to the timing of their mothers' emotional *attunement* in their two-way exchanges. These attuned exchanges indicate the development of *primary intersubjectivity* – the rudiments of turn taking, sensitive timing and responsiveness to the other's behaviour, especially facial expressions. Intersubjectivity is thought to be the foundation of early social interaction. Such early, playful interactions are called 'proto-conversations' and they gradually offer the young child opportunities for anticipating and predicting and they form the basis for social and cognitive advances that occur during the first year (Trevarthen and Aitken, 2001).

Naturally, attachments change over time (Belsky et al., 1996; Dunn, 1993). As Dunn's research shows, this is unsurprising, since even mothers can change their attitudes/approach towards their children at different ages, preferring particular phases of development.

Attachment theory has been used to encourage mothers to stay at home, rather than seek employment outside the home, and it has induced guilt in several generations of women, because it has been used politically at certain times, with warnings of dire consequences for babies – *maternal deprivation* – if their mothers are unavailable as primary attachment figures because they go out to work for long hours. Recent research demonstrates, however, that not only can babies form attachments to a number of people, it may be that they are better protected and better equipped to form subsequent relationships by having several primary attachment figures rather than the sometimes claustrophobic (and unnatural in human terms) relationship which can result from long hours spent in the company of only one adult, their mother. For example, in the event of the mother suffering from postnatal depression, the attachment process and the baby's emotional development are disrupted (Cooper and Murray, 1998; Kumar, 1997).

Bowlby (1988) himself stated that attachment research had shown up flaws in his theory and that instead of the idea of specific, crucial phases of development he had come to prefer a theory of developmental pathways. Despite these reservations, attachment remains a useful concept in trying to understand babies' need to relate positively to the people closest to them and in recognising the ways in which early interactions provide the building blocks for the sense of self and models for later social competence.

The bedrock of emotional development

According to Roberts (2002), Goldschmied and Jackson (1994) and Selleck and Griffin (1996), responsive, loving attention in the years between birth and three provide children with opportunities to develop a positive personal identity, self-concept and interdependent relationships. To achieve all these young children are said to need unconditional acceptance from the significant people in their lives. To such young children these people are important and powerful and they learn they are acceptable when one of these people smiles at them or comes in response to their call. This is how they learn to instigate pleasurable interactions and every interaction at this stage is a learning experience. A baby's first language is body language and they learn about themselves and their world through what they can feel, taste, hear, smell and see.

Babies and young children are also able to recognise mismatches between what they hear and a person's body language. Such incongruities confuse them. In the worst cases of insensitivity to babies, when abuse is being perpetrated, even very young children will try to make themselves acceptable by negating feelings of pain, anger and fear, by shutting down their emotions. This can have a negative effect on their emotional health and it can also impact on their physical growth and brain development.

Of course, even sensitive parents cannot respond to every cue from their children but we know from research (Aber and Allen, 1987; Lyons-Ruth and Zeanah, 1993) that babies who experience success in re-establishing contact with a key adult who was previously preoccupied gain a stronger sense of self-efficacy and a growing feeling of being successful. Additionally, emotionally sensitive parents and carers who encourage young children to explore and enjoy 'their world' find these children take greater pleasure in goal-directed task persistence, and as a result are socially and cognitively more competent in later life, whereas babies whose key adults constantly fail to support them can develop 'learned helplessness'.

So we can conclude that emotional well-being is the bedrock on which all later development depends. Happily, human brains and human beings generally are 'plastic' – they never stop learning and they can change, given the right conditions, as the research on resilience shows.

Children and adults who have factors in their lives enabling them to cope with any adverse circumstances which may beset them are said to be resilient. The research indicates that the factors relevant to this chapter which appear to foster resilience in children include: a positive disposition; a positive self-concept; good social skills; a balance between independence and interdependence; good relationships with other children; strong attachment relationships; competent parents who model competence for the child; household rules and parental monitoring; a stable relationship between parents; family expectations about positive social behaviour; supportive adults outside the family; family participation in a religious community; not being poor; positive alliances between local workers and the community; positive attitudes on the part of professionals; neighbourhood stability and policies which result in increased resources (Breton, 2001; Chenoweth and Stehlik, 2001; Clarke, 2001; Davies, 1999; Gilgun, 1996; Masten and Coatsworth, 1998; Pedro-Carroll, 2001). Above all, according to Werner (1996), who studied a group of high-risk children through to adulthood, the most important 'ingredient' is a significant person in the child's life to whom that child and what they do 'matters'.

A growing sense of self: personal development

One of the most striking changes during the transition from babyhood to early childhood is a child's growing sense of self (Dunn, 1993). Individual children become aware of how others view them and, as emphasised earlier, it is usually the parent-child relationship that provides the basis for fostering a sense of self-competence and worth. Along with this growing sense of self, the child will be trying to gain a sense of independence, wishing to be seen as capable by others – and told so in words and actions when attempting to be independent (Karmiloff-Smith, 1994).

As Hutchins and Sims (1999) point out, children develop self-awareness and social awareness in conjunction with a sense of their own agency. When they have parents and practitioners who allow them to assert some power and control over their own lives, they learn to be self-regulating and autonomous.

By eighteen to twenty-four months old, young children usually recognise themselves in mirrors, begin to use 'I', 'me' and 'mine' and use their own name. They also start to assert their own wishes. A few more months on and they begin to develop their gender identity, and to show awareness of racism in their society. Iram Siraj-Blatchford (2001) suggests strategies for dealing with discrimination, because 'A positive self-concept is necessary for healthy development and learning and includes feelings about gender, race, ability, culture and language. Positive self-esteem depends on whether children feel others accept them and see them as competent and worthwhile' (Siraj-Blatchford, 2001: 104).

Children with special needs

Parents who have been informed soon after their baby's birth that their child has identifiable special needs are often left to deal with powerful emotions which may impact upon the attachment process (Herbert, 1994; Herbert and Carpenter, 1994). According to Doyle (1997), despite the Children Act 1989, which required different professionals to work together more effectively in the 'best interests' of children, the United Kingdom still lags behind other countries in its ability to ensure this in practice. She maintains that research, training and resources in this area have been neglected and her view is supported by more recent research about multi-professionalism by Atkinson et al. (2002).

Disruption to the attachment process is also more likely if a baby needs in-patient hospitalisation or many visits in the first few weeks of life, and Menzies Lyth (1995) emphasises the importance of staff in institutions such as hospitals being aware of the potential effects of lack of continuity in early relationships and their key role in supporting parents.

Another group who require special support are children with autism, who appear aloof and indifferent and who do not seek out meaningful interactions with other children or with adults. This is because they do not perceive their world in the same way that other children do (Trevarthen et al., 1998).

Children born to parents who did not themselves experience warm and sensitive parenting, or who are experiencing high levels of stress, also tend to have attachment difficulties (Siegel, 1999; Steele et al., 1995) and babies described as irritable or difficult, whose parents (usually the mother), because of anxiety, respond aggressively rather than being able to calm them, tend to have low resilience later in life (Hagekull et al., 1993).

Mind-reading experts

Towards the end of their first year, most young children will begin to point to things and they will also be able to follow someone else's gaze when they are pointing. Such pointing activity involves referencing by looking back at the other person's face, to check they are looking at the same object, and this tells us that the child has some understanding about other people's viewpoints (Gopnik et al., 1999). Even babies younger than six months old have been observed using *social referencing* strategies, searching their parent's face for reassurance when something surprising and strange (to them) happens (Channel 4, 1992, and the allied text, Konner, 1991; for further information on social referencing see for example Moses et al., 2001; Striano and Rochat, 1999).

During the second year, too, young children begin feigning crying (showing they are aware of its effect) and they are also more likely to make caring gestures when someone else is upset or hurt. They also begin to engage in pretend play with adults or other children. As Judy Dunn (1999) points out, being able to agree on what is happening in fantasy play, even for a short bout, shows they can take account of the play partner's thoughts, and by playing in this way children develop the ability to collaborate and develop narratives.

This is important, because, as Gopnik et al. (1999) remind us, one of the main tasks of childhood lies in understanding the difference between their own minds and those of others. Interactions with other young children, who will not make allowances for different views (or with the 'zany uncles', advocated by Urie Bronfenbrenner, who challenge through unconventional behaviour), are vital to the young child's developing brain, because parents and carers will often try to minimise such differences of opinion, scaffolding a child's attempts and looking for commonality. The challenges from other children, meanwhile, help them begin to understand that other people do not necessarily always think as they do and this is when their ability to 'mind-read' begins to come into play. Parents, grandparents, siblings, educators and others will then become subject to the child's attempts to manipulate them through this ability, because they will know what makes them loved and acceptable to these important people. For example, Joe (four years) and Sam (three years) were playing with the large blocks in their nursery, building a space rocket, when Tom (three years) tried to join them. They rejected his involvement and started to make threatening gestures, Sam at one point even taking a swing at Tom – clearly intended to miss but nevertheless threatening – with a large torch in his hand. Few words had been exchanged and almost all the conflict was expressed through behaviour on the part of all three. However, after swinging the torch, Sam had caught the eye of a member of staff and he suddenly handed the torch to Tom, gesturing to him to join the play. Children use various cues, such as facial expressions, but also language, to read the minds of others and they usually try to be in the 'good books' of the people who matter to them.

When they are between the ages of two and three years, children's narratives through pretend play begin to proliferate (Bruner, 1990; Feldman, 1992). These narratives are at their most sophisticated when they are concerned with emotional events – particularly negative ones involving fear, anger or distress – and they are sequentially and causally accurate (Dunn, 1999). Both Bruner and Feldman argue that narratives are used to generate a person's sense of self, to make sense of their lives and to explain the actions of ourselves and others.

'Belonging'

Wrapped up in the process of emotional, social and personal development is the child's sense of belonging. Families today are very different from the families of even a generation ago, and as Jagger and Wright (1999: 3) point out, 'The family is neither a pan-human universal nor a stable or essential entity ... Families and family relations are, like the term itself, flexible, fluid and contingent.' However, since research shows how important familiar, loving, significant people are to babies and young children, it is vital that, as a society, we explore ways of ensuring that they feel they are part of a 'family', however it is constituted.

Nancy Boyd Webb's (1984) research highlighted the ways in which certain behaviours gave children messages about themselves and their place in their 'family'. She observed twenty-four children aged under four, who had experienced multiple caring in their earliest years. She found that the most socially competent, confident and self-assured children had parents who 'bugged and nudged' them (to do, show or share something they had achieved to another of their significant adults); they had pet names, and they had rituals that the children had devised and which were respected (for example, 'He always has his "snuggly" and a cup of water at bedtimes').

While it does not appear to matter who does what, or whether one's parents are a cohabiting heterosexual couple, since what matters is the act of 'mothering/fathering/parenting', we live in a gendered society and research has often explored the roles taken up by mothers and fathers. Apparently, most fathers behave differently towards their children compared with the mothers. However, as Anderson (1996) points out, it can be the mother who acts as a gatekeeper, either including or excluding the father and thus encouraging or discouraging a meaningful relationship between a father and his child. According to Belsky (1996), fathers whose infants are securely attached to them are usually more extrovert and positive about their home lives than fathers whose children are insecurely attached to them. In fact, research by Fox et al. (1991) suggests that the strength of attachment to one parent is usually a good indicator of attachment to the other. Additionally, the relationship between a mother or father and their first-born appears to set the tone for the attachments of later offspring (Volling and Belsky, 1992).

Young children's ambivalence towards new siblings is common (Dunn, 1984) but with parental support and encouragement they soon show that, even before they are three years old, they can adapt the way they talk and behave, for example using terms of endearment towards a baby that a parent, grandparent or other significant adult has modelled. For Kieran, having new twin brothers when he himself was still not quite two years old could have been a tremendous upheaval. However, as a result of his parents' sensitive and loving approach to all their sons, Oliver and Sam quickly became family members, and sometimes when they cried, and Kieran's mum was preparing a bottle or food, he would suggest that he would like some music on so he could dance to cheer them up – and he did, because his brothers were entranced by this wonderful, agile and entertaining little person.

Of course, all siblings have their quarrels – and sometimes fights: the incidence of fighting between sisters and brothers is higher than that between friends outside the home, although the incidence for boys is roughly the same as that with peers. As Dunn (1984: 144) adds, 'It is because they understand their siblings so well, and because they feel so strongly about them, that their relationship is so significant and so revealing.'

For ECEC settings, the issues related to staff relationships with children and the difficulties of shifts, holidays and other complications require debate. Elfer et al. (2002) advocate the key worker system, to enable close relationships, which the babies and young children need, to develop. While Dahlberg et al. (1999) argue that one should not create 'false closeness'; they too advocate a concept of intensity of relationships with a small network of familiar adults and children, and Rutter (1995) has demonstrated the benefits to children of closeness and continuity.

Attendance at an ECEC setting affords babies and young children opportunities to make friends and to play with other children. Again, Judy Dunn (1993) tells us that young children's friendships are important to them and often children as young as four have friends they made when only two. Friends are also important when children move to a new ECEC setting or group (Howes, 1987). Those who, on transition, had a friend who moved setting with them fared much better in comparison with those who did not move with a friend, and Dunn (1993) found that they remembered that it was the presence of the friend that made them happy in a new setting.

Children's relationships with their friends were also the focus of research into whether the ways in which family members related to one another were reflected in interactions in nurseries. Importantly, children who enjoyed high levels of involvement with their mothers were more likely to be conciliatory and to compromise with friends. They also engaged in longer and more elaborate bouts of shared fantasy play and conversations (Dunn, 1993).

A similar effect was found when Howes and her colleagues (1994) explored children's relationships with their ECEC practitioners. Where the practitioners modelled socialisation the children seemed to be more accepting towards each other and when they felt secure in their setting they displayed complex play with other children, with whom they were also more gregarious than children who did not experience positive relationships with staff. Sally Lubeck's (1986) fine-grained account of two very different settings in an American city also showed the influence the style of interactions between staff and children, as well as those involving staff with other staff, can have on how children relate to one another and how this affects their learning. In one setting the staff related very much to individual children and there was little if any staff–staff interaction in the presence of children, while in the other group staff discussed problems together (modelling for the children) and they used a much higher level of group activities with the children. As a result, the children from each setting were losing out to some extent, since some had few opportunities to experience co-operation and interdependence, while those attending the other rarely experienced independence.

The New Zealand Ministry of Education (1996: 54) argues that all children need to have a feeling of belonging, because it 'contributes to inner well-being, security and identity. Children need to know that they are accepted for who they are. They should know that what they do can make a difference and that they can explore and try out new activities.' McGuire (1991) found that nursery staff in the United Kingdom often failed to give additional support to withdrawn children to help them become integrated into a group or to engage in play activities and Anning (1999) observed that three-year-olds struggling to make sense of themselves as members of a family and a group setting were given insufficient support in dealing with discontinuities between the two contexts.

Harris (1989) explains how different cultures build on what may be a universal, innate ability to recognise positive and negative emotional states. He also discusses the ways in which the emotions of guilt and shame are used to socialise children and different cultures use these to varying degrees. By the time they are two years old children are learning the 'scripts' assigned to different emotions by their family or community, that are learned to make one acceptable. Sometimes they will use 'transitional objects' to help them in this regulation of the emotions. These might be dummies, favourite soft toys, comforters that have been self-chosen.

Children who have warm, affectionate relationships with their parents have been found to be more likely to have high self-esteem, to be better socially adjusted and to achieve academically (Mortimer, 2001). Siegel argues that if parents – and one might surmise this could also apply to practitioners – did not enjoy warm, close relationships with their own parents, then encouraging them to reflect on their narratives of their own childhoods and to understand how they feel, can help them become more positive, so that they are able to engage in the loving, sensitive interactions which will benefit their children's emotional well-being and personal and social development.

Conclusion

The main points debated in this chapter have been as follows. Early relationships with sensitive, loving others form the model for later relationships; pleasurable interactions during the first two years provide the scripts which children adopt in their later friendships – i.e. adults and older children act as models. Children who, early in life, have been encouraged by emotionally sensitive parents and carers to explore and enjoy their world will take greater pleasure in goal-directed behaviour later in life and they will persist at difficult tasks; they will also be more competent socially and cognitively. Resilient people tend to have, or have had, at least one person in their life to whom they feel they (and what they do) matter. Staff in ECEC settings sometimes need to help children integrate into the group and they need to be aware of how friendships can help children cope with transitions. Most important, babies and young children need to experience unconditional acceptance, continuity of relationships – these can be with several key people – and to bask in interactions and play with those who love them.

3
Language Development in the Young Child
Stephanie James

Contents

- The behaviourist perspective
- The nativist perspective
- The semantic perspective
- The interactionist perspective
- Conclusion

How do children learn to talk? That is the central question that this chapter addresses. It traces the development of key theories about the process of language acquisition that dominated the second half of the twentieth century and indicates some influential pieces of research that supported or challenged those theories.

Parents the world over have always marvelled at their infants' rapid accomplishment of the power of speech, and one of the major milestones in a young child's development is the utterance of the first recognisable words. For centuries, philosophers, psychologists, linguists and others have also taken an interest in children's seemingly effortless acquisition of their first language. However, it was not until the middle of the twentieth century that the debate about how children learn language really came alive. Four major perspectives on early language acquisition and development have contributed to our understanding of how children learn to talk:

1 *The behaviourist perspective*, which emphasises the role of nurture, imitation and repetition in language acquisition
2 *The nativist perspective*, which emphasises the role of nature and the child's innate capacity to understand and use the grammar of any language
3 *The semantic perspective*, which emphasises the link between cognitive development and language development
4 *The interactionist perspective*, which emphasises the essentially social and communicative nature of language.

Before discussing each perspective in detail, it is important to emphasise that they are not mutually exclusive. For example, the last two perspectives are often

Questions and exercises

1   Reflect on your own feelings as an adult, when thwarted, spurned or hurt. How do you react and why? What helps you cope? What prevents you from coping? What do you think both adults and children need if powerful feelings about negative experiences are not to overcome them and become destructive?
2   Think of an observation you have recorded (in your mind or on paper) of an incident in an ECEC setting, when a child has been upset. How was it dealt with? Did the event or incident contribute to that child's, or other children's, learning about emotions, and if so, how? If you think the event was handled in a negative way, how would you like it to have been different?
3   What can be done to help shy or isolated children gain entry to a group?

Reading

Dowling (2003), 'All about resilience', *Nursery World* 103, includes clear explanations about what we know from research about *resilience* and how to foster this important characteristic through our practice, in interactions with babies and young children. Roberts, *Developing Self-esteem in Young Children* (2002), deftly combines findings from research with insightful examples from real life. David, Gooch, Powell and Abbott, *Birth to Three Matters* (2003), a review of over 500 research references for the DfES project 'Birth to Three Matters', includes a chapter called 'A strong child', focusing mainly upon children's emotional and social development. However, the review also points out that children's development is not compartmentalised, it is interconnected. Gopnik, Melzoff and Kuhl, *How Babies Think* (1999), is first, a really good read – it provides a mass of neuroscientific research evidence in such an accessible way! Second, the authors give those of us in the ECEC field extra support in arguing for humane, loving and exciting contexts for babies and young children.

considered as one, but for the sake of clarity they are discussed separately here. It is also important to make it clear that, although the four perspectives are considered chronologically, each new perspective did not simply replace the old one. Rather, each perspective has helped to fill in another part of an enormous and very complicated jigsaw puzzle, so that we know far more about the process of language learning at the beginning of the twenty-first century than we did fifty years ago. However, the puzzle is still far from complete.

The behaviourist perspective

This view of how children learn to talk could be regarded as the commonsense view; that children hear language and simply copy and repeat what they hear. In 1957 B.F. Skinner, a well known scientist of animal behaviour, published a book called *Verbal Behavior* in which he outlined his views on how language is acquired. He based his theory on his studies of how animals learn. For example, he described how rats in a cage learned to press a bar when a light flashed in order to obtain food. Central to his account of how animals learn are the three processes of stimulus, response and reward (or reinforcement). In the case of the rats, these three processes worked as follows. The rats received a stimulus in the form of a flashing light and learned that if they gave the correct response by pressing a bar they would receive a reward in the form of food. If the rats gave an incorrect response then they were not rewarded.

You may wonder what rats doing clever things in cages has to do with children learning to talk, but in *Verbal Behavior* Skinner applied behaviourist theories of learning in general to the specific context of learning language. According to Skinner, learning language is no different, in essence, from any other form of learning and we learn through the same mechanisms that control animal learning. For example, the parent stimulates the child by playing and talking to her. The child responds by imitating and repeating the parent's language. If the child imitates and repeats correctly her response is rewarded and reinforced through, for example, praise, smiles or saying something like 'Yes, that's a dog!' However, if the child's response is incorrect or inappropriate it is not reinforced; it is ignored or corrected. So correct responses are reinforced. Incorrect responses are not reinforced. Children gradually learn to talk, therefore, by listening, imitating and repeating correctly the language they hear.

This explanation must be right, up to a point. Obviously children *do* listen and they *do* copy what they hear. Anyone who has listened to young children talking knows that this is the case. An example that supports the behaviourist explanation of language learning based on reinforcement of correct responses comes from Daniel, aged fifteen months. He would raise his arms towards an adult whenever he wanted to be picked up and say 'Get down!' This apparently contradictory request and gesture can be explained by the fact that as a very active toddler he frequently heard his mother saying to him, 'Daniel, get down!' when he was climbing on the furniture and in imminent danger of hurting himself. He had heard the phrase on many occasions but had not yet learned that 'down' indicates only one direction. He had interpreted it as meaning movement in either direction, up or down. The significance of this example is that all the adults who knew Daniel very well thought that this was highly amusing and actually reinforced his inaccurate request by picking him up! So this example supports a behaviourist explanation: that the child copies the adult and is rewarded when he copies a phrase correctly even, in this instance, when he has interpreted it incorrectly. After hearing more examples of the phrase, in context, he had learned the distinction between 'up' and 'down' by the age of eighteen months.

So anyone who has ever listened to children talking knows that they copy words and phrases they hear. Therefore the behaviourist view of language acquisition, with its emphasis on the role played by nurturing adults, must be valid. However, anyone who has ever listened to children talking also knows that they say things like 'I rided my bike', 'I hurted my foots' and 'I catched the ball'. You can immediately see that a theory based on the idea that children learn language simply by listening to and imitating adult speech must have great difficulty in explaining examples of children's language such as these. Whoever heard an adult say 'I hurted my foots!'? A linguist who was to have a profound influence on our understanding of language, Noam Chomsky, tackled this phenomenon of children saying original things they can never have heard adults say. In 1959 he wrote a highly critical review of Skinner's *Verbal Behavior* in which he effectively demolished a view of language learning based on the behaviour of rats in cages. Not only did he believe that rats were irrelevant to the study of language learning, but he also claimed that Skinner misunderstood the nature of language. Pinker (1994) identifies two fundamental facts about language highlighted by Chomsky.

> First, virtually every sentence that a person utters or understands is a brand-new combination of words, appearing for the first time in the history of the universe. Therefore a language cannot be a repertoire of responses.... The second fundamental fact is that children develop these complex grammars rapidly and without formal instruction and grow up to give consistent interpretations to novel sentence constructions that they have never before encountered.
>
> (Pinker, 1994: 22)

The major theory Chomsky proposed to explain these two fundamental facts was that humans are born with an innate predisposition to learn language. He called this innate predisposition the Language Acquisition Device, or LAD, as it quickly became known. So in direct contrast with Skinner's baby, who is an 'empty vessel' waiting to be filled up with language through the nurture provided by his parents, Chomsky's baby is a vessel which nature has already partly filled with language learning potential. This is the heart of the nature-nurture debate as it applies to language learning.

The nativist perspective

Chomsky focused particularly on the idea that children are not only learning words when they learn to talk, but they are also learning something else – how to put words together and in the right order. They are learning the grammar of the language. A major aspect of his theory was that every sentence has an inner hidden deep structure and an outer, evident surface structure. For example, 'The dog bit the man' has the same deep structure, the same underlying meaning, as 'The man was bitten by the dog' but it has a different surface structure. Conversely, 'The dog bit the man' and 'The man bit the dog' have the same surface structure but very different deep structures. Of course, any language can usually express the same deep structure with more than one surface structure, which is one of the problems we encounter when we learn a foreign language. We may have learned a particular way of saying something in a foreign language class, a particular surface structure, only to find, when we visit that country, that native speakers have alternative ways of expressing the same meaning and we have difficulty understanding them. Aitchison (1998: 98) provides a helpful illustration of the way in which several sentences which have quite different surface structures are all related to a similar underlying deep structure:

> Charles captured a heffalump.
> A heffalump was captured by Charles.
> It was a heffalump which Charles captured.
> What Charles captured was a heffalump.

So any one language can express the same deep structure with a variety of surface structures. Different languages such as English, Chinese, Swahili, whilst obviously having different sounds, words and rules of grammar, nevertheless share the potential for the same underlying deep structures, otherwise translation from one language to another would be impossible. Chomsky proposed, therefore, that there is a universal grammar and that children from every language community in the world somehow have an innate awareness of deep structures and how to transform them into the surface structures of their particular language.

The idea that children are learning not only words when they learn to talk, but also the rules for putting words together – a grammar – created a huge amount of interest in the academic community and beyond. It is important to note, however, that Chomsky did not suggest that children learn the grammar of their language by sitting down and receiving lessons in grammar. Of course not! Whoever heard of an English-speaking parent trying to teach her three-year-old that you must place the adjective *before* the noun – 'white house' – whilst a French-speaking parent tries to teach his child that you put the adjective *after* the noun – 'maison blanche'? That is not how it works. What Chomsky suggested was much more exciting than that. He claimed that the child is an 'intuitive grammarian'. Children infer the underlying rules of the language from the linguistic evidence they hear all around them.

If we now return to the typical child utterances that posed a problem for a behaviourist account of language learning, we can see how children infer particular rules of grammar. When children say things such as 'I rided', 'I hurted' and 'I catched' they are over-generalising the rule for making the past tense in English. They have learned the rule that in English you add a 'd' sound to the end of the word whenever you want to say that something happened in the past. What they have not yet learned is that there are also exceptions to that rule. Similarly, when children say 'foots' or 'sheeps' they have learned the rule that to make the plural in English you add an 's' sound to the end of the word, but again they have not yet noted exceptions to that rule.

The impact of Chomsky's theories was overwhelming. They became known as the 'Chomskyan revolution' and his ideas spawned thousands of studies into children's language development. Pinker (1994: 23) gives us some idea of Chomsky's importance in creating a mind-shift in the field of linguistics and related areas of study:

> By now, the community of scientists studying the questions he raised numbers in the thousands. Chomsky is currently among the ten most-cited writers in all of the humanities (… trailing only Marx, Lenin, Shakespeare, the Bible, Aristotle, Plato and Freud) and the only living member of the top ten.

We will now consider a few pieces of research which followed in the wake of Chomsky's ideas and which sought to confirm that children are not parrots when they learn to talk but are creative, 'intuitive grammarians.'

In 1958 Jean Berko devised a number of ways to test children's implicit understanding of English grammar, particularly plurals and verb tenses. A very famous example is 'The Case of the Wug' in which she showed a group of young children a picture of a strange bird-like creature called a 'wug', followed by a picture of two of the creatures. She then asked them to complete the following sentences: 'This is a wug. Now there is another one. There are two of them. There are two …' As you would expect, nearly all the children said 'wugs', as you probably did yourself as you read the sentences! What is the point here? How did you know, just like the children, that the missing word is 'wugs'? The point is, of course, that you have never met the nonsense word 'wug' before, and yet you were able confidently to supply the missing plural form, not because you had heard it before and had memorised and repeated it (as in a behaviourist explanation) but because you simply applied your implicit knowledge of the rule for forming the plural in English – add an 's' sound to the end of the word.

Numerous researchers also showed that children find it incredibly difficult to imitate correctly grammatical structures which they have not yet acquired, despite the best efforts of adults explicitly to teach them. Courtney Cazden (1972: 92) for example, tried in vain to teach a child to use the correct form of the past tense of the verb 'to hold':

> *Child*: My teacher holded the baby rabbits and we patted them.
> *Adult*: Did you say your teacher held the baby rabbits?
> *Child*: Yes.
> *Adult*: What did you say she did?
> *Child*: She holded the baby rabbits and we patted them.
> *Adult*: Did you say she *held* them tightly?
> *Child*: No, she holded them loosely.

Children are impervious to grammatical correction before they are ready to understand that there are exceptions to rules that they have learnt and over-generalised. Another example was overheard in a nursery class of three to four-year-olds. A little girl had been icing her birthday cake and announced to the teacher:

> *Child*:   I writed my name in icing.
> *Teacher*: You mean you wrote your name in icing.
> *Child*:   Yes, I writed my name in icing.
> *Teacher*: Say 'I *wrote* my name in icing.'
> *Child*:   I … wroted my name in icing.

Evidence such as that provided in these few examples steadily accumulated to support Chomsky's theory that children are endowed by nature with the ability to infer the rules of the grammar of any given language. Such examples also challenged the behaviourist view that nurture, the environment, including the contribution from significant adults, enables children to listen, memorise and repeat language they hear all around them. As the nativists pointed out, apart from routine greetings, every time we speak we produce a unique string of words never heard before 'in the history of the universe' (Pinker, 1994: 22). It would be an impossible feat of memory for children to remember all the possible combinations of words needed to create precise meanings, so the powerful force of an innate potential to learn any language must be responsible for the miraculously rapid achievement of fluency in our first language.

However, the nature versus nurture debate is not the end of the story by any means. People increasingly accepted many of Chomsky's ideas and also acknowledged the behaviourist view that children must be exposed to language in the environment to provide the catalyst for speech. Others, however, began to feel that the emphasis on children's developing understanding of grammar, fascinating and revealing though it was, neglected other important aspects of their linguistic development.

Here is a sentence that may pose some difficulties for you to understand: 'The notes were sour because the seams were split.' What is causing the problem here? Do you need to consult a dictionary for the meaning of any individual word? Almost certainly not! Do you think it is ungrammatical in any way? No, that is not the problem, either. So why don't you immediately understand it, if language is concerned only with words and grammar? If you can play the bagpipes, or know someone who does, the sentence may have made immediate sense to you – that the notes played by the pipes were off-key because the seams of the bag were split! This apparently trivial example points to another important feature of language that has not so far been considered – that any sentence needs to be in an arena of shared meaning if it is to make sense. This brings us to the third perspective on language acquisition and development.

The semantic perspective

Whilst acknowledging the huge debt we owe to Chomsky in deepening our understanding of language learning, people began to question whether an innate Language Acquisition Device could sufficiently explain the process of language acquisition. Surely other cognitive and social factors must be important too? This perspective sees the child as a meaning maker, actively seeking to make sense of the world and of the language that is an intrinsic part of it. The late 1960s saw the first systematic investigations of the meanings young children try to express in their speech.

Lois Bloom (1970) conducted one of the best known pieces of research in which she made 'rich interpretations' of the intended meanings of young children's two-word utterances. The two-word stage of language development is particularly interesting because as soon as children put two words together they demonstrate the presence of an emerging grammar; they are making choices about which words to select, which words to omit and what order to place them in. Bloom gives the example of how a little girl called Kathryn, then aged twenty-one months, said 'Mommy sock' twice in the same day but in two quite different contexts. The first context was when Kathryn picked up her mother's sock. The second context was when her mother was putting Kathryn's socks on Kathryn. In the first instance, 'Mommy sock' means 'This sock belongs to Mommy' and in the second instance it means 'Mommy is putting my sock on me.' This example shows that Kathryn understands the relationship between her mother, the two different socks and herself long before she has the language for expressing the relationship precisely. At this stage she just has the two words that have to stand for a number of meanings and relationships between people and objects. To use Chomsky's terminology, the phrase 'Mommy sock' has the same surface structure in each instance but is expressing an entirely different deep structure.

The significance of this example is that it strongly suggests that cognitive development precedes language development; that some form of thought is present before children have adequate language to express their understanding. This brings us to the heart of the debate about the relationship between language and thought, a very complex debate which can only be touched on in this chapter. The debate raises many questions. For example, does the child acquire the concept of an object or action before learning an appropriate word for that object or action? Does knowing the word for an object or action actually help develop the concept of it? These are difficult ideas to untangle. The views of Jean Piaget, Lev Vygotsky and Jerome Bruner have been particularly influential in this area. These authorities hold differing views about the nature of language and thought and the kind and degree of relationship between them. (For a concise summary of their views see Whitehead, 1997.) The debate continues, but the consensus is that there is a very strong link between thought and language.

From the semantic perspective, language development is dependent on children's more general cognitive development, an idea which is expanded by Margaret Donaldson in her seminal book *Children's Minds*. She says that this idea virtually stands Chomsky's Language Acquisition Device on its head. Now, instead of saying that language development happens because the child has an innate LAD, rather, language development happens because the child has other cognitive skills, one of which is a highly developed capacity for making sense of human situations. Donaldson gives an anecdote to illustrate how this may occur (1978: 37).

> An English woman is in the company of an Arab woman and her two children, a boy of seven and a little girl of thirteen months who is just beginning to walk but is afraid to take more than a few steps without help. The English woman speaks no Arabic, the Arab woman and her son speak no English.
> The little girl walks to the English woman and back to her mother. Then she turns as if to start off in the direction of the English woman once again. But the latter now smiles, points to the boy and says: 'Walk to your brother this time.' At once the boy, *understanding the situation* though he understands not a word of the language, holds out his arms. The baby smiles, changes direction and walks to her brother. Like the older child, she appears to have understood the situation perfectly.

She then makes the point that the thing to notice is that all the participants in this interaction understood one another's intentions and the situation was 'highly predictable in the human context of its occurrence. What the people meant was clear. What the words meant could in principle be derived from that' (Donaldson, 1978: 37).

So, from the semantic perspective, language development is possible because of children's ability to grasp the meaning, to 'make sense' of human situations. An analogy with children's ability to infer the rules of grammar is evident here. We might say that they can also infer the meaning in human situations; that they are 'intuitive meaning makers', to paraphrase Wells (1986). They are not passive recipients of experience (as in the behaviourist explanation), nor are they simply blessed with an innate ability to learn language (as in the nativist account), but they are active participants in the world around them, eager to seek out an understanding of the people, objects and events they encounter. Bruner (1983: 34) put it well: 'children ... needed to have a working knowledge of the world before they acquired language'.

We have considered how children make sense of, and impose meaning on, the world around them but the role of adults in helping children to develop language has barely figured in the account so far. Equally, the discussion has concentrated on the stages of language acquisition beyond the production of the first few words and has not yet considered the importance of the pre-verbal period in laying the foundation for later language learning. Our fourth perspective will now redress that imbalance.

The interactionist perspective

The social interactionist interpretation of language development is that both biological and environmental factors are important. This perspective is very closely linked with the last one, but its focus is much more concerned with children's early social interactions with the important people in their lives and their early attempts at communication. By the 1970s the main focus of the study of language acquisition had begun to shift away from grammatical structures and towards an investigation of the functions that language serves for the infant. Bruner (1983) has argued strongly that any attempt to shed light on early language development *must* deal with the period of pre-linguistic communication.

One of the first researchers to look at the interpersonal functions which the child's early utterances seem to serve was Michael Halliday (1975). He carried out an intensive study of his own son, Nigel. Instead of waiting until Nigel was producing recognisable words, Halliday started his investigation when Nigel was only nine months old. He sees language as having a vast meaning potential, realised primarily through interaction with other human beings. As far as Halliday is concerned, as soon as there is 'meaningful expression' there is language. By 'meaningful expression' he refers to sounds that the baby makes consistently in similar contexts on similar occasions. For example, when Nigel made the sound 'Nyaaah! Nyaaah!' Halliday interpreted his intended meaning as 'Give me that'. When he made the sound 'Ah-dah!' he interpreted the meaning as 'Look – a picture!' You may think that such interpretations are highly fanciful, but Halliday says that in fact he found it extremely easy to interpret what Nigel meant. The important point to note here is that the child understands the functions of language long before he can produce recognisable words himself. Parents all over the world perform such exercises in interpretation all the time, although a stranger may find it difficult to understand what the baby is 'saying'. What this suggests is that the earliest language utterances are primarily interpersonal and their main function is to communicate with other people.

In 1977 Catherine Snow wrote a paper called 'The development of conversation between mothers and babies'. In it she describes how mothers respond to the behaviour such as coos, burps and yawns of infants as young as three months as if they were *intentional*. The mother initiates what Snow calls 'conversation-like exchanges' in which the turn-taking characteristics of conversation are gradually refined.

It has long been observed that adults modify the language they use when interacting with babies. They use simpler language, are more repetitive and change their pitch and intonation. This special language for talking to babies first became known as 'motherese'. Later on the term 'parentese' was adopted, in recognition of the fact that fathers also modify their language in similar ways. 'Parentese' is used by adults particularly in very familiar, routine settings such as mealtimes, playtimes, bathtime and bedtime and provides for the child what Bruner (1983) calls a Language Acquisition Support System, or LASS. He contends that:

> The infant's Language Acquisition Device could not function without the aid given by an adult who enters with him into a transactional format.... In a word, it is the interaction between LAD and LASS that makes it possible for the infant to enter the linguistic community – and, at the same time, the culture to which the language gives access.

> (Bruner, 1983: 19)

Gradually, from the late 1970s, and with the aid of huge advances in video technology, younger and younger infants became the subjects of research, going right back to the first few moments after birth. For example, Colwyn Trevarthen (1979) made video recordings in the laboratory of mothers' interactions with their babies. He observed that within a few weeks, almost all mothers and babies establish patterns of interaction involving gaze, gesture and often vocal sounds as well: what he called 'proto-conversations'. A perhaps surprising, but extremely interesting, feature of this early communication between parent and child was that it was often the baby who initiated the interaction, and decided when it would end, though the mother supported it with sensitive and appropriate responses.

Later evidence (Murray and Andrews, 2000) reveals the social skills of newborn babies. Within one minute of birth babies can identify their mother and are more comforted by her than by a stranger. Within two minutes they strain their neck to study her face and within fifteen minutes they study the father's face, actively imitating his facial movements. Within half an hour the baby recognises an abstract pattern of dots as more similar to a human face than another and prefers to look at it.

So the interactionist perspective sees the child as an active partner in a communication process rather than a passive recipient of other people's linguistic output. Probably the most important factor urging children into speech is their desire to communicate their intentions more precisely. From birth, then, children initiate communication as well as respond to the communications of others.

Conclusion

So, over the last fifty years, an increasingly complex picture emerges: from the behaviourist view of the child as an 'empty vessel' who listens to the language used by people all around him and imitates it, and who, if he imitates it correctly, is rewarded until the 'vessel' is eventually filled; to the nativist view of the child born with an innate Language Acquisition Device who makes increasingly accurate hypotheses about the rules for constructing sentences until she gets them right; to the view of the child as actively seeking to make sense of the world generally, and language is an inextricable part of that world. All these perspectives concentrate on different aspects of language and learning – imitation, grammar and meaning – but with the final interactionist perspective we can put a few last pieces into the jigsaw. We see that without people, without a social context, language has no place. All four perspectives have something to offer our growing understanding of the fascinating process through which infants become fluent speakers of the language, or indeed languages, of the community into which they are born.

Questions and exercises

1 What is the evidence for the role of nature in children's language acquisition and development?
2 What is the evidence for the role of nurture in children's language acquisition and development?
3 How can parents, carers and other significant adults in children's lives most effectively support and extend their language development?
4 How do differing views about the nature of language and thought influence different accounts of early language acquisition?
5 How can our knowledge of the processes involved in learning a first language inform our understanding of the experiences of children who are brought up in a bilingual setting from birth, or who learn a second or third language at a later stage in their lives?

Reading

Aitchison, *The Articulate Mammal* (1998), is a very accessible introduction to the field of psycholinguistics. Jean Aitchison explains complicated topics in a clear and entertaining manner. Amusing chapter headings and lots of interesting examples enliven the key ideas she addresses. The topic of bilingualism was outside the scope of this chapter. Colin Baker's *A Parents' and Teachers' Guide to Bilingualism and Bilingual Education* (2000) provides a readable introduction to the subject. It poses questions frequently asked about raising bilingual children and offers some clear answers. Fromkin, Rodman and Hyams, *An Introduction to Language* (2003), an American text, is very widely used as a general and comprehensive introduction to the subject and is in four main parts: 'The nature of human language', 'grammatical aspects of language', 'the psychology of language' and 'Language and society'. *The Language Instinct* (1994) is a challenging but fascinating book in which Steven Pinker, one of the world's leading scientists of language and the mind, explains how language works, how children learn it, how language changes, how the brain computes it and how it evolved.

4
Young Children and Gender
Trisha Maynard

Contents

- Gender and sex
- Gender stereotypes
- Gender as biologically determined
- Psychoanalytical theories
- Social learning theories
- Cognitive development theory
- Gender schema theory
- Gender script theory
- Feminist post-structuralist theory
- Conclusion

Gender is a – if not *the* – primary category by which the social world is organised (see Sheldon, 1990). As is often pointed out, when a baby is born, one of the first questions asked is whether it is a boy or a girl. The division of the social world by gender is so embedded, so 'obvious', that we are often oblivious to its influence on who we are and how we see ourselves. But the initial labelling as male or female will have had an impact on almost every aspect of our lives: not only on our physical bodies but also on our thinking, behaviour, language, expectations, relationships and life chances.

This chapter focuses on the process of young children's gender development. Having considered the significance of the terms 'gender' and 'sex' and the nature of gender stereotypes, we will then examine a number of theories that have attempted to explain when and why young children begin to demonstrate *gender-typed* behaviour and an identity as female or male.

Gender and sex

The first issue in need of explanation is the term 'gender' and how it differs from the term 'sex'. Some writers use 'sex' to refer to differences between females and males that are seen as purely biological whereas 'gender' is used to refer to differences that are socially learnt. Unfortunately, as we shall see, this distinction is simplistic. In reality it is impossible to separate the biological from the social, as the two continuously interact with and impact on each other. For example, an awareness of the biological sex of an infant will influence how adults respond to the child and this, in turn, will have an effect not only the child's sense of identity as a male or female but also on the child's developing brain and body. In this chapter, therefore, the terms 'sex' and 'gender' are used interchangeably and do not imply that gender difference is either exclusively biological or social in origin.

Gender stereotypes

There is also a need to consider the nature of gender stereotypes. Whether we are aware of it or not, stereotypes are a part of our day-to-day thinking. The world is a complicated and confusing place and, in order to make sense of it, we devise (or learn) categories that can be used to interpret what we see and what happens to us (EOC, 1992). Gender stereotypes provide useful 'shorthand' ways of categorising our observations and experiences. However, while they are central to the formation of an individual's sense of self as male or female they can also be limiting and con-straining. A notion of the stereotypical male and female, while not necessarily lived out in practice, can shape individual and collective expectations of what is deemed appropriate and acceptable for males and females.

What, then, is a gender stereotype? In simple terms, it is a set of assumptions, beliefs or expectations about what it means to be male and female. In our culture and time, the stereotypical male is often seen as aggressive, competitive, dominant, rational, ambitious, active and adventurous while the stereotypical female is com-pliant, affectionate, emotional, nurturing, compassionate, talkative and gentle. (Stop for a moment to consider how far these stereotypes relate to others ... and to you.)

Are gender stereotypes supported by research? A seminal study that explored the psychological and behavioural differences between boys and girls was published by Eleanor Maccoby and Carol Jacklin in 1974. Maccoby and Jacklin considered a large body of research evidence concerning sex differences and came to the following ten-tative conclusions. First, it appears that girls develop verbal abilities more rapidly than boys while boys excel on visual-spatial ability and mathematical ability (although not in early childhood). Compared with girls, boys are more aggressive both physically and verbally; this sex difference is found as soon as social play begins – at age two or two and a half. There is some tentative evidence to suggest that boys are more com-petitive and, during the pre-school years at least, more active than girls are, particu-larly when in the presence of other boys. When playing in single-sex groups boys tend to make more 'dominance attempts' than girls do and more often try to dominate adults. In addition, there are indications that compared with boys girls are more timid, anxious and compliant to the demands and directions of adults – although not to the demands of their male and female peers. Finally, some research suggests that girls of six to ten years are more likely than boys to demonstrate nurturing behaviour.

But are Maccoby and Jacklin's conclusions accurate? And even if they are, where do these gender differences come from: are they biological in origin or are they learnt from others? In other words, is gender development a case of 'nature' or 'nurture'?

In the next section we will consider the key theories put forward to explain gender differences and the development of *gender identity*: psychoanalytical theories, social learning theories, cognitive developmental and gender schema theories, and post-structuralist feminist theories. We begin, however, with an exploration of gender as 'biologically determined'.

Gender as biologically determined

Halpern (2000) maintains that in order to understand biological determinism it is necessary to consider three interrelated systems: chromosomes, sex hormones and the structure, organisation and function of the brain. For, as Halpern (2000) explains, our chromosomes determine the type of sex hormones secreted and these sex hormones influence the development of the brain.

As humans, most of us have forty-six chromosomes, forty-four of which are organised into twenty-two fairly similar looking pairs. The twenty-third pair is the sex chromosome which determines our genetic sex. The sex chromosome provided by the female egg is always an X while that provided by the male can be either an X or a Y: thus a genetically female baby is XX and a genetic male is XY.

Regardless of whether it is XX or XY, the initial development of the foetus is identical. At about six weeks following conception, embryos containing the XY chromosome will begin to excrete hormones that cause the male embryo to develop testes. The presence of testes leads to the secretion of androgens (male sex hormones) and the eventual development of male reproductive organs. In the female foetus, the absence of male sex hormones (without the need for female sex hormones) results in the development of the female internal reproductive organs.

It is reasonable to conclude that as well as influencing changes in the body, sex hormones will also have an impact on the structure and organisation of the brain. We know that the brain is divided into two hemispheres and that, in 'right-handers' at least, areas relating to language and speech are primarily located in the left hemisphere and those relating to visual spatial skills are primarily located in the right hemisphere. It is argued that the presence of testosterone has an impact on the structure and function of the male brain: the adult male brain is more lateralised or specialised than the female brain. That is, in men, the area associated with language is located solely in the left hemisphere and the area for visual-spatial abilities is located solely in the right hemisphere. Women, on the other hand, tend to have areas for language and visual spatial abilities represented in both hemispheres (Brannon, 2002).

It is suggested that a further difference to be found in the structure and function of the male and female brain is in the corpus callosum – the thick band of neural fibres that connect the right and left hemispheres of the brain. Some researchers have claimed that in the female brain the corpus callosum is larger and, in part, more bulbous than it is in the male brain (see Halpern, 2000).

These differences are said to have certain consequences. For females, the presence of areas for verbal ability in both hemispheres, along with the greater number of neural connections between these hemispheres, is said to explain their superior verbal fluency. But differences in the brain structure are also used to explain females' inferiority – and males' superiority – in solving spatial problems. That is, when faced with a visual-spatial problem the less lateralised female brain may use language in an attempt to reach a solution. This, Halpern (2000) notes, is neither efficient nor effective.

Other than in verbal and spatial abilities, it is often suggested that males and females differ in terms of aggression, males being seen as more aggressive than females. A higher level of aggressive behaviour in males has been linked with the prenatal and postnatal impact of male sex hormones, in particular with testosterone. Kimura (1992), for example, referring to research on the effect of sex hormones on the behaviour of rodents, claims that these hormones account for the higher incidence of aggression in males and in their tendency to engage in rough-and-tumble play. But, as Brannon (2002) points out, in relation to babies and very young children, aggression is virtually impossible to define. That said, Brannon notes that researchers who have adopted alternative definitions of aggression, such as activity level or physical action, have concluded that boys are more aggressive than girls.

Biological theories can sound convincing and offer a neat solution to the question of gender differences. However, a great deal of this research has been challenged and the findings remain inconclusive. Brannon (2002), for example, points out that while some gender differences in brain lateralisation are generally accepted, in reality these differences are extremely small. Similarly, Fausto-Sterling (1992) maintains that there is little evidence that girls speak sooner than boys do or that older girls have superior verbal ability. While she acknowledges that research does indicate male superiority in visual-spatial ability (post-adolescence), she attributes this, at least in part, to boys' and girls' different play experiences. She claims that 'typical' boys' activities such as model construction, ball games, tree climbing, running and throwing are likely to have a significant impact not only on boys' physical development but also on the development of certain cognitive abilities, including the development of spatial skills.

Research which claims that aggressive or impulsive behaviour in males is the result of relatively higher levels of testosterone is also considered problematic by some researchers. Fausto-Sterling (1992) cites anthropological research that indicates.that the different gender roles assigned to boys and girls may have an impact on the development of aggressive behaviour. Indeed, as Brannon (2002) points out, it may be that aggression causes an increase in testosterone and not the other way round.

In conclusion, therefore, while biological determinism has become popular in recent years, research findings that claim that gender differences are 'natural' or purely biological remain tentative and inconsistent.

Psychoanalytical theories

Linked with the view that gender differences are biologically determined are those theories that focus on the unconscious processes of mind. This group of theories appears to be built on or around Freud's theory of psychosexual development. (See Beal, 1994; Brannon, 2002; Golombok and Fivush, 1994; Stainton-Rogers and Stainton-Rogers, 2001, for a more detailed explanation and evaluation of Freud's theory of psychosexual development.)

Freud maintained that instinctive and unconscious drives and impulses are fundamental to personality development and also to the development of a gender identity. He claimed that as part of this development, at three to four years of age children enter the 'phallic stage' of psychosexual development: they begin to focus on their genitals, gain pleasure from masturbation, and experience feelings of sexual attraction for the opposite-sex parent.

At this stage, Freud stated, boys realise that not everyone has a penis. Thus, while the young boy (unconsciously) feels hostility towards his father – the rival for his mother's affections – he also fears that his father may punish him for these feelings by castrating him (the Oedipus complex). According to Freud, boys resolve this conflict by strongly identifying with their fathers. Moreover, given the severity of this psychological trauma, compared with girls boys develop a stronger superego and, because of this, a stronger sense of morality.

This is not to say that girls go through this stage unscathed! Freud noted that girls also notice the anatomical differences between males and females and begin to experience penis envy. The young girl believes that, like her mother, she has already been castrated and assumes that her mother must somehow be to blame. She therefore develops feelings of hostility towards her mother while also turning her affections towards her father (the Electra complex). Eventually girls relinquish their feelings of desire for their father and identify with their mother although for girls these feelings of identification with the same-sex parent are not as strong as those experienced by boys. According to Freud this is the reason that females' superego – their conscience – is not as well developed as the superego of males, resulting in the moral inferiority of females.

Freud's ideas have been reinterpreted by a number of researchers – many of whom (unsurprisingly) have looked at this theory from a feminist standpoint. Chodorow (1978), for example, focused on the mother-child relationship at an earlier stage – during the pre-Oedipal period. Chodorow maintains that initially both female and male babies closely identify with their mothers although, because they are both female, this sense of identification is stronger between a mother and daughter. When the young girl begins to separate from her mother and to develop a sense of self she therefore retains a sense of continuity with her mother, her mother's female identity being much like her own (Brannon, 2002). Boys, however, need to develop an identity that is not only separate but also completely different from that of their mother: this is a much more difficult task (Brannon, 2002). For boys, then, this process demands that they inwardly repress the feminine and outwardly reject all that is associated with the female.

Freud's theory portrays females as essentially inferior to males and unsurprisingly, therefore, has been widely critiqued. Chodorow's theory has also been questioned: Golombok and Fivush (1994), for example, note that there is little evidence that the emotional bond between mothers and daughters is different from the bond that exists between mothers and sons. That said, psychoanalytic theories do have the advantage of focusing on the importance of the unconscious and emotional aspects of young children's gender development.

Social learning theories

Some theorists have proposed that, rather than having a biological origin, gender differences develop as a result of the individual's interaction with her or his environment: that is, they are socially learnt. Social learning theory builds on classic learning theory, which defines learning as a change in behaviour brought about by the application of reinforcement and punishment. Proponents of social learning theory also maintain that children learn what it means to be male and female through the reinforcement of gender-appropriate behaviour but, in addition, they recognise the significance of observation and the imitation of same-sex role models – in particular, the same-sex parent (Golombok and Fivush, 1994). Importantly, social learning theory differs from learning theory in that it sees learning as cognitive rather than behavioural.

According to social learning theory, then, children are seen as active participants in the development of their gender identity. Even so, this process is not straightforward. Children are surrounded by many different images of males and females and many different versions of masculinity and femininity. In addition, children will find that the same behaviour can provoke entirely different responses from the adults who care for them. Through their observations, however, young children differentiate between males and females, identify which behaviours are normally associated with each sex, and recognise how others respond to these behaviours. Thus, they begin to imitate those behaviours that they recognise as being strongly connected with their own gender and which tend to provoke a positive response from others. Rather than simply modelling themselves on any one individual, therefore, children imitate the behaviour of a composite and possibly idealised female or male role model.

This is not to underestimate the role of parents in this process. That parents interact differently with their daughters and sons has been well documented by numerous research studies (see Golombok and Fivush, 1994). Research has shown, for example, that parents tend to dress girls and boys in different colours and types of clothes (which in itself can have a significant impact on children's physical development), give them different toys to play with, encourage different activities and interests, interpret their behaviour differently and respond to that behaviour in different ways. In addition, Golombok and Fivush (1994) note that boys are more likely to be discouraged from engaging in cross-gender interests and activities than girls are, although this kind of intervention peaks when the child reaches about eighteen months old (Fagot and Hagan, 1991) and thereafter decreases (Lytton and Romney, 1991) – possibly when parents are satisfied that 'appropriate' patterns of behaviour have been established.

Differential reinforcement is particularly true of fathers, who may play a particularly significant role in gender-typing their children (Weinraub et al., 1984). Of course, reinforcement may be subtle rather than overt; parents may demonstrate their approval of gender-typed toys through, for example, simply joining in with the child's play (Golumbok and Fivush, 1994).

As the young child becomes more independent, messages about gender and gender-appropriate activities will come not only from the child's family but also from a whole range of additional sources, including the packaging on toys, picture books, comics, advertisements and television programmes (see Marsh and Millard, 2000).

Children also 'police' gender-typed behaviour for themselves (Paechter, 1998); they ensure that gender boundaries are carefully delineated and that other children adhere to appropriate gender roles. It is interesting to note, again, that compliance is more rigidly enforced on boys than girls. Lloyd and Duveen (1992) point out that a girl may participate in male-typed activities without other people finding the behaviour at all odd. When boys engage in female-typed activities, however, this is not usually tolerated by peers. For example, dressing up in girls' clothes is something that boys can do only if they make a joke out of it, otherwise it is likely to draw negative comments from the other children. Thorne (1993) similarly notes that the term 'tomboy' is associated with some of the positive qualities associated with the masculine whereas the label 'sissy' suggests a failed male: 'that a boy has ventured too far into the contaminating "feminine"' (Thorne, 1993: 111).

According to social learning theory, therefore, the actions of parents, peers and the outside world have a significant impact on children's (particularly boys') behaviour. Research has shown that in the first year of life infants have learned to differentiate between males and females (Bussey and Bandura, 1999). By around two years of age most children seem to prefer activities that are seen as appropriate to their gender (Bussey and Bandura, 1999) and have developed a basic understanding of adult male and female gender roles (Weinraub et al., 1984). Smith et al. (2003) point out that by school age both boys and girls tend to select same-sex partners for play, with boys preferring outdoor play involving competition and risk taking (often in large groups) and girls preferring indoor, sedentary activities involving collaboration and sharing (often in pairs). Gender-typed behaviour seems to peak when children are around five years old and, as Paley (1984) notes, 'no amount of adult subterfuge or propaganda deflects the five-year-old's passion for segregation by sex' (1984: ix).

Social learning theory has been criticised. Some researchers have pointed out that this theory does not adequately explain why young boys tend to imitate other males when it is females who are usually their primary care takers (Stainton-Rogers and Stainton-Rogers, 2001). Beal (1994) maintains that this theory does not explain why boys and girls adopt different ways of being masculine and feminine and not necessarily those that are demonstrated by their parents. Moreover, as Beal (1994) comments, we all know children often do things for which they know they will be punished and fail to do things which promise a reward! This is especially true of boys, who are reluctant to engage in feminine behaviour even if they see another boy or adult male perform this behaviour.

Cognitive development theory

Cognitive development theory, based on the work of Lawrence Kohlberg (1966), views gender development as starting not with biology or with the social world. Rather, it is seen as part of children's cognitive development and maturity. Drawing on Piagetian theory, Kohlberg claims that rather than being gradual and continuous (as in social learning theory), children pass through three separate stages in developing a gender identity. These stages are seen to parallel children's cognitive development in other areas.

According to Kohlberg, at around two years of age, children begin to label first themselves and then others as either female or male. However, this labelling is based on external, physical characteristics such as the length of hair, type of clothes worn and so on. In the second stage, at around three to four years of age, children learn that gender is stable across time: the girl believes she will grow up to be a woman and the boy to be a man. However, at this stage children still believe that gender can change, depending on the situation. For example, if a boy puts on a dress or plays with female gender-typed toys then he may become a girl. Gender constancy – an understanding that gender is constant despite any apparent changes – is reached somewhere between five and seven years of age.

What it is important to note here is that Kohlberg maintains that it is gender constancy that acts as the trigger for gender-typed behaviour. In other words, Kohlberg asserts that it is only when children have developed a gender identity that they become interested in and influenced by gender-appropriate 'norms' and begin to imitate and perform gender-appropriate behaviours.

While it is generally agreed that children do pass through each of these stages in developing an understanding of gender, the ages attached to each of these stages have been criticised (Golombok and Fivush, 1994). Kohlberg's notion that gender constancy is the trigger for children's gender-typed behaviour has also been questioned. Studies show that children demonstrate some gender-typed behaviour even before they can consistently label by gender (see Bussey and Bandura, 1999). As Golumbok and Fivush (1994) point out, an understanding of gender begins very early in life and may influence children's behaviour even before they are consciously aware of gender as a social category. Thus, the development of gender identity may begin long before children reach the stage of gender constancy.

Gender schema theory

Kohlberg's ideas are developed and extended by the notion of gender schema: the developing content and structure of gender knowledge. As soon as young children can accurately assign a gender label they begin to form a gender schema (Martin and Little, 1990) – first of their own and then of the other sex. In many ways a schema is like a stereotype – it is a framework or set of principles which organises and guides perceptions (Hyde, 1985, in Halpern, 2000).

According to Golombok and Fivush (1994) the young child's gender schema is simple and rigid: if an individual is assigned the label 'boy' – usually on the basis of visual cues such as hairstyle and clothes (Bem, 1989) – then, it is assumed, he must also have particular (stereotypically male) interests and characteristics. Moreover, at a time when they are trying to develop a clear understanding of gender it seems that children pay more attention to information that confirms rather than challenges their schema (Golombok and Fivush, 1994) and demonstrate a particular intolerance of peers who stray from what are seen as appropriate gender norms. Such gender stereotyping appears to peak at about five years of age and begins to diminish as the child's schema becomes more complex and flexible in middle childhood (Golombok and Fivush, 1994). In terms of gender schema theory, then, children gradually develop more detailed and more complexly organised knowledge first about their own and then the other gender (Golombok and Fivush, 1994).

Gender script theory

More recently, gender schema theory has been extended to include gender script theory. This theory suggests that children's knowledge about gender may be organised as an ordered sequence of actions or events. Brannon (2002) notes that it is likely that children develop such scripts about various aspects of their day: they will develop scripts relating to getting up, getting ready for nursery, and so on. The significance of a gender script is that embedded within that script is a representation of who, stereotypically, performs a particular sequence of events: for example, who does the cooking and who mends the car. Similar to the development of a gender schema, it appears that children (particularly boys) are more accurate in both remembering sequences of behaviour that relate to their own gender than the other gender and that younger children are more rigid than older children in adhering to the gender script (Brannon, 2002).

Feminist post-structuralist theory

Feminist post-structuralist theory is complex and has been interpreted and reinterpreted in different ways. In this chapter, therefore, I will only touch on some of the most significant ideas.

Those who adopt a feminist post-structuralist perspective also reject the notion that the social world moulds and shapes the passive child. These theorists argue that social values and norms cannot be imposed on children, as the individual and the social world do not simply interact but are 'interdependent and mutually constructing' (MacNaughton, 2000: 24). In other words, as MacNaughton points out, we are 'always and inevitably social' (ibid.).

A key idea here is that of discourse. According to post-structuralist feminism we are produced by, and exist within, a complex web of different discourses: those of parents, children, students, rappers, runners, early years practitioners, and so on. As Kenway and Willis (1997) note, this multitude of discourses means that we (as subjects) are offered many ways of being – some more powerful than others. Post-structuralist feminists thus reject the idea that there is a single way of being male or female and focus instead on the differences between individual males and between individual females.

Through their interactions within these various discourses children learn what it means to be male and female. Language plays a crucial role in this learning. In making sense of their worlds young children actively make use of categories – binary pairs such as good/bad, strong/weak and pretty/ugly. One of the most significant of these binary pairs relates to gender – male/female. As with other binary pairs, however, the elements that make up this pair are not seen as of equal value (Paechter, 1998). We live in a society where males hold power, and, in most contexts, masculinity is prized above femininity. Within most discourses, therefore, 'male' is positioned in dominance over 'female'.

But while young children receive messages about their own and others' gender from many sources and processes – from a whole market place of ideas – (MacNaughton, 2000) they also learn that, within our society, there are dominant views of what is seen as 'normal' and 'desirable'. Connell (1995) notes that for boys, hegemonic masculinity (associated with the stereotypical male or 'lad') is the most prized version of masculinity and serves to marginalise or subordinate others. For most males, however, hegemonic masculinity is an 'idea' of masculinity (Davies, 1989) it is not something that is lived out in its entirety. For younger boys a commitment to this ideal of masculinity may be demonstrated through mucking or clowning around, fighting, rejection of girls and anything they see as associated with the feminine, and, for older boys, through sport – particularly playing football.

Girls may also have a gender ideal: that of emphasised femininity (Connell, 1987, 1995). Ochsner (2000) notes that 'emphasised femininity' was displayed by the five and six-year-old girls in her study through, for example, their body movements, clothes and through the discourse of 'make-up': this was a theme that emerged in the children's talk, actions, drawing and writings.

While these dominant and stereotypical ideas of masculinity and femininity can be resisted, it is extremely difficult because, as part of their learning, children tend to make an emotional investment in getting their gendered practices 'right', taking up as their own the particular 'patterns of desire' relevant to their gender and what are seen as proper ways of being male and female (Davies, 1989).

Conclusion

At first sight, it might appear that the theories that attempt to explain gender differences are often in tension with each other. In one sense this is true; certainly these explanations emerge from different theoretical perspectives and suggest difference mechanisms and processes for the development of a gender identity. However, when viewed together, these theories can provide us with complementary insights and contribute to a more complete understanding of gender development. In other words, gender development can be seen as a process of continuous interaction between biology and the environment: 'nature' and 'nurture'.

An understanding of the development of gender identity is clearly important for all those working with young children. But we need to keep in mind that, as early years practitioners, we are also gendered beings; any consideration of gender development must therefore incorporate an acknowledgement and evaluation of societal norms, and importantly, of our own gendered understandings and beliefs.

Questions and exercises

1 How accurate are gender stereotypes? Do you conform to a gender stereotype?
2 Why are boys much less likely than girls to cross gender-boundaries?
3 Should young children's gendered behaviour be challenged?
4 Undertake a number of observations of children in an early years setting. Note any examples of girls' and boys' gender-typed behaviour. In terms of each of the theories outlined above, what are the reasons for such behaviour and what would be an appropriate response?

Reading

Beal, *Boys and Girls* (1994), provides an accessible account of gender development. It adopts a developmental approach and includes chapters on children's early gender development, different theoretical perspectives (psychoanalytical theory, social learning theory and cognitive developmental theory) as well as the influence of peers, the school and the media. Brannon, *Gender: Psychological Perspectives* (2002), is a comprehensive text which focuses on a wide range of issues pertaining to gender which extend beyond those specifically related to the young child. Nevertheless, the book provides a wealth of relevant information. Golombok and Fivush, *Gender Development* (1994), is an extremely useful text which should provide students with a sound knowledge of the field. The authors adopt a developmental perspective, tracing gender development from conception to adulthood. The text provides detailed information on various theoretical perspectives as well as examining how gender relates to play and friendships, families and school. MacNaughton, *Rethinking Gender in Early Childhood Education* (2000), explores early childhood teachers' perspectives and concerns about gender issues through the adoption and exploration of feminist post-structuralist theory. This results in an interesting mix of theory and practice.

Website

Equal Opportunities Commission   www.eoc.org.uk

Part II
Perspectives on Childhood

This part of the book is concerned with perspectives on childhood and on how children grow up. If there is one message from all that has been written about childhood in the last twenty years, it is that childhood is not at all the same thing in different times and places. That childhood is in important ways different according to where in the world we are, what period of history we are in, or which social group we are considering, is not in dispute. What is sometimes disputed is whether we can use the same words 'childhood' and 'children' to apply to what we find in different times and places or among different social groups. Some authors now prefer to speak of a multiplicity of 'childhoods' rather than a single 'childhood'.

It is now generally accepted that childhood is, in a significant sense, socially constructed – that is, it is something produced in social interaction and discourse rather than being a purely natural phenomenon. That is not to say that there is not a physical and biological base to some of the important characteristics that distinguish children from adults – but the form which these differences take is a social production. In no way is this more evident than in the enormous variation between the appearance of childhood in different times, places and social settings. The following three chapters approach the issue of differences in childhood from three different angles.

In Chapter 5 Bob Sanders focuses on the study of child development and child rearing in different cultures: he explains why we should study child development from a cross-cultural perspective and explores what we mean by 'culture'; he also introduces the twin pitfalls of *ethnocentrism* and *cultural relativism* and looks at the implications of a shrinking world for cultural diversity.

In Chapter 6 Roy Lowe turns his attention to the history of childhood and considers how the pioneering work of Ariès and others has redefined the way in which we understand childhood. Key themes in this chapter are the tension between views of children as innocent or corrupt, how far childhood is socially constructed or biologically given, and how far childhood in history differs in different places. Lowe looks in particular at the significance for childhood of key social changes that took place in Britain during the sixteenth century in domestic life and in education.

In Chapter 7 Nigel Thomas reviews developments in the sociological study of childhood, and the potential of sociology for advancing our understanding in this area alongside other disciplines. He shows how theoretical models such as Corsaro's 'interpretive reproduction' help us to understand how children can be at the same time determined by their culture and society and active in making meanings and transformations. A strong message is that children do not simply exist in relation to the family or the school, but may have to be understood differently in different settings. This echoes the point made earlier that there is not one 'childhood' but a multiplicity of childhoods, and that children themselves help to define and make those childhoods what they are.

5
Childhood in Different Cultures
Bob Sanders

> ## Contents
>
> - Why study the development of children in a cross-cultural context?
> - Culture, ethnocentrism and cultural relativism
> - Globalisation
> - International conventions
> - Conclusion

This chapter asks why it is important to understand how different the experience of being a child can be, depending upon where in the world a child is growing up. It begins by considering why we should study childhood in different cultures – not only because it helps us provide better care for children, but also because we need to understand the power issues that lead to the definition of childrearing patterns in some parts of the world as 'proper' whilst those in other parts are seen as failing to live up to Western notions of what all children should aspire to. The chapter goes on to discuss the concept of culture in more depth, and introduces an issue which has long provided a challenge for anthropologists, that of finding the right balance between *ethnocentrism* and *cultural relativism*.

Why study the development of children in a cross-cultural context?

There are many reasons for studying the cross-cultural context of children's development. First, there are practical reasons. Trawick-Smith (1997) gives an illuminating example, of a relatively experienced care provider who encounters difficulties in her new post in a large urban child care centre, when trying to soothe a young child from a different cultural background. The usual things that she has tried in the past do not seem to work with this child. He asks the question: 'How is it that this lesson had escaped her until now?' (p. 577). The answer he suggests is:

> Children in her previous family child care home were of very similar cultural and socio-economic backgrounds. They were primarily sons and daughters of white middle-class professionals. Their family lives were very much like her own. Her new child care setting includes children of many different cultural and social economic backgrounds.
>
> (Trawick-Smith, 1997: 577–8)

To operate effectively with young children, the worker needs not only to learn 'what works' but 'what works for this particular child, from this particular socio-economic and cultural background'.

Another reason for studying children's development across cultures is to appreciate the value of, and the necessity for, diversity in adaptation to different environments. Darwinian principles apply not only to the physical adaptation of living organisms to their environment, but also to their social adaptation. Harkness and Super (1994) have suggested the concept of 'developmental niche', which is conceived in terms of three basic components: the physical and social settings of the child's everyday life, the culturally regulated customs of child care and child rearing, and the psychology of the care takers. It is important to remember that child-rearing patterns vary from culture to culture and represent an adaptation to different environments (physical and social). Given the dynamic nature of the adaptation, they may represent the optimal survival patterns within that particular environment. This also emphasises child development as a continuing dynamic of an individual interacting with, and adapting to, his/her environment – an 'ecological' model of child development that has gained considerable attention in recent years (Barrett, 1998; Bronfenbrenner, 1979).

A third reason is to remind us that the process of attaching values to different cultural practices, whether in relation to child rearing or in relation to other customs and practices, contains a *power* component. In this sense there is a postmodern construction of cultural differences. The 'discourse' within cross-cultural child rearing can be construed as a set of events and circumstances defined and evaluated by those with power, in relation to those without (or with less). Sanders (1999) for example looks at child abuse in a cross-cultural context, and argues that it is essential to understand the power to make definitions about *how* 'abuse' is defined. There is a danger that Westernised concepts of child abuse are taken on board in other cultures and societies where there may be far more urgent threats to children's well-being and survival, certainly dangers that are at least as pressing as the risks posed by intra-familial abuse. Related to this is the importance of beginning to understand the concepts of 'ethnocentrism' and 'cultural relativism', both of which contain inherent difficulties when taken to extremes.

A fourth reason for studying culture in relation to children is to gain a new perspective on our own society. As Rogoff and Morelli put it:

> An important function of cross-cultural research has been to allow investigators to look closely at the impact of their own belief systems ... Working with people from a quite different background can make one aware of aspects of human activity that are not noticeable until they are missing or differently arranged, as with the fish who reputedly is unaware of water until removed from it.
>
> (1993: 18)

It is helpful to experience just how different child upbringing can be, so that one's own cultural approach can be set in the context of a range of different approaches. It provides a kind of 'You are here' marker in relation to a world map of diverse cultural child rearing.

Related to this is a fifth and final reason – the value of a 'decentring' exercise, so that one's own experience of being on the receiving end of child rearing does not become the yardstick against which other methods of child rearing are compared. There are other yardsticks for looking at differing child-rearing approaches, which will be discussed below, but using one's own upbringing is a potential pitfall to be avoided. It should be remembered that differences are just that – differences. They should not be seen or interpreted as deficits.

This chapter does not describe the different patterns of child rearing throughout the world; there is simply not enough space to address in a chapter what many books have addressed. Instead, it considers some of the issues around looking at child-rearing patterns across cultures. The chapter considers the issues of culture, ethnocentrism and cultural relativism, globalisation, and the development of international conventions to promote the welfare of children. There is, however, a wealth of information available for students to consider in depth the experiences of growing up in particular societies and cultures.

Not all of this is in the form of textual material, and students are also advised to look at the portrayals of children and childhood in film. Childhood has long been a favourite theme of film makers, and they will often use children as the protagonist in films to highlight issues such as the impact of large-scale adversity (for example, war and political turbulence) on children, or use the 'uncontaminated' eyes of the child to present to the audience a particular view of society. Such films can be seen to contain profound themes in relation to the social construction of childhood, a theme of this book, but on a more immediate level, they contain depictions of everyday life involving children in other societies and cultures.

The following are all highly worthwhile films:

The Blue Kite (China)
My Life as a Dog (Sweden)
Kolya (Czech Republic)
The Bicycle Thieves (Italy)
The 400 Blows (France)
The Boy Who Stopped Talking (Netherlands and Kurdistan)
Ma Vie en Rose (France)
The Spirit of the Beehive (Spain)
Pather Pachali (India)
Whistle Down the Wind (Yorkshire, Britain)
Hope and Glory (Britain)
The Gods Must Be Crazy II (Kalahari, Africa)
Yaaba (Africa)
Los Olvidados (Mexico)

For some of these films the societal context is peripheral to the theme of the film, and we see an unselfconscious depiction of a child in a particular culture at a particular time as conveyed through the eyes of the director. In others – for example, *The Boy Who Stopped Talking, The Blue Kite, Kolya, Ma Vie en Rose, Pather Pachali, Los Olvidados* – the focus is on the interaction between a young child and some powerful influence of the society within which he or she is growing – for instance, war, political ideology, sexist ideology or Third World poverty.

Culture, ethnocentrism and cultural relativism

So how are we to understand culture? At its most basic, culture can be understood as the 'rules and tools' of a society, a definition which has the advantage of being memorable and at the same time encompassing both the tangible and non-tangible aspects of a society. An early definition of culture is in Tylor (1958): 'that complex whole which includes knowledge, belief, arts, morals, law, custom and any other capabilities and habits acquired by man as a member of society'. White (1959: 3) defines culture as comprising 'tools, implements, utensils, clothing, ornaments, customs, institutions, beliefs, rituals, games, works of art, language, etc.' (cited in Kottak, 1994: 36).

Kottak also describes a number of aspects of culture which provide us with a clearer understanding. Culture is *learned* and relies on symbols to convey meaning. Culture is imposed upon nature ('Natural lakes don't close at five, but cultural lakes do'). It is both general and specific: all people have culture, but individuals have different cultures. It is all-encompassing, in the sense that it includes everything that people do, not just the more 'aesthetic' activities. Culture is *shared*; it is learned through interaction with others in the society. Consider for example children who have not had that experience – so-called 'feral' children brought up by animals away from human society (Newton, 2002). Not only do they miss out on learning human language, and that part of thinking that is dependent upon language, but they have also not been *encultured*; they have not engaged in that process through which babies and young children acquire culture. Culture is *patterned* in the sense that aspects of it are linked, so that if one cultural institution changes, for example employment practices, other connected institutions, such as domestic roles within families, may change as a result.

On the other hand, Kottak reminds us that although people may be clear about the requirement to live within a particular culture, people don't always follow the rules, reflecting the tension between the individual and society identified by child development theorists. Likewise, the cultural practices themselves may not be conducive to the well-being, and indeed the long-term survival, of the culture; consider the heavy use of fossil fuels and other environment-threatening practices within the developed nations of the world.

Another aspect of culture described by Kottak (1994) is that it has universality, particularity and generality at the same time. By *universality* is meant those cultural aspects that distinguish human beings from other species and which are present in all people. *Particularity* refers to the uniqueness of every culture; it is like no other. *Generality*, on the other hand, refers to aspects of culture that may link some cultures together into groupings, but not all. In relation to people, there is an expression:

'Every person is, at any one time, like all other people, like some other people and like no other people.' The same could be said to apply to cultures.

Cultures do not exist in a vacuum. They live in a social world within which there is increasing contact at all different levels (see discussion of globalisation below). The early anthropologists were aware of the dangers of imposing external cultural values on the societies they were studying. They began to articulate such notions in the concepts of ethnocentrism and cultural relativism, which may be seen as opposite ends of a continuum. These are difficult concepts to fully understand, and indeed because one (ethnocentrism) has tended to become value-laden as a 'bad thing', and the other (cultural relativism) as a 'good thing', it is sometimes difficult to appreciate that extremes at either end can be unhelpful. After defining the concepts, some examples will be considered.

What is ethnocentrism?

Schultz and Lavenda (1990: 32) offer the view that ethnocentrism is 'the opinion that one's own way of life is natural or correct, indeed the only true way of being fully human'. Seymour-Smith (1986: 97) offers as a definition 'the habit or tendency to judge or interpret other cultures according to the criteria of one's own culture', and considers it to be a universal tendency. Applebaum (1996) considers that one of the greatest achievements of multiculturalism has been a better understanding of the 'indignity' of ethnocentrism, arguing that appreciating diversity and finding value in other cultures do not imply belittling one's own culture. Kottak (1994: 48) describes it as 'the tendency to view one's own culture as best and to judge the behaviour and beliefs of culturally different people by one's own standards'. In connection specifically with child-rearing practices, Barnes (1995: 102) refers to the 'ethnocentric fallacy', which holds that 'what any one culture considers to be optimal child-rearing practices (for example, firm control with clearly explained reasons embedded in a climate of warmth: the authoritarian style ...) will also be optimal for every other culture'. In the same vein Sprott (1994) observes, 'Polarized ideas about parental control dominate the Anglo Dominant Culture's value orientations, reflected in both popular and scientific literature. Parental permissiveness is cast into an opposing category of "noncontrol", imbuing it with negativism.' Prejudice against Eskimo child rearing as being over-indulgent is examined in that context and a method is offered to 'loosen' the grip of Anglo beliefs about parenting.

Kincheloe and Steinberg (1997: 3) write of 'conservative multiculturalism/ monoculturalism', which for our purposes is similar to ethnocentrism. 'Everyone ... would be better off if they could be exposed to the glories of Western Civilization ... From this colonial mind-set Africans and indigenous peoples have been categorized as lower types of human beings devoid of the rights and privileges of the higher (European) types.' However, it is not as simple as it might seem to avoid some degree of ethnocentrism. It can be tantamount to trying to achieve a completely value-free perspective, or a viewpoint that is not based on the history of one's own experiences. Barrett (1996: 20), for example, writes with reference to anthropologists:

Yet the very fact that they have been socialized into a particular culture, a culture which encompasses specific values and institutions and occupies a particular moral and political niche in the world order, inevitably suggests, without even considering the individual anthropologist's personality, that some amount of ethnocentrism must always creep in.

A particular dilemma posed by Seymour-Smith (1986) is how anthropologists should deal with ethnocentrism encountered in the populations they study. He asks: 'should "native ethnocentrism" be respected as part of the indigenous world view, or should the anthropologist combat prejudice and misinterpretation in the community by providing more information about the values and customs of other people?' (p. 97).

What is cultural relativism?

If ethnocentrism is an evil to be avoided, what then is cultural relativism? 'Cultural relativism involves understanding another culture in its own terms sympathetically enough so that the culture appears to be a coherent and meaningful design for living' (Greenwood and Stini, 1977: 182; cited in Schultz and Lavenda, 1990: 32). Kottak (1994: 48) defines it as 'the position that the values and standards of cultures differ and deserve respect. Extreme relativism argues that cultures should be judged solely by their own standards.' Seymour-Smith (1986: 63) defines it as 'An approach or theory in anthropology [in which] each culture or each society possessed its own rationality and coherence in terms of which its customs and beliefs were interpreted'. In all three of these definitions we see a pattern of internal consistency emerging as a defining characteristic. If then, indeed, a culture was to be understood in its own terms, and not according the standards and dictates of other cultures, 'what business did members of one culture have telling those of another what to do?' (Gardner and Lewis, 1996: 28).

But as with ethnocentrism, there are dilemmas. Seymour-Smith (1986: 64) notes, 'One of the major problems in the concept of cultural relativism when held dogmatically is that it leaves the anthropologist without a theoretical basis for comparative generalizations regarding human societies or cultures.' Korbin (1981), in her anthropological examination of child abuse, notes that 'a stance of extreme cultural relativism, in which all judgments of humane treatment of children are suspended in the name of cultural rights, may be used to justify a lesser standard of care for some children'. Barrett (1996: 21) also addresses the issue of abusive cultural practices:

The time-honoured way in which anthropologists have attempted to avoid ethnocentrism is relativism. It has generally been assumed that there are no good or bad cultures or cultural practices. This approach carries with it the danger of slipping into the more radical position of amoral relativism, in which there are no standards whatever. In other words, under the guise of culture, anything goes, because moral judgment is ruled out. This seems to be one of those problems incapable of rational solution. If we criticize someone else's cultural practice, such as clitoridectomy (female circumcision), we would seem to be guilty of ethnocentrism; but if we fail to do so, where do we draw the line? The obvious way around this dilemma is to articulate a set of universal values, but that is easier said than done.

How then is one to approach the issue of cultural practices, particularly as they apply to children, which might be acceptable within the context of one culture but unacceptable when judged by another? At a time when there was much less contact between different cultures, when that contact was limited to anthropologists from Westernised developed nations visiting so-called 'primitive' societies, the issue might have been less significant than it perhaps is today when most nations now have majority and minority ethnic groups, and many countries have a significant number of different cultural groups establishing communities within national borders. These globalising trends place different cultures in contact with each other much more than previously, and this trend is likely to continue. As I have noted elsewhere:

> it would be an oversimplification to say that ethnocentrism is an unmitigated evil, and that cultural relativism is an unequivocal good. One simply has to look at the extremes of both positions to realise that a balance needs to be struck; one which does not go too far towards one or other end of the spectrum. The dangers of an ethnocentric perspective are relatively clear. It is a manifestation of the exercise of power imbalances between different cultures and societies. With ethnocentrism one has cultural hegemony; however, with cultural relativism one lacks a foundation from which to censure female circumcision, the internment of Jewish children (and adults) in concentration camps, the historical practice of foot-binding in China, and ultimately, the practice of child sacrifice as practised in some societies in former times. At its most extreme, cultural relativism would imply the acceptance of such practices on the basis of being only comprehensible within the culture in which they are/were practised, and not susceptible to external judgement.
>
> (Sanders, 1999: 27–8)

Are there, as suggested by Barrett (1996), universal standards which one can apply? One may perhaps consider the UN Convention on the Rights of the Child as such a set of universal standards. However, as noted by Hodgkin (1994), implementation of the convention can produce difficulties when violations of the rights of children are justified on the basis of cultural practice.

Globalisation

What is globalisation? According to Tomlinson (1999: 2) it is 'the rapidly developing and ever-densening network of interconnections and interdependencies that characterize modern social life'. McGrew (in Hall, 1992) describes it as 'those processes, operating on a global scale, which cut across national boundaries, integrating and connecting communities and organizations in new space–time combinations, making the world in reality and in experience more interconnected'. In both of these cases, it could be argued that the writers, by emphasising the intercommunication aspect, are describing the causes of globalisation rather than the consequences, and as such only focusing on a part of the definition. Pugh (1997) describes it as a 'process in a world in which time and space have become compressed because of the operation of modern transport, communications and the increasing internationalisation of economic activity. Thus, actions in one part of the globe have consequences elsewhere' (p. 101, cited in Pugh and Gould, 1999).

Among these other usages, the concept reflects the increasing trend of cross-influence between different cultures on a world level. It also reflects power differentials within that process of reciprocal influence, which mean that the traffic is predominantly one-way. Despite the proliferation of exotic restaurants within Western societies (very frequently beginning with previously colonised nations – for example British-Indian, French-Vietnamese, Dutch-Indonesian), there is arguably more influence of Westernised, developed and industrialised countries on non-Westernised, non-developed and non-industrialised countries than the other way round. In large part this is because of the desire for overseas markets on the part of multinational companies. Hirst and Thompson (1996: 1) observe:

> It is widely asserted that we live in an era in which the greater part of social life is determined by global processes, in which national cultures, national economies and national borders are dissolving. Central to this perception is the notion of a rapid and recent process of economic globalisation.

With others being more influenced by us and vice versa, one aspect of concern about globalisation is the trend from a planet of diverse societies and cultures towards a planetary cultural homogeneity. It is possible, however, to overstate this. For example, Hall (1992) provides a number of reasons why the concept of cultural homogeneity is 'too simplistic, exaggerated and one-sided' (p. 304). Reasons include the continuing fascination with difference, and the fact that this kind of globalisation is 'unevenly distributed around the world', affecting more so countries in the Western world (in contrast perhaps to what I have argued above). Further, although there is a fascination with difference, our current fascination may be rooted not only in the exotic, but also in the disappearing. In like manner, one might be interested in a Komodo dragon (or indeed any endangered species) not only because one has never encountered it before, but also equally because if the environment continues to change in the way it has, we may be faced with never seeing one in the future.

A perhaps more powerful argument against the ultimate threat of cultural homogeneity emerges when we consider the reasons why we have different cultures. From a Darwinian perspective, it could be argued that one reason human societies differ from each other in the first place is that the world consists of tropical rain forests, vast plains, mountainous areas, deserts, areas of permafrost, and so forth. Culture is perhaps largely a reflection that human species have been compelled to adapt to different environments, thereby reflecting a diversity at least as wide-ranging as the ecological niches within which people are born, grow, live and die. The argument against the threat of eventual cultural homogeneity therefore would be that as long as the world has a variety of different environments within which people can and do survive, and as long as people continue to derive an advantage from living in social groupings rather than in isolation, there will continue to be a wide range of variations in cultures. However, whilst this may reassure us about the threat of the eventual demise of all cultures but one, it does not necessarily reassure us about variations in the levels of cultural diversity around the world.

Let us now consider some further aspects of this concept. It would not be possible to have such a worldwide trade in culture without the incredibly rapid technological advances of the twentieth century. Transport and communication developments in particular have effectively made a reality of the phrase 'It's a small world' – and becoming smaller all the time. Whereas at the beginning of the century it would have taken a month to cross the Atlantic, now one can do it in a matter of hours. Communication technology over the last two centuries has gone from telegraph systems (1837) to transatlantic cables (1858) to the invention (1876) and subsequent development of the telephone, the development of wireless radio (1895), and the subsequent development of public broadcast radio, the development and marketing (1936–8) of televisions, the large-scale distribution of personal computers and the development of the internet during the 1990s. During the same time cars have revolutionised the ability of people to move around within and between countries, and air travel, once the prerogative of the affluent elite, has developed into a widespread necessity of life, enabling people to live and work farther and farther afield from the place where they may have originated.

These technological advances have also contributed to another facet of globalisation, which has been highlighted through 'McDonaldization' and 'Coca Colaization' metaphors: 'Wherever you go in the world you will find a McDonald's.' Apart from wonder at the successful marketing of a product that is less than forty years old, and aside from the astounding economic success of the product, there are other cultural implications. First, it is not only bringing an American product, but an American ideology (entrepreneurial enterprise) to many other countries. As noted by Fukuyama (1991, cited in Pugh and Gould, 1999), 'For some writers, globalisation marks the triumphal spread of the capitalist free market influence over the world's economic and political systems.' Nothing exports capitalism nearly so effectively as the fast-food delivery of a Big Mac. The product is both standardised and adapted to the local customs: in Spain one can get shrimp meals at McDonald's. However, with the dominance of McDonald's in the ecosystem of localised fast-food markets, one is tempted to speculate on the disappearance (or non-appearance), through competition, of more locally and culturally derived forms of food that might have been able to fill the particular niche for fast foods. The success of McDonald's draws on the love-hate relationship with the United States throughout the world. Whilst people may have deplored the engineered involvement of the United States in numerous overseas conflicts, protested outside American embassies over a range of political activities, etc., there has ever been a deep fascination with American cultural symbols, and companies in the United States have been quick to exploit these. Levi and Wrangler Jeans, Hollywood icons such as James Dean, Marilyn Monroe, Humphrey Bogart, entertainers such as Elvis Presley, Chuck Berry, Buddy Holly are all 'products' that have been deliberately marketed overseas and have been voraciously devoured by consumers of various nationalities, eager to import American culture, if not American imperialism, into their part of the world.

Let us now briefly consider the role of language in globalisation. The biblical story of the Tower of Babel tells of the origin of different languages; it was God's punishment for the arrogance of mankind, that they should contemplate building a tower that would reach to heaven. To punish them he made them all speak in different tongues, and with that, the ability, and necessity, to collaborate in the building of the tower was lost and the tower was abandoned. The tale highlights the necessity to be able to communicate, and the ability to sell products and services overseas has historically required the ability to communicate in local languages. However, English had become the 'lingua franca' of the world by the end of the twentieth century. In Wales a Welsh-language social work training pack was given the title *They All Speak English Anyway* (Davies, 1994), a sentiment that can be said to apply more and more to the rest of the world. Europe provides a very interesting illustration of the ethnocentric orientation of the English language. In virtually every Western European country except the United Kingdom, children are taught a second and sometimes a third language at an age when they are most receptive – in primary school, usually starting around age seven. By the time European children are eight or nine they are frequently proficient in English. In the United Kingdom other European languages are not taught until children enter secondary school (although in Wales children learn Welsh in primary school). In effect, children of other countries are expected to learn English, but English-speaking countries make little effort to teach their children European languages. Nor is there a likelihood of change; rather it is likely that British participation in European affairs will continue to rest on the assumption that others will learn English.

Elsewhere (Sanders, 1999) I have given examples of models of child protection being influenced across national boundaries, in ways that reflect linguistic similarities (United States and United Kingdom; Belgium, Netherlands and France). If the models adopted to address social problems are indeed, as suggested, derived predominantly from interaction with countries speaking the same language, and if English appears to be headed towards being the Esperanto dream of a language spoken around the world, regardless of what other language is spoken, then it would seem to follow that there is a likelihood, and I would argue a danger, that the future holds the prospect of more and more solutions to social problems being derived from the English-speaking nations.

International conventions

International conventions such as the UN Convention on the Rights of the Child also have implications for the consideration of childhood in different cultures. The UN convention, now ratified by all countries in the world except Somalia and the United States, sets minimum standards against which the treatment of children in different countries can be judged. Provisions such as the right to life, to a name and a nationality, the prevention of kidnapping and abduction, the right to free primary education, the prohibition of torture, cruelty, capital punishment or life imprisonment for children, and protection from the effects of war, appear to relate to issues that are not of pressing concern within the United Kingdom. However, it would be a mistake to be complacent or regard the convention simply as a tool to promote minimum standards in non-Western countries. The United Kingdom is a long way from adequately addressing children's right to express views on matters concerning them. It has a very poor track record when it comes to providing protection for refugee children; the United Kingdom was singled out in a European report as providing poor services in this respect (The *Guardian*, 3 April 2001). Even the articles requiring countries to provide support to both parents to bring up a child, and to promote a child's right to an adequate standard of living, could be said to have been dramatically undermined during the last twenty years in the United Kingdom as more and more British children found themselves growing up in impoverished households.

Likewise, if we look at the European Convention of Human Rights, we see that there are significant differences within Europe in the extent to which children are treated as citizens in their own right (for instance, by countries banning corporal punishment), or the extent to which the state is seen as having a role in the care of children (for instance, by countries providing pre-school programmes for young children). In these ways the interpretation of international standards is coloured by each country's own cultural values.

The final point to be mindful of when looking at provision across countries is whether rich and powerful countries are using their power and economic influence to coerce others to adopt their standards. In other words, the process of implementing international conventions also brings us back to the tension we identified earlier, between ethnocentrism and cultural relativism.

Conclusion

This chapter has focused on themes arising from a better understanding of children's development that students will derive from considering it in a cross-cultural context. It has not attempted to describe the range of different child-rearing approaches in different cultures, as that would be too extensive to be covered in a single chapter, but the student is referred to other sources that can begin to help the student appreciate how different the experience of rearing children can be in a global context.

Rather, the focus in this chapter has been to provide a rationale for studying child rearing in different cultures, an examination of issues of power in defining 'normality' in child development (with particular reference to discourses concerning ethnocentrism and cultural relativism), a discussion of globalisation, and a brief reference to international conventions affecting the welfare of children.

Questions and exercises

1 What are the most important reasons for studying the cross-cultural context of children's development?
2 How can we find out about cultural differences in child rearing?
3 What do we mean when we talk about culture?
4 What is 'ethnocentrism' and what is wrong with it?
5 What is 'cultural relativism' and what are the problems with it?
6 What is 'globalisation' and what are its implications for child rearing and child development?
7 What is the impact of international conventions on the upbringing of children? Can such conventions help us to overcome the problems we have identified with 'ethnocentrism' and 'cultural relativism'?

Reading

Bronfenbrenner, *The Ecology of Human Development* (1979), is indispensable as an introduction to thinking about global differences in children's upbringing. Trawick-Smith, *Early Childhood Development* (1997), is a useful starting point for understanding what sort of differences there are, and provides a particularly good critique of traditional child development theories, when examined from a multicultural perspective. Konner, *Childhood: a Multicultural View* (1991), is an excellent source (with a range of interesting illustrations), highlighting cross-cultural variations in specific aspects of child rearing. Likewise, Keats, *Culture and the Child* (1997), focuses on specific aspects of different societies. Tomlinson, *Globalization and Culture* (1999), is helpful on the issue of globalisation and its implications for culture. Harwood, Miller and Lucca Irizarry, *Culture and Attachment* (1995), and Kağitçibaşi, *Family and Human Development across Cultures* (1996), both reflect powerfully on precisely what difference culture makes in the way children develop, and finally Valsiner, *Culture and Human Development* (2000), describes the relatively new field of cultural developmental psychology and provides interesting cultural contexts of various aspects of children's lives and development.

6
Childhood through the Ages
Roy Lowe

Contents

- Origins
- Underlying issues
- A framework for understanding the history of childhood
- Conclusion

This chapter examines the ways in which childhood has been studied by historians. It looks at the origins of the historical study of childhood, picks out some of the issues which have been seen as important and then goes on to give one account of the changing nature of childhood in the period since the Middle Ages.

Origins

Two books can be identified as starting points for the study of childhood in history. First and most significantly, Philippe Ariès's *Centuries of Childhood* was initially published in French in 1960 and was translated into English in 1962. Its appearance marked the beginning of the systematic study of the history of childhood.

It is perhaps hardly surprising that this sub-discipline should have originated in France. After the Second World War the *Annales* school of history, which was extremely popular in France, stressed the need for new approaches to the study of society by historians. Ariès was a leading protagonist of this school and sought to open up a whole new field of enquiry by turning his attention to the history of childhood.

In the book, which remains influential today, he came up with several hypotheses. First, he stressed the extent to which there was little precision during the medieval period in respect of counting things such as years of age. One result of this was that the idea of childhood remained ill defined, if recognised at all, and was not in any sense quantified with reference to any particular age or stages of development. He found numerous examples of the brutal treatment of children and of their being introduced to an adult world at a very early age through both sexual play and exploitation and as a commodity within the labour market. Ariès went on to argue that during the early modern period, most probably the seventeenth century, although most social groups continued to be very imprecise in their use of the term 'child', it became possible to discern a new usage, first among the middle classes, by which 'childhood' began to assume some of its modern meanings. Ariès argued that somewhere between the thirteenth century and modern times 'childhood' was discovered. Whereas during the Middle Ages children were depicted and seen as being small adults, by the eighteenth century there was a general understanding that 'childhood' meant a stage of life which was widely recognised in a number of ways. This involved the coming of children's clothing, distinct from that of adults, an end to their being depicted as small adults in books and illustrations, as well as the appearance and wider recognition of children's games and pastimes and a growing sense of the innocence of childhood.

There were several reasons why Ariès's arguments proved persuasive and are still taken seriously. First, as he pointed out, it was the common lot of humankind that a significant proportion of infants did not survive to adulthood. In many societies more than a half the child population was lost through one cause or another. He suggested that the likelihood of losing children made it very difficult for parents in earlier times to draw too close to their children or to sentimentalise them lest they suffer emotional torment at their likely loss. Although this argument is conjectural, it carries some weight for earlier historical periods.

It should be remembered too that in most societies children were needed as part of the work force to sustain the economy. In this context it would have been an inappropriate luxury to spend too much dwelling on the particular needs of childhood. Only with the coming of affluence and the appearance of a more comfortable middle class did it become possible to postpone the entry of some children to the labour market, thus allowing a growing number of parents to consider their offspring as 'children' in the modern sense. In brief, Ariès located the appearance of childhood within the sixteenth and seventeenth centuries.

Ariès's work sparked off an interest in the history of childhood among historians and a growing number of authors began to focus on the phenomenon. In 1974 an American scholar, Lloyd deMause, brought together a collection of essays under the title *The History of Childhood*. Here, in a lengthy introductory chapter on the evolution of childhood, DeMause developed his 'psychogenic theory of childhood' and set about turning Ariès's ideas on their head by suggesting that childhood, in particular the way in which children were treated by adults, was central to any understanding of the human past. He argued that the habits and practices which were imposed on children throughout history offered the only meaningful explanation of how they subsequently performed as adults. Therefore, DeMause argued, it was not possible to understand human history without first understanding how the main protagonists had been reared, the kind of childhood they had experienced. He extended this argument to suggest that the maltreatment of children was a constant factor in human history and explained much of the social involvement of adults at a later stage in their lives.

DeMause remains active to the present day and continues to disseminate his ideas. He is actively involved in debates in a website exchange on the history of childhood and is still seeking, almost thirty years after his initial pronouncements, to publicise the importance of understanding child psychology in history. His ideas have been enormously influential and certainly have had the effect of 'psychologising' the study of childhood.

Underlying issues

As the study of childhood developed during the years that followed a number of underlying issues quickly became evident. It is important for anyone approaching the history of childhood to have some awareness of these issues and to have thought through their own beliefs in respect of each of them.

First, running through European history there is a tension between two opposed views of childhood which appear to contradict each other. On the one hand, there is a vast literature which suggests that the child is at birth intrinsically evil, or at least in need of improvement, and that it is the duty of parents and adults to school the child, to get rid of unfortunate characteristics and behaviours and, in brief, to redeem it so that it can become an effective adult. This view is, of course, underpinned by much Christian literature which stresses the need for redemption and the extent to which humankind is innately evil. The idea that humankind is innately wicked is an enduring and pervasive one and it has underpinned much of the thinking about childhood during the last two millennia.

Set against this, quite contradictorily, is the view which also is frequently found in European literature that children are born innocent but are corrupted by their growing experience of and acquaintance with the adult world. Ironically, this thread can also be discerned within the Christian church. For example, during the Middle Ages, it was usual at religious ceremonies to dress children in white as a symbol of their innocence.

During the eighteenth and nineteenth centuries in particular a school of literature appeared which stressed the innocence of the child. Jean Jacques Rousseau's novel *Emile* (1762) took this view, as did Wordsworth, who subscribed to the Neoplatonist view that it was possible to look back to an age of innocence during which various insights into the nature of being were possible which were denied the corrupted adult:

> There was a time when meadow, grove, and stream,
> The earth, and every common sight,
> To me did seem
> Apparelled in celestial light,
> The glory and the freshness of a dream.
> It is not now as it hath been of yore; –
> Turn wheresoe'er I may,
> By night or day,
> The things which I have seen I now can see no more.

In his 'Ode on intimations of immortality from recollections of early childhood', from which these lines are taken, Wordsworth reflected on the loss of childish innocence and the loss of insight and understanding that went with it. These two views of childhood appear to be mutually contradictory, and yet they have stood against each other for the best part of two millennia.

A second underlying issue is the question of the extent to which childhood has been socially constructed in history or whether it is a stage of life which all human beings necessarily pass through. On the one hand, much recent child psychology, such as the work of Piaget, would suggest that there are stages of development through which all children must pass on their journey to adulthood. Against this is the consideration that in many contexts childhood has necessarily been abbreviated and curtailed, allowing no possibility of a childhood in the form that we understand it. In these historical contexts, does it make sense to talk of childhood as though it were comparable, for the vast majority of children, with the experiences undergone by a modern-day child? Equally, there is in recent times, an idealisation of childhood in books, films and on television which suggest to any thinking observer that childhood may be being redefined as well as described by these treatments. The possibility of the social construction of childhood has to be to the fore in the thinking of any historian of childhood.

A third issue is the question of what adult characteristics are socially constructed during childhood. Central to this is the question of gender. Are the differences and distinctions in male and female adult behaviour and the differing roles ascribed to them within society the result of differing hormones and a differing genetic endowment or are they the result of the social conditioning which takes place during the early years? What other adult characteristics and attitudes can be shown to be, to some extent at least, moulded during childhood? Is personality ultimately genetic or socially conditioned? These are all questions which can be illuminated by the study of the emergence of childhood as a historical phenomenon.

Fourth, it is important to bear in mind the extent to which childhood may differ and may have differed in history in differing locations. There are today very clear contrasts between the developed world, the developing world and the Third World in respect of experiences which children undergo. It is likely that this has always been the case. Such variations in experience exist both across continents and countries and within individual nations. In Britain, for example, during the period of industrialisation, childhood meant different things in differing locations, depending upon particular local patterns of industrialisation. These contrasts persist to the present time and some would say have always been there. It is important for anyone approaching the history of childhood to bear this consideration in mind and to have a sense of the limits which have to be placed on any generalisation. This also gives rise to the possibility of fascinating local studies which unearth local experiences of childhood which have been lost or are as yet unknown to historians.

A framework for understanding the history of childhood

As the study of the history of childhood has become more extensive during the past thirty years, it has become possible to distinguish a number of key elements in the historical development of childhood which, together, constitute a framework which helps us to conceptualise childhood over the past four or five centuries. First, a number of detailed studies have thrown far greater light than ever before on the relative ill treatment of children across Europe during the medieval period (Shahar, 1990; Schultz, 1995). This work has led us to a greater realisation of the significance for childhood of key social changes that took place in Britain during the sixteenth century. The growth of the wool trade and the swift growth of a number of towns in response meant that a growing number of merchants and yeoman farmers could afford, for the first time, to build larger homes than had been usual throughout the Middle Ages. These buildings often incorporated a first floor to enable separate sleeping arrangements for parents and children. This kind of domestic arrangement was unknown before and was critical for the development of the family and of childhood since it instituted in a growing number of homes for the first time a con-cept of privacy. It also made it easier for the children to be separately identified and treated differently in a number of respects within the home. This subtle but very significant shift tied in with other changes that were going on in society. A restruc-turing of apprenticeship and a complete restructuring of the education system meant that the preparation for work became far more codified and far better organ-ised during the sixteenth century than had ever been the case before. Society was beginning to put in place the mechanisms for the codification and organisation of childhood. It is no coincidence that in 1545 Thomas Phayre wrote the first English book on paediatrics, *The Regiment of Life*. Also, at this time, the Reformation meant not only the redirection of the religious life of Northern Europe but also that education itself became far more secular than had previously been the case. This too had a massive impact upon the lot of many children. Another key development at the end of the century was the 1598 Poor Relief Act, which, for the first time, made poor children the responsibility of the parish. The parochial overseers of the poor became for the next three centuries those who took responsibility for the welfare of children whenever parenting failed or was absent. This was to determine for ever the way in which children were perceived and treated in Britain.

Nonetheless, although there was a prospect of some kind of schooling for a minor-ity of the luckier ones, for the vast majority of children life remained hard. In many rural areas over the next two centuries gang systems of agricultural labour developed, with women and children being used for weeding, stone picking, root gathering and other menial tasks. In other parts of Britain local trades such as lace making, hosiery, straw plaiting, glove making and shoe making each generated a demand for unskilled child labour. Some industries, such as the making of straw hats in Bedfordshire and other parts of the Home Counties, were almost entirely dependent upon child labour. The textile industries placed particular demands on children, whether it was woollen manufacture in West Yorkshire, East Anglia or the West Country or lace manufacture in some Midland towns. The well established tradition of out-working by which much of the manufacturing took place small-scale in the homes of weavers and spinners led to a situation in which children were notoriously exploited for their nimble fingers and their availability. By the end of the eighteenth century there was hardly any corner of Britain in which children were not being exploited on a vast scale for one form or other of cheap labour (Horn, 1994).

Set against this, the responsibility of the parish to care for orphaned and penuri-ous children resulted in a significant network of charity schools. From 1699 these were co-ordinated and founded by the Society for Promotion of Christian

Knowledge, with a welter of new foundations in England down to 1740. By the mid-eighteenth century there was hardly any middle-sized town in England which did not have its 'blue coat' or charity school, the blue uniforms being a token of the poverty of the children who were being cared for. Without exception the supporters of these schools stressed the need for a basic education to be provided. Isaac Watts wrote in 1724:

> there are none of these poor who are, or ought to be, bred up to such an accomplished skill in writing and accounts as to be qualified for superior posts: except here and there a single lad whose bright genius and constant application and industry have outrun all his fellows.

The tradition that the education of the poor should not extend beyond the 'three Rs' and the catechism was well established in these charity schools during the eighteenth century.

If the lot of the poor child was hard during the early modern period, the coming of industrialisation served only to make it worse. Industrialisation, involving the appearance of factories and a rapid increase in population and in the size of towns and cities, generated a situation which was too tempting for unscrupulous employers to resist. In large towns such as London clergymen and parish officers realised they had a new opportunity to solve the problem of child pauperism. Equally, factory owners saw the possibility of gaining a new and remarkably cheap labour force from the towns. The consequence was that literally thousands of young orphaned children were taken long distances from their homes and confined in near prison conditions for long hours of industrial labour. At the start of the nineteenth century this traffic in children had passed its peak, but still during the first decade of the century over 2,000 pauper apprentices were sent from London to work in a variety of textile mills, three-quarters of them going into the cotton industry. Most of these children were below the age of eleven (Horn, 1994: 18–34). Parish children were a key source of labour, enabling the swift expansion of industrialisation between 1750 and 1850. Many of the tasks they did were dangerous and the conditions in which they lived, usually in apprentice houses, were overcrowded and unhealthy. Survival rates were dreadful and those that did make it to adulthood were often stunted, puny and unhealthy. Conditions in other industries such as mining were hardly any better and in some cases worse.

All of this led to a relatively new construction during the nineteenth century: the child as the object of pity or of philanthropy. A growing number of reformers such as Peel and Wilberforce, alarmed at the conditions in which children were working in the factories, set about the establishment of legislation which would control such practices. The outcome was, by the end of the century, a plethora of Acts of Parliament which made it increasingly difficult for unscrupulous employers to exploit children as had been the case 100 years before. This was the first serious engagement of the state in its modern form with children. By controlling the conditions of their employment and seeking to set minimum standards, the state, perhaps unwittingly, set itself up as the ultimate arbiter of the well-being of children. The other leg of this nineteenth-century reform movement was the drive to establish systems of popular education which would be increasingly accessible to all and ultimately universal. By 1870 provisions were in place for every child in England

and Wales to be served by elementary schools and by 1891 schooling was *de facto* compulsory for all except the children of itinerant workers such as bargees and travelling showmen (Stephens, 1998).

But for much of the century the emphasis was on a schooling that was basic and confined in reality to reading, writing, arithmetic and the catechism. As Andrew Bell, one of the founders of the monitorial system of elementary education, observed in his book *The Madras School* in 1808:

> it is not proposed that the children of the poor be educated in an expensive manner or be taught to write or cypher. Utopian schemes for the universal diffusion of general knowledge would soon realise the fable of the belly and the other members of the body and confound that distinction of ranks and classes of society on which the general welfare hinges ... There is a risk of elevating by an indiscriminate education, the minds of those doomed to the drudgery of daily labour above their conditions and thereby rendering them discontented and unhappy in their lot.

Thus, in practice, the coming of popular education seems to have been driven as much by determination to impose some kind of social control as by any spirit of charity. It is surely no coincidence that regular hours, submission to the demands of the bell, and the ready acceptance of a system of rewards and punishment (all characteristics of the industrial system) were central elements in what was offered to children through elementary schools throughout the nineteenth century. Only towards the end of the century, with a series of extensions to the revised code which had been introduced in 1862, was there a prospect of a fuller education for the ordinary child.

It is impossible to overstate the significance of universal schooling for under-standings of childhood. First, schooling enabled childhood to be perceived as a set of stages through which young people progressed naturally: nursery, infant, junior and secondary. The processes of transition defined and identified what was thought to be taking place. Further, schooling in this way involved a standardisation of child-hood which otherwise would not have happened. It became increasingly easy for commentators, policy makers and critics to identify templates of childhood to which 'template' solutions could be applied. One spin-off from this was the identi-fication of the 'normal'. In 1956, C.W. Valentine wrote a book entitled *The Normal Child* reflecting these perceptions.

Also, schooling enabled a heightening and codification of the gendering of child-hood. Boys and girls were separated from an early age in classrooms, into different schools and into differing curricula routes. All this made it far easier to fashion 'little women' and 'little men' through the education system. An extreme version of this was the code of masculinity which was perpetuated in the boys' preparatory schools and public schools (Heward, 1988). These schools developed during the Victorian period and have persisted. They provide an elite education for a privileged few (roughly 7 per cent of the population) who, among other things, acquire dis-tinct perceptions of their gender roles through their schooling. Conversely, schools for girls, which grew greatly in number at the start of the twentieth century, marketed their own versions of 'domesticity' and 'femininity' in order to prove attractive to fee-paying parents (Dyhouse, 1989). Thus, schooling meant gendering.

The processes that were set in train with the coming of industrialisation appear, in retrospect, to be almost irreversible.

A third concomitant of universal schooling was the discovery of child poverty towards the end of the nineteenth century. The success of school attendance officers appointed by the School Boards after 1870 in getting the vast majority of the child population into school meant that teachers were brought face to face with the spectre of urban poverty. It was an issue that was seized on by the nascent socialist movement. Two investigators, Charles Booth, a Liverpool shipowner, and Seebohm Rowntree, a chocolate manufacturer, independently investigated the extent of poverty in London and York. Their findings, which were published at the turn of the twentieth century, were shattering in their impact. In both cities they found that about one-third of the population were living below the poverty line but, equally significantly in our context, that it was possible to identify cycles of poverty during one individual's lifetime. Those families most likely to fall into poverty were those with a large number of children. Hence the number of children living in poverty at the beginning of the twentieth century was disproportionately higher than the overall percentage of people in poverty. These findings coincided with the realisation of the ill health of the urban proletariat during the recruiting campaign for the Boer War. Even worse, it became evident that child poverty correlated with ill health. Children in poverty were far more likely to be suffering from tuberculosis, to die of scarlet fever or to suffer dental caries. All this became evident as a direct result of universal schooling and of politically inspired, privately funded research projects (Englander and O'Day, 1995).

The outcome was a permanently changed view of the ways in which the state should deal with the child. At the beginning of the twentieth century the medical inspection of schoolchildren was introduced. At the same time, a school meal programme was allowed by Parliament. Also, it became clear that the process of educating children was to involve far more than instruction in future. A number of welfare initiatives were intended to alleviate the lot of poor and unhealthy urban children. The first of these was the Open Air School movement, which took off during the Edwardian period and resulted, by the time of the First World War, in most large cities having Open Air Recovery Schools (usually for tubercular children) in rural locations away from the urban centres.

One other significant result of the discovery of child poverty was the appearance of a child study movement in the late nineteenth century. In 1895 James Sully produced a book entitled *Studies in Childhood*. This appeared at exactly the moment that organisations were being set up in both England and America to study children and the child's mind. Between 1889 and 1906 the medical profession organised five large-scale inquiries into the condition of children in London alone. In 1894 the Child Study Association was set up. Two years later, the more medically oriented Childhood Society was established. This immediately launched a journal, *The Paidologist*. During the Edwardian period these two organisations merged and in 1907 they formed the Child Study Society (Hendrick, 1994). In these initiatives we can see the origins of child psychology in modern Britain. Many of the early leaders in the child psychology movement were members of one or other of these organisations.

However, in Britain the child study movement took a particular slant as a result of the foundation of the Eugenics Society, a London-based organisation committed to racial improvement. Founded by Charles Galton at the turn of the century, this quickly became the basis of an international movement. The Galton Laboratory was established in 1905 at University College London, where Galton's collaborator, Karl Pearson, set about experimental work on the human mind. Several of the pioneers of child psychology were attracted to the eugenics movement, perhaps most notably Cyril Burt. Within a few years Burt and his associates, working from within the Eugenics Society, had shifted child psychology in Britain to a position where it was very firmly focused on intelligence testing and on the separation and streaming of children rather than on the identification of a whole range of psychological needs (Hearnshaw, 1979). Britain became one of the 'stamping grounds' for early intelligence tests and over a forty-year period before the Second World War most local education authorities were beginning to use intelligence tests to diagnose children for entry to schools of one type or another (Wooldridge, 1994). It is possible, to greater or lesser degree, to show that each of these initiatives stemmed in large part from the coming of universal schooling.

Meanwhile, other agencies were appearing which would work to stereotype and to idealise childhood. The popular press emerged in its modern form in the years following the foundation of the *Daily Mail* in 1896 and universal schooling, leading to universal literacy, resulted in a mass reading public which enabled a vast growth in book publishing at the dawn of the twentieth century. Books were written about children and for them (Turner, 1976). A number of authors from the mid-Victorian period onwards established their reputation on writing at least some of their major works for children: G.A. Henty, Rudyard Kipling, Jack London, C.M. Ballantyne, Robert Louis Stevenson, Anna Sewell, to name but a few. They conjured a world in which children were brave, adventurous, loyal and patriotic. They provided the stereotypes which enabled children to have an image of what they were meant to be and which at the same time offered the adult world a stereotype of childhood which it found acceptable and worthwhile. This stylisation of childhood has continued apace during the intervening 100 years. New agencies such as radio, television, popular film and, more recently, the record, tape and CD have all offered images of childhood which are widely admired and extremely influential. In brief, during the period since the 1880s agencies have appeared which are deeply influential in determining society's view of childhood. If schooling began the process of standardisation and stereotyping, the media have extended and confirmed it.

More recently, the range of areas in which the state has felt it appropriate to intervene towards children has expanded dramatically. Perhaps the first signals of this were apparent when schemes to send orphaned Dr Barnardo's children to Australia and Canada became popular during the inter-war years (Bean and Melville, 1990). This preparedness to arbitrarily move large numbers of children in what was perceived to be their own interest was followed by the evacuation scheme introduced in 1939 to save urban children from the perils of a German bombing campaign. This scheme proved largely ineffective, since thousands of children and their parents simply returned to their own homes rather than sit the war out in strange rural locations, but it was evidence of the preparedness of the state to take far wider responsibility for the well-being of children. Since then the expansion of the work of Juvenile Courts, the 'statementing' of children with emotional and behavioural difficulties in schools, the accretions to the powers of the Youth Service and the introduction of Young Offender schemes are all clear tokens of the preparedness of the state to take responsibility for more or less every aspect of the life of the child (Pilcher and Wagg, 1996).

Conclusion

Thus, in brief, what emerges from this sketch of key developments in the history of childhood over the last 200 years is that childhood does appear to have changed irreversibly, that the powers of society to govern and control childhood have been greatly enhanced, and in the process childhood itself seems to have become irreversibly stereotyped. All this has generated a vast research literature, some of which is hinted at in the references.

This phenomenon of the emergence of childhood as a historical phenomenon also raises questions for anyone embarking on a study of the early years. Whatever aspect of childhood is being examined, it is always important to bear in mind the historical context within which we work today and the historical influences which have come to bear on childhood. These are still working themselves out in adult perceptions of children and in the self-images that children acquire as they grow up. The study of the history of childhood is necessarily central to any proper understanding of what it means to be a child at the beginning of the twenty-first century.

Questions and exercises

1   Explore the books in the reading list which deal with the history of childhood to find out how far you agree with the ideas in this chapter. Be ready to incorporate your growing knowledge of the history of childhood into your other work on this course.
2   Consider how far and in what ways childhood as you know it today has been conditioned by this historical legacy.

Reading

Ariès, *Centuries of Childhood* (1962), is in some ways the best introduction to the subject – after all, this was the book that established the discipline. DeMause, *The History of Childhood* (1974), is a stimulating exploration of the psychological aspects of the subject, with links to other elements of early childhood studies. Heywood, *A History of Childhood* (2001), is the best recent summary of the field.

7
Sociology of Childhood
Nigel Thomas

Contents

- Sociology and childhood
- What is sociology?
- Socialisation theory
- Psychologists, sociology and childhood
- Anthropologists, sociology and childhood
- The 'new paradigm'
- Studying children in society
- Conclusion

The aim of this chapter is to introduce some key elements of the sociological study of childhood, and to see how it can help us to a better understanding of childhood and children's lives. We will look first at how sociologists have traditionally studied childhood (or more often, have failed to). We will consider some of the problems with socialisation theory and with views of childhood as a preparation for adult life, and consider the critique of socialisation theory from an interactionist perspective. We will also look at some recent work in psychology and anthropology which has dealt with some of the same issues. We then review what has been called the 'new paradigm' of the sociology of childhood. The final part of the chapter looks at a number of areas of children's lives to see what can be learned about them through sociological research. This part includes some simple exercises based on research texts, which you can do by yourself or with a partner.

What is sociology?

In general terms, sociology is concerned with the study and understanding of *social processes* and *social structures*. These may be studied at a number of different levels:

1   The *macro* level is concerned with demographic patterns (population and so on) and with global changes in social patterns and relations.
2   The *meso* level looks at social institutions – the family, work, leisure, schooling, and so on.
3   The *micro* level studies social interaction – sometimes in a very detailed way.

The key organising concepts used by sociologists include:

1   Ideas about social relations – authority, social cohesion, conflict.
2   Social categories such as class, ethnicity and gender.
3   Broader social processes – for instance, 'modernisation'.

Early European sociologists such as Emile Durkheim and Max Weber, at the beginning of the twentieth century, were interested in social organisation and in the relationship between the individual and society. They asked questions such as 'What binds people together in social groups?' 'How do people come to share belief systems, and why are belief systems different?' 'Why do people obey authority?' In the middle of the century the dominant voices were American – sociologists such as Talcott Parsons who aimed to build a comprehensive theory that would explain everything from global social structures to the detail of social relations in terms of *function*, and critics such as C. Wright Mills who were more interested in the conflicts of interest between different groups in society. In the 1960s a branch of sociology developed that was concerned much more with social interaction – for instance, Erving Goffmann, who studied how individuals present themselves in society, and Harold Garfinkel, who focused on the minute detail of interaction such as the rules governing conversations.

More recently the dominant voices have included Michel Foucault, with his complex exploration of power and knowledge, and in Britain Anthony Giddens. Giddens's central preoccupation is with one of the key tensions in social theory, which he characterises as the relationship between *structure* and *agency*. On the one hand, our lives are governed by social structures and social processes, so that it might be said that we have no existence outside society. On the other hand, these social structures and processes are nothing but the result of human activity. So which is prior – do individuals create society, or does society create individuals? Are we free agents, or are our lives determined? A moment's reflection may suggest to us that in some way both statements are true – but the task then is to explore the relationship between them.

So what has all this to do with childhood? From a cursory reading of much of the sociological literature, one might say, 'Very little.' Many of the standard texts have in the past had no index entry for childhood, or if they have it has been simply a cross-reference to 'the family' or 'education'. This has begun to change, but only slowly, and it is rare to find any book of general sociology with a chapter on childhood. The questions about social structures and social processes have not been asked specifically in relation to childhood; the questions about social relations, authority and power have not been applied to adult–child relations; and the social categories used – class, ethnicity, gender – have not been extended to include childhood. Where we do find books in the past about 'the sociology of childhood' they tend to be specifically about the process of *socialisation* (for instance, Bossard and Boll, 1966). Children are studied, not as actual and participating members of society, but as *prospective* members. What is interesting about children, from this perspective, is the process by which they are made into adults.

Socialisation theory

> A child is born into a world that already exists. From the point of view of society, the function of socialization is to transmit the culture and motivation to participate in established social relationships to new members.
>
> (Elkin, 1960: 7)

The central idea of classical socialisation theory (note: it is often spelt 'socialization', especially in American texts) is that we are in effect *produced* in childhood by social conditioning. It is only through this process that we become *social*, and because human beings are essentially social animals, this means that it is only through this process that we become fully human. More specifically, we are socialised into understanding and accepting the conventional norms and values of our particular society, and into becoming part of a culture; we are socialised into our particular role(s), social status and social class; and, according to some, our own individual personality is also the result of a socialisation process. The idea that individual personality is the result of socialisation was put forward most strongly by the behaviourist J.B. Watson, who wrote:

> Give me a dozen healthy infants, well-formed, and my own specified world to bring them up in, and I'll guarantee to take any one at random and train him to become any type of specialist I might select – doctor, lawyer, artist, merchant-chief and, yes, even beggarman and thief, regardless of his talents, penchants, tendencies, abilities, vocations, and race of his ancestors.
>
> (From 'Behaviorism', 1930; quoted in Elkin, 1960: 46)

Socialisation theory identifies a number of socialising institutions or 'agencies of socialisation': principally the family, the school, the peer group and the mass media. Some theorists distinguish between *primary* socialisation, which includes the laying down of fundamental characteristics of personality, basic values, and so on, and *secondary* socialisation, representing the continuing effect of group interaction and culture on our habits, thoughts and values throughout life. Most of the attention tends to be on primary socialisation; some conceive of this as taking place throughout childhood and into adolescence, whilst others confine it to early childhood. For instance, Bossard and Boll argue that 'the social conditioning of the personality during the first years of life is of primary importance ... the basic patterns of personality are laid during the period of childhood', and that 'the sociological processes of personality formation can best be studied during the earlier stages' (1966: 7–8). From this perspective the family is clearly the most important socialising institution.

Socialisation theory came under increasing criticism in the 1970s from sociologists who took an *interactionist* approach such as Norman Denzin. Studies of adult–child interaction and child–child interaction, and reflections on them, led to dissatisfaction with 'socialisation' as a model for what was observed to take place. Mackay (in Waksler, 1991) uses the example of an observed interaction between a child and a teacher about the child's understanding of a story, to show how the teacher treats the child as incompetent throughout in respect of the task, and how an analysis of the interaction shows that it presumes a high degree of competence on the child's part to make it work.

Matthew Speier puts the criticism forcefully. He argues that traditional interests in development and socialisation have neglected 'the interactional foundation to human group life':

> The traditional perspectives have overemphasised the task of describing the child's develop-mental process of growing into an adult at the expense of a direct consideration of what the events of everyday life look like in childhood ... the intellectual and analytic position of sociol-ogists is essentially ideological in the sense that they have used an adult notion of what children are and what they ought to be that is like that of the laymen in the culture.
>
> (Speier, 1976: 170)

Psychologists, sociology and childhood

The key organising concepts of developmental psychology are very different from those used by sociology – concepts such as *learning, conditioning* or sometimes *unfolding*. Most discussions of child psychology start with Piaget, whose key insight was that the child learns to understand the world better as s/he progresses through a series of developmental stages characterised by increasingly sophisticated concep-tual schemes. Margaret Donaldson and others revised Piaget, using research that showed that children were able to understand concepts that had been thought to be beyond their reach if the tasks were presented in a way that 'made sense' to the child. This linked with the ideas of Vygotsky, an early contemporary of Piaget, about the 'zone of proximal development' – the area into which the child is able to move on with support.

There are other differences between Piaget and Vygotsky. Piaget is sometimes thought to view the child as a solitary learner, and Vygotsky seen as adding a social perspective on the process of development. In fact Piaget did emphasise a social element in learning, but he also seemed to see what was learned as in some sense *natural* – there is a natural progression from one conceptual framework to another, which it is the child's task to discover. For Vygotsky what the child learns is above all a culture, and therefore the role of other people in learning is indispensable. Building on these ideas, a number of psychologists including Jerome Bruner, Martin Richards and Paul Light began to explore the social dimension of psychological development in more depth.

It might on the face of it appear that psychology has converged with socialisa-tion theory, in that it has gone from seeing development as a natural process of 'unfolding', or of the child discovering what is already there in the world, to a focus on the process of transmission of cultural norms and ways of seeing and doing things. In fact the new psychology is very different from traditional socialisation theory precisely because of what Piaget taught us about the child's active participation in learning, and Vygotsky's revelation of the processes of dialogue and negotiation inherent in cultural learning. These strands in the theory are much more convergent with, for instance, the interactionist perspective of Denzin than they are with classical socialisation theory. Barbara Rogoff (1989) writes of 'the joint socialization of development by young children and adults'; she argues that the child from the earliest age is an active participant in the socialising processes of development.

Anthropologists, sociology and childhood

Anthropology is literally 'the study of people'. It developed as an academic discipline in the late nineteenth and early twentieth centuries. First in the field was physical anthropology (the study of variations in physical types around the world), followed closely by cultural anthropology (the study of habits and mode of life), from which developed modern social anthropology with its focus on kinship relations and belief systems. From the beginning anthropology developed a distinct method based on close observation and detailed recording in 'field notes', known as *ethnography*. The focus was very much on 'primitive' or 'tribal' societies – people who are 'different' from 'us' in what were thought to be significant ways, although in recent years the same methods and concepts have been applied to Western societies.

Like sociologists, anthropologists for many years were backward in applying their concepts and methods to children and childhood. Anthropologists tended to rely on adult informants, to study adult behaviour and adult beliefs, to be interested in the social networks of adults, and to share adult concerns with their subjects. In 1973 Charlotte Hardman argued that children were a 'muted group' who had been ignored by anthropologists and given no voice in the anthropological record. She suggested that children deserved to be studied in their own right as a group with their own *culture*, their own network of relationships, their own beliefs and their own values. Gradually more and more anthropologists have turned their attention to childhood and the lives of children. This has been important for the study of childhood for the following reasons:

1 It implies looking at children not just as developing adults or adults-to-be, but as people in their own right.
2 It implies looking at children not just in their families or at school, but in their peer group, in work, in interaction with other children and with adults both within and outside their family group.
3 It implies taking children's own explanations and their beliefs seriously, in the same way that anthropology respects adults' accounts of their own culture.

The 'new paradigm'

The contemporary sociology of childhood is distinguished by two central ideas. The first is that childhood is a social construction. Historical and cross-cultural studies have shown us that the 'nature' of childhood is enormously variable according to the social context, and that childhood is in a sense socially defined and created. The biological processes involved in growing up and getting older are real; but the pattern and the meaning of these changes is structured and mediated by society and culture. The second idea is the increasing recognition we have seen in sociology, psychology and anthropology that children must be seen as social actors in their own right. Children's lack of active presence in society has been mirrored by their lack of active presence in theory.

These two insights, that childhood is a social construction and that children are social actors, are the key elements in what has been called a new *paradigm* for the sociology of childhood. (A paradigm is a theoretical framework, a fundamental way of understanding reality that underlies specific theories; for instance when Newton's physics based on gravity was overturned by Einstein's physics based on relativity, a new paradigm was created in which different questions were asked and different kinds of answers were given.) This new sociological paradigm was clearly articulated by Alan Prout and Allison James (1990). They describe it as an 'emergent' paradigm, because it is not yet fully developed but still in the process of formation. Prout and James identify the distinctive features of the new paradigm as follows:

1 Childhood is understood as a social construction. As such it provides an interpretative frame for contextualising the early years of human life. Childhood, as distinct from biological immaturity, is neither a natural nor a universal feature of human groups but appears as a specific structural and cultural component of many societies.

2 Childhood is a variable of social analysis. It can never be entirely divorced from other variables such as class, gender, or ethnicity. Comparative and cross-cultural analysis reveals a variety of childhoods rather than a single and universal phenomenon.

3 Children's social relationships and cultures are worthy of study in their own right, independent of the perspective and concerns of adults.

4 Children are and must be seen as active in the construction and determination of their own social lives, the lives of those around them and of the societies in which they live. Children are not just the passive subjects of social structures and processes.

5 Ethnography is a particularly useful methodology for the study of childhood. It allows children a more direct voice and participation in the production of sociological data than is usually possible through experimental or survey styles of research.

6 Childhood is a phenomenon in relation to which the double hermeneutic of the social sciences is acutely present (see Giddens, 1976). That is to say, to proclaim a new paradigm of childhood sociology is also to engage in and respond to the process of reconstructing childhood in society.

(Prout and James, 1990: 8–9.)

This perspective has produced a great deal of stimulating research, much of it in Northern Europe and Scandinavia. At the same time sociologists in North America have continued to develop research and theoretical work in understanding childhood. Corsaro (1997) made a substantial contribution to thinking about the relationship between *structure* and *agency* in childhood, with his concept of *interpretive reproduction*. The idea behind this concept is that children work to reproduce themselves, their culture and their social relationships, but that in doing so they interpret them for themselves. As he puts it:

1   Children actively contribute to cultural production and change.
2   They are constrained by the existing social structure and by societal reproduction.
3   Within these constraints, children's participation is *creative* and *innovative*.

Studying children in society

The methods used by sociologists to study children in society vary in relation to a number of different factors, in particular the level of analysis:

1   At the *micro* level research is concerned with the study of children as individuals or in social interaction. Research at this level may be qualitative or quantitative, but is more likely to be qualitative. Such research often favours the use of methods of communication that are accessible to children and elicit their competence – for instance drawing, writing and using stories.
2   At the *meso* level research is concerned with the study of children's lives on a larger scale, in relation to institutions such as school, family or the media, in activities such as leisure, sport or travel, or in terms of 'problems' such as poverty, illness, disability, homelessness, divorce and separation, crime, abuse, pornography, war and famine. Such research tends to use survey methods, statistical data, or the compilation of findings from a number of 'micro' studies.
3   At the *macro* level research is concerned with the study of children's lives on a larger scale. This might include historical changes in the nature of childhood and in patterns of child–adult relations, or global and generational relationships between children and adults. This research uses statistical data, or analytical and theoretical work based on existing theory or research.

Most of the research we will consider in this chapter is at the *micro* level, because that is where most of the work in the 'new paradigm' is done. However, there is also some important work being done at the other levels.

Children and their peers

Corsaro uses his concept of 'interpretive reproduction' in studying children's *peer cultures*. For Corsaro, peer culture is defined in interaction, but this takes different forms at different ages. Children's early participation in peer culture is mediated by adults – for instance, it takes place in pre-school settings to which parents arrange access for their children. In these settings children first encounter ideas of sharing and collective ownership, and of friendship. The central themes in children's 'initial peer cultures', according to Corsaro, are: attempts to *gain control* of their lives, attempts to *share* that control with each other, and the importance of *size* and of the idea of 'growing up'. He explores these themes through studies of play routines, of children's protection of their interactive space, and of sharing routines and rituals. Corsaro shows how children learn about autonomy and control through challenging and mocking adult authority and by confronting fears and conflicts in fantasy play. In contrast to the traditional psychologists' view of children's innate capacities unfolding as they mature, or the traditional sociologist's view of roles and values being inculcated by external social institutions and processes, he emphasises the importance of viewing such phenomena like conflict and friendship as *collective* and *cultural* processes.

In later age stages Corsaro focuses on social differentiation: gender differentiation, status hierarchies, core groups and 'rejected, neglected or controversial' children. He advises caution about assuming that these processes are the same everywhere, arguing that cultural differentiation is always important. However, some themes tend to be consistently present; for instance in pre-adolescent peer cultures he notices the different patterns and issues that typically emerge in the seven-to-thirteen age group, the greater stability of friendship patterns and the phenomena of 'best friends', of friendship groups and alliances and of gossip.

Children in families

Sociologists may ask different kinds of questions about children in families, depending on what paradigm they are using. For instance, someone using a *socialisation* paradigm might ask questions like: How are children socialised? How do families 'raise' children? What difficulties do parents encounter in 'raising' children? What are the different patterns of family socialisation? How does family socialisation interact with school and peer culture?

Someone working within a *family sociology* paradigm might ask questions such as: Why do parents have children? What is the significance of changes in family composition? What are the different patterns of family life and how are they experienced?

On the other hand, for those following the new paradigm of the sociology of childhood the salient questions might be: What is the meaning of 'family' to children? How are the lives of children in families negotiated? What is the relationship between children's lives in their families and children's other social worlds? What is the relationship between how childhoods are negotiated in families and the social construction of childhood?

Regardless of the approach taken, some features will be important from any perspective, illustrating common concerns of all sociologists:

1   Changes in family life.
2   Changes in family composition.
3   Children's place in families.
4   Children who are outside families.

Children in school

Now let us look at the kind of questions that sociologists might ask about children in school. The socialisation paradigm produces questions like: How are children socialised in schools? How do schools inculcate social values and norms in children? How does school socialisation interact with family socialisation?

Traditional sociology or social policy approaches, on the other hand, might lead one to ask: What is the nature of the school as an institution – how does it operate, where does the power lie? What are the objectives of schooling, and how are they effectively achieved? What is the effect of schooling on social inequalities (in terms of class, gender, ethnicity)?

In the new paradigm the questions that are asked tend to be: What is the meaning of 'school' to children? How are the daily lives of children in schools patterned? How is the experience of children in schools structured in terms of e.g. age, gender, ethnicity? How is meaning negotiated in the classroom between children and teachers? What is the relationship between children's lives in the classroom and in the playground? How does school have an impact on transitions in children's lives? What is the relationship between how childhoods are negotiated in schools and the social construction of childhood?

Children and work

If we consider the questions that sociologists in different paradigms might ask about children and work, we find a different picture. Within the socialisation paradigm very little attention has been paid to this subject, although someone using this paradigm might ask questions about the role of work experience in socialising children into adult culture and values. Nor are questions about children and work often asked within traditional sociology and social policy approaches. However, sociologists working in the new paradigm have looked at this aspect of children's lives more fully, asking questions like: What counts as children's work? What is the meaning of 'work' to children? What is children's experience of work? What are children's views of work? Why do children work? What are the benefits and losses to children from working?

Morrow (1994) studied work done outside school by children aged eleven to sixteen. She collected children's written accounts of their everyday lives outside school, and followed these up with interviews and classroom discussions. She found that the work done by children outside school fell into four categories: wage labour, marginal economic activity such as baby sitting, car washing and odd jobs, non-domestic family labour (e.g. helping in a family business) and domestic labour (including housework, household maintenance and repair, caring activities). Some older children held positions of responsibility involving safety, money, animals or valuable equipment. Many children took responsibility for the care of their siblings, and some took responsibility for the care of adult family members with disabilities. Many older children looked after other people's young children. Morrow comments:

> It is interesting that supposedly 'incompetent' children are given responsibility for looking after younger children and babies. Thus, the social construction of childhood and the reality of children's activities do not correspond, with the result that children who do assume responsibility are hidden from view, and occupy an ambiguous, and unacknowledged, place between adulthood and childhood.

(Morrow, 1994: 137)

Morrow's conclusion was that there is a need for a re-evaluation of childhood in relation to ideas of dependence and responsibility, in the light of the evidence of their experience of work.

Conclusion

We have seen, I hope, how sociology can help us to understand children's lives and children's place in society in a fuller and more rounded way – especially if it is a sociology that takes as its starting point that children are people and participants in social life, not just 'adults in the making'. The insights being developed by sociologists have a lot in common with recent work in psychology and anthropology, and to some extent there has been a convergence between the disciplines. However, the distinctive sociological emphasis on social structures and social processes remains important.

It has been possible in this chapter only to introduce some of the ideas behind contemporary sociological research in childhood, and to look at a few examples of the work that is being done. If you want to find out more about the ideas contained in this chapter, do make use of some of the further reading suggested below.

Questions and exercises

1   Take an example of research into children's peer culture and relationships – for instance the paper 'Children's negotiation of meaning' by Nancy Mandell (1991). Ask yourself (or your partner, if you are working in a pair) the following questions:

   (a)   What aspects of children's lives does the study address?
   (b)   What is the main purpose of the study? (What is the author trying to achieve?)
   (c)   What concepts or categories are used in the paper?
   (d)   How might we develop this analysis further?

2   Read an account of some research into children's experience of families – for example, chapters 1 and 3 in *Understanding Families: Children's Perspectives* by Virginia Morrow (1998), or chapter 3 of *Connecting Children: Care and Family Life* by Brannen et al. (2001). Ask yourself (or your partner, if you are working in a pair) the following questions:

   (a)   What are the main aims of this research?
   (b)   What concepts or ideas do(es) the author(s) start with?
   (c)   What are the principal methods used in the research?
   (d)   What are the most important findings of the research?
   (e)   What questions are left unanswered (or unasked)?

3   Read a research paper on children's lives in school – for instance, the chapter 'Making sense of school' by Margaret Jackson in Pollard (1987). Ask yourself (or your partner, if you are working in a pair) the following questions:

(a)   What are the main aims of this research?
(b)   What assumptions does the researcher start with concerning children's lives in school?
(c)   What methods does the researcher use?
(d)   What are the most important findings of the research?
(e)   What questions deserve exploring further?

Reading

For sociology in general there are many sound introductory texts, such as Giddens, *Sociology* (1993). For the sociology of childhood specifically, the most useful sources are probably James and Prout, *Constructing and Reconstructing Childhood* (1990, revised edition 1997); James, Jenks and Prout, *Theorizing Childhood* (1998); Corsaro, *The Sociology of Childhood* (1997); Jenks, *Childhood* (1996); Waksler, *Studying the Social Worlds of Children* (1991) and *The Little Trials of Childhood and Children's Strategies for Dealing with Them* (1996). There are useful research collections edited by Mayall, *Children's Childhoods* (1994), Pollard, *Children and their Primary Schools* (1987), and Qvortrup, Bardy, Sgritta and Wintersberger, *Childhood Matters* (1994). A good general book on childhood in society is Hill and Tisdall, *Children and Society* (1997). For a brief overview of recent trends in developmental psychology see Woodhead (1999), 'Reconstructing developmental psychology', *Children and Society* 13. For those interested in exploring some of these issues further, Thomas, *Children, Family and the State* (2002), links the sociological understanding of childhood to issues of children's rights and participation.

Part III
Policy and Provision for Young Children

In this part of the book the focus is on policy and provision in relation to the education, health and welfare of young children. Readers will find that a number of themes recur through the chapters that follow. Several of these are related to the general theme of difference and change over time and across cultures, which we noted in Part II. Here, however, we see how difference and change not only affect perceptions of children and childhood but also impinge on policy and practice. This is well illustrated in the contrasts made by several of our authors between 'medical' and 'social' models: for example, disability can be seen as an individual deficiency or as a problem of societal attitudes; ill health can be viewed in terms of physical symptoms in need of treatment or alternatively within a broader framework of social factors such as housing, poverty and diet.

The significance of changing perceptions and values is very apparent when we think about young children's education. More than one author shows how early years policy and practice in education have varied in different times and places to an extent that compels us to consider how we understand childhood, the purposes of education, how children best learn, and what constitutes 'quality' of provision.

Two further elements of change over time feature in more than one chapter. One is a shift from family or community responsibility for children towards a greater degree of state responsibility and control. This trend is uneven, interrupted as it is from time to time by calls for greater parental or shared responsibility, and currently by a greater recognition of the need to take into account the views of parents. Nevertheless the extent of official intervention, both in the lives of individual children and in the setting and monitoring of standards for all, seems to advance inexorably. This is evident in relation to all the services described in Part III.

The other element of change which needs emphasis is the recognition that children's views and opinions also matter. Beginning in child welfare, but now also in health, education and other areas of policy, there is increasing emphasis on hearing 'the child's voice' – even the voices of very young children. Increasingly, early years policy and practice are viewed not as something done *to* the child but as something done *with* the child. This is linked with our general theme of children's rights, which is also a feature of several chapters in this part of the book – in particular Chapter 9 by Nigel Thomas and Chapter 11 by Kate Wall.

Children's rights have become an increasingly important part of social and political discourse in the last century, especially since the adoption by the United Nations of the Convention on the Rights of the Child in 1989. There are important legal and philosophical questions about what it means to talk about children's rights. We do not propose to examine those questions here, but readers who are interested in exploring them further might consult Archard (1993) or Thomas (2002). Children's rights both in theory and in practice are frequently divided into *provision* rights (such as the right to basic welfare or to education), *protection* rights (such as the right to freedom from physical abuse or economic exploitation) and *participation* rights (such as the right to a voice in decision making). For a discussion of the practice of children's rights it is worth looking at the Children in Charge series edited by Mary John (John, 1996a, b, 1997; Flekkoy and Kaufman, 1997).[1] Much debate on children's rights has tended to concern older children and young people, but there is now a small but growing body of work on the rights of young children; a good introduction to the topic is Alderson (2000).

A final theme to which we draw attention, and one that runs powerfully through these chapters, is the need for the integration of services dealing with young children's care, health, welfare and education. Several writers point to the dangerous fragmentation of services in the past and argue for the adoption of a more unified or 'holistic' approach. This, as we shall see later in this book, makes inter-agency collaboration extremely important. In fact it has recently been argued that to think in terms of 'children's services' and 'children's needs' at all militates against a holistic approach, and that we should rather think of 'children's spaces' in which children are enabled to develop their strengths (Moss and Petrie, 2002).

In Chapter 8, Sonia Jackson reviews early years policy and services in the United Kingdom. She outlines the development of early years policy and the factors which have shaped it, considers the wide (or fragmented) range of services that have developed in the name of diversity and in response to local need, and looks at the impact of the shift in policy since 1997 in relation to the care of young children.

In Chapter 9, Nigel Thomas provides an introduction to key aspects of the law in England and Wales as it affects young children. He argues that the history of child care law is marked by an increasing emphasis on children's welfare, on mutual accountability between families and the state, and more recently on the child as a person with wishes and feelings. He also considers the relationship between the law relating to the care of children and the UN Convention on the Rights of the Child.

In Chapter 10, Branwen Llewelyn Jones considers the increasing focus on early childhood education – prompted both by research findings about early brain development and by the increasing number of working mothers who need provision for young children. Jones argues for greater integration of early years education with services concerned with young children's health and social development, and argues for the training and education of all those working with our youngest children to reflect a similar sense of coherence.

In Chapter 11, Kate Wall looks at policy in relation to services for disabled children in the early years. She takes as her starting point the right of all children to an education 'directed to the development of the child's personality, talents and mental and physical abilities to their fullest potential', as provided for in the UN Convention on the Rights of the Child,[2] and argues that the Convention also demands inclusion in mainstream education. Wall shows how policy has developed in stages, from segregation through 'integration' to 'inclusion'. Whilst acknowledging that the demands on providers to keep up with changing policy and practice can be challenging, Wall makes a strong argument for insisting on the highest standards precisely because it is every child's right.

In Chapter 12, Bob Sanders examines the role of social work services in providing support for children 'in need' and protection for those 'at risk'. He highlights concerns over the impact of child protection procedures with families who are in need of support with social problems, and points to the importance of understanding family context and of practitioners establishing good relations with parents and other family members.

In Chapter 13, Anne Kelly focuses on child health. She argues for health to be seen positively in terms of *well-being*, rather than simply the absence of disease. She reviews medical and social models of health care, and shows how the social model leads us to focus on the impact of environmental factors such as housing, unemployment, diet, poverty, parenting and social exclusion. Kelly argues that all agencies concerned with families must recognise the interrelationship of these factors and the impact that they have on children's well-being and life chances.

Notes

1 It is also a good idea to look at websites such as those of the Centre for Europe's Children (http://eurochild.gla.ac.uk/), Childwatch (http://www.childwatch.uio.no/), the Child Rights Information Network (http://www.crin.org/) and UNICEF (http://www.unicef.org).

2 Article 29.

8
Early Childhood Policy and Services
Sonia Jackson

Contents

- Historical overview
- Changing times
- Influences on early childhood policy
- Choice and diversity
- Services mainly for children under three
- Childcare as a social service
- Early Excellence Centres
- Learning from other countries
- Conclusion

This chapter discusses the development of early years policy in the United Kingdom and the influences that have shaped it. Having reviewed the range of early childhood services, it concludes that, despite considerable progress, there is a long way to go before all young children have access to high-quality services appropriate to their age and family circumstances. Comparisons with other Western European countries highlight the effect of years of political neglect and under-funding and the damaging split between care and education (see Cohen et al., 2004).

There are increasing signs of divergence between the four nations of the United Kingdom, and a bewildering succession of new initiatives, with hardly time for one to be absorbed before it is overtaken by another. However, there is a tendency for England to set the policy framework, with the other countries taking time to consider how best to adapt it to their own circumstances. For this reason the main focus in this chapter is on developments in England, referring to the rest of the United Kingdom when there are important differences. Because the picture is changing so rapidly at the time of writing, the best source for up-to-date information is the internet, and a number of useful websites are listed at the end of the chapter. The chapter begins, however, with a brief historical overview.

Historical overview

During the last thirty years of the twentieth century provision for young children in Britain fell far behind that of other European countries. The main characteristics of early years services during those years were:

1   No coherent national policy.
2   Continuing division between care and education.
3   Part-time nursery education, in some areas only.
4   No publicly funded child care except for children 'in need'.
5   Limited training opportunities.
6   Little attention to quality or curriculum development.

Despite the new initiatives discussed below there are still striking historical continuities in early years policy and provision which continue to shape services today, for example the short hours of publicly provided nursery education, early entry to primary school, the limitation of funded day care to 'deprived' areas or poor families and the low pay and inadequate training of the work force.

Changing times

The election of a Labour government in 1997 was a significant turning point. For the first time the state recognised a responsibility towards its youngest citizens and announced a National Childcare Strategy. This also introduced an important change in terminology, with the term 'childcare' (one word) largely replacing 'day care' in official documents. In contrast, 'child care' (two words) refers to substitute care for children unable to live in their own families.

A series of new initiatives followed, supporting developments already in progress and stimulating new forms of provision. At the same time a falling child population created free places in infant schools, which in many areas were filled by admitting four-year-olds to full-time education. In Wales almost all four-year-olds were in school by the year 2000, and there is a government undertaking to provide funded part-time nursery places for all three and four-year-olds in England whose parents want them. The inadequacy of this limited commitment is tacitly acknowledged by the official Department for Education and Skills website, which states, 'Working parents may need to arrange for other childcare to fit round the hours.' It falls far short of the universal full-time nursery education, with extended hours of childcare if needed, available to all children aged three to six in Nordic countries and in many other parts of Europe (Moss, 2001).

Sure Start

The largest new component of the Childcare Strategy was Sure Start, the first government programme ever to be targeted at the birth-to-three age group. Originally set up as an independent agency, Sure Start was later absorbed into the Department for Education and Skills in England and the Children and Families Division of the

Scottish Executive. In 2003 Sure Start Wales was amalgamated with the Children and Youth Partnership Fund and the Childcare Strategy to form the Children and Youth Support Fund, Cymorth. Cymorth is administered through local Children and Young People's Partnerships within each local authority. Sure Start Northern Ireland is administered through the Education and Library Boards.

Sure Start is an area-based programme providing funds for a variety of different early education, childcare and family support services for children under four in the most disadvantaged areas. An important economic and political motive for the generous funding provided by the Treasury was to enable mothers, particularly single mothers, to work instead of being dependent on welfare payments, so that every Sure Start scheme had to include day care. One principle of the scheme that differentiates it from previous projects is that inclusion is based on living in the catchment area and not on a social work assessment of individual needs, so that attendance does not imply any suggestion of difficulty in parenting, unlike local authority day nurseries or some family centres.

Sure Start has already been through many changes since it was set up but is generally regarded as one of the major successes of the Childcare Strategy. Evaluation has shown small but significant improvements in outcomes for children – for instance, in improved language development in two-year-olds and reduction in parental anxiety (Harris et al., 2003). The main criticism is that it reaches only a third of children in poverty and that services are still fragmented rather than joined up. The government's long-term aim is for integrated children's centres providing early education, childcare, health services, family support and help into employ-ment in every community, but in the short term these will still be targeted at the most disadvantaged areas (government Green Paper, 2003).

Childcare

Despite Sure Start the level of publicly funded provision of childcare in the United Kingdom continues to be obstinately low. There is still only one childcare place for every seven children under the age of three. The Daycare Trust estimates that there are only 42,000 subsidised places even for disadvantaged families (with 600,000 children in the relevant age group living in poverty: Daycare Trust, 2004).

Day care for children of working parents remains largely in the private sector, provided either by childminders or in childcare centres run for profit and increas-ingly by commercial chains. There are estimated to be over 8,000 private day nurs-eries in the United Kingdom, and the number continues to grow. Private childcare centres largely serve families where both parents have professional jobs and the mother returns to work after maternity leave. The fees charged by private nurseries put them out of reach of ordinary families. Mothers with fewer educational qualifi-cations are much more likely to work part-time and turn to relatives, especially grandmothers, for childcare. However, Brannen (2003), researching four-generation families, found that this supply of childcare was drying up, with grandparents increasingly unwilling to provide full-time day care on a regular basis.

The present state of early childhood provision in the United Kingdom is proba-bly transitional, with more changes still to come. There is a clear intention to create a more integrated system. In 1998 the government took the radical step of moving responsibility for all early years services from the welfare system (social services) into the education system. Only three other countries, Sweden, Spain and New Zealand, have abandoned the traditional split between welfare and education, though the immediate effect, as Moss (2001) has pointed out, depended very much on the previous situation.

Influences on early childhood policy

Early Years policy in any country is shaped by a complex interaction of different factors. These include: demographic trends; economic conditions; prevailing ideology; historical factors; educational theories. We can see all these elements in the development of early childhood services in Britain, and they go some way to explain why provision evolved on different lines from that of the rest of Europe from 1945 onwards.

Demographic factors

Children have never been greatly valued in British society. The prevailing fear, going back to the nineteenth-century economist, Malthus, has always been of overpopulation, of being 'swamped' by the underclass, and more recently by immigrants and refugees. By contrast countries with a lower population density are concerned to encourage childbearing and larger families. They therefore pursue pro-natalist policies and introduce measures to make life easier for families with children (Jackson, 1992). Anxiety becomes acute when the birth rate falls below the level needed to sustain the population and the proportion of older people begins to rise steeply, as is now happening in the United Kingdom. It is no accident that this has coincided with a greatly increased interest in young children and parenting among policy makers (Brannen and Moss, 2003).

Economic and political factors

Early years policy is strongly influenced by the wider demands of society. The most striking example was the creation of wartime day nurseries caring for young children for long hours while their mothers worked in munition factories. These closed very quickly when the war ended and there was concern about availability of jobs for returning servicemen if women continued to work outside the home. A small number of these nurseries survived to provide day care for working mothers, but increasingly only if they could prove financial need – having no male breadwinner to support them – or were thought to be providing inadequate care for the child (Jackson, 1993). Political pressure for increased provision of day care did not start to develop until the rise in home ownership, coupled with increased housing costs, made it more and more difficult for families to manage on a single income. Until then it was uncommon for mothers of young children to work outside the home except for part-time work. Factories ran 'twilight shifts' so that the wife could go out to work as soon as the husband came home. Alternatively one or other of the parents might work permanent nights. Many working-class couples in industrial areas saw very little of each other (Jackson and Jackson, 1979). In the absence of affordable childcare this work pattern still persists in some places (Moss and Penn, 1996).

Middle-class women often did not work outside the home at all between the birth of their first child and the last one leaving home. That has now changed completely. Fifty-four per cent of mothers of under-fives had a job in 2000 as compared with only 27 per cent in 1984. Better educated women and those in professional occupations are now *more* likely to be in employment and to work full-time than women in low-income households (Mooney, 2003).

Economic pressures have coincided with a resurgence of feminism after a period when the campaign for gender equality was denigrated and ridiculed (Abrams, 1996). Responsibility for home making and childcare is still very unevenly divided, with women taking by far the major part of the work, but there is increasing emphasis on the father's role in bringing up children, with parents taking a more equal share of housework and childcare, though not of organisation and decision making (Lamb, 1997).

At the same time educational and job opportunities for women have expanded, and many now want and expect to continue their careers after their children are born. Since maternity and parental leave provision is far less generous in the United Kingdom than in most other European countries (Deven and Moss, 2002), this creates a strong demand for childcare, which has largely been supplied by the huge increase in privately run day nurseries discussed above (Brannen and Moss, 2003; Goldschmied and Jackson, 2004). There is much more general acceptance of mothers working when their children are young. The idea that it is invariably harmful has been largely discredited, with the debate now centred on the form and quality of the provision, especially for infants and toddlers (Melhuish and Moss, 1991).

There is still a question mark over full day care for babies under one year. Following a very comprehensive review of all the evidence available at the time, Belsky (2001) concluded that early, extensive and continuous non-maternal care is associated with less secure attachment and increased incidence of aggression and problem behaviour in pre-school and early school years. This is an important finding, since some private day care nurseries offer care for babies as young as seven weeks. However, it only applies to children looked after away from home for more than twenty hours a week.

Findings from evaluation of Sure Start projects show positive effects of good-quality child care and early intervention both in social and in cognitive development (Sylva et al., 2003).

Historical factors

The shape of early years provision in Britain can be traced back to the mid-1960s with the publication of the enormously influential report commissioned by the then Minister of Education, Sir Edward Boyle, and named after the chair of the committee, Lady (Bridget) Plowden (Central Advisory Council, 1967).

The more radical members of the committee, led by Michael Young, recognised that educational success was largely determined by social class, and the report proposed two ways of tackling educational under-achievement. One was by greatly expanding nursery education, the other was by creating 'educational priority areas' in parts of the country suffering from social deprivation. Both schemes were designed to make the most effective use of scarce resources at a time of economic stringency. The emphasis was on the compensatory function of nursery education, which was still seen as an optional extra rather than an integral part of the national education system.

The pattern of early years provision set by the report persisted for the next thirty years. At the time its recommendations were seen as an advance by campaigners for nursery education. In retrospect it was disastrous. In the first place it perpetuated the damaging split between care and education. The report shows almost no interest in children under three, not deemed to be the concern of educationists. Day care was dismissed as a necessary evil; nothing should be done to encourage or enable mothers of young children to go out to work. It was implied that those who did so were selfish and irresponsible. Childcare was perceived as purely custodial, designed to provide better physical care than could be supplied by the mother, with no idea that it might have any educational purpose. 'Some mothers who are not obliged to work may work full-time, regardless of their children's welfare. It is no business of the educational service to encourage these women to do so' (Plowden report, 1967: 127).

Ideology

The strongly negative view of working mothers certainly had an ideological basis, which has been rather unfairly attributed to the influence of John Bowlby, a key figure in the development of the theoretical concept of attachment (Bowlby, 1965). Bowlby made an enormous contribution to our understanding of childhood by drawing attention to the emotional needs of children, which until his pioneering work, dramatically illustrated by the films of James and Joyce Robertson, had been largely ignored. But his linking of early separation from mother with later delinquency and mental ill health referred to much longer periods of separation with unsatisfactory substitute care.

However, his research as misinterpreted was widely used to support what became a fixed official orthodoxy, constantly repeated in official circulars and guidance (Jackson, 1993). As a result the Plowden Committee decided that the best interests of young children and economic constraints conveniently coincided. They recommended that any expansion of nursery education should be part-time, allowing for double shifts, and concentrated in areas of economic deprivation.

Thus the pattern of nursery education was set to the end of the century and beyond. In contrast to other countries, almost all nursery education in the United Kingdom is delivered in sessions lasting two and a half hours, morning or afternoon, making it completely useless as a service for working mothers and of limited value as a form of family support. At the time it had the perverse effect of ending most existing full-time nursery provision and making nursery education inaccessible to the most needy children, whose mothers had no choice but to go out to work (Jackson and Jackson, 1989). The persistence of the Plowden philosophy in official circles was remarkable. As late as 1991 the Education Minister, Angela Rumbold, stated in a parliamentary debate, 'In no way should [nursery education] be regarded as a mechanism to enable women to work' (Moss and Penn, 1996).

Educational theories

Books about child development usually begin by expounding the contrasting views of the philosophers John Locke and Jean-Jacques Rousseau, to which many existing schools of pedagogical theory can be traced. Locke believed that a child's mind at birth was a *tabula rasa*, a blank slate, and that all human knowledge and abilities were acquired by learning. Rousseau, on the other hand, thought that, given the right environment, the child's innate capacity would simply unfold through exploration, discovery and imagination.

The nature–nurture debate, as it became known, is now considered rather irrelevant, since contemporary advances in the study of very early brain development have shown that an infant is learning not only from the moment of birth but even while still in the womb (Selwyn, 2000). Genetic and environmental influences are so enmeshed that the attempt to ascribe any individual child's characteristics to one or the other is a fruitless exercise. Factors such as the mother's diet in pregnancy as well as more obvious negative influences such as drug addiction, alcohol misuse or smoking have been shown to have long-term effects which are difficult to disentangle either from genetic or postnatal environmental influences.

Few people would now dispute that children's earliest experiences have a profound, though not irreversible, influence on their ability to take advantage of opportunities to learn, but the persistence of two distinct schools of thought can still be seen in Britain and the United States, more than in most European countries.

Charles Dickens's novel *Hard Times* caricatures the school of education that discounts imagination, exploration, fantasy and the natural world in favour of attempting to stuff children's heads with information which is divorced from their everyday experience and therefore meaningless to them. The book opens in a schoolroom where Mr Gradgrind is expounding his theories to the schoolmaster and the government inspector: 'Now what I want is, Facts. Teach these boys and girls nothing but Facts. Facts alone are wanted in life. Plant nothing else and root out everything else.' This approach was firmly rejected by the pioneers of nursery education in Britain, though it persisted in some pre-war elementary schools. However, it is always hovering in the wings, ready to re-emerge in response to every wave of panic about 'falling standards'. The prescriptive emphasis on literacy and numeracy in primary schools may be seen to belong to the same tradition.

Cultural influences

Another way of looking at these two views of childhood is suggested by Gunilla Hallden (1991). They are 'the child as project' and 'the child as being'. In the first view the child is seen in terms of the future, someone to be moulded by parents and society. Parents set goals for their child and have a firm belief in expert knowledge as relayed by teachers and psychologists. The 'child as being' implies that the young child develops autonomously as an individual with his or her own driving force to learn and grow, needing adults as supporters, not instructors.

Historical and cultural influences usually remain invisible but they are very important in understanding why things are the way they are. For example the 1939–45 war had a different impact on countries that experienced it at first hand. One of the strengths of the much admired Reggio Emilia early childhood service is the political support it has enjoyed. The mayor, Bonacci, explained to Gunilla Dahlberg that the Fascist experience had taught them that people who conformed and obeyed were dangerous. In building a new society it was imperative to nurture and maintain a vision of children who can think and act for themselves (Dahlberg, 2000). This is very different from the prevailing official idea of early years education in England (though not in Scotland and Wales), seeing it mainly as preparation for formal schooling with a considerable emphasis on learning to sit still and obey adult instructions.

Choice and diversity

The range of early childhood services

The failure to develop a national early years policy before 1997 was always justified by official spokespeople in the name of allowing local services to develop in response to local needs and requirements. This lack of central direction resulted in a bewildering variety of different forms of provision for under-fives, but the idea of choice was largely illusory and remains so. Table 8.1 gives an indication of the distribution and intake of the different services. This section then goes on to discuss some of them in more detail.

Moss and Penn (1996: chapter 4) provide a vivid illustration of what this 'diversity' may mean for families living on a council estate on the edge of a northern city. In theory there are enough places for all the children who might use them. In practice the forms of provision and their hours of working are a poor fit with the needs of either parents or children.

The nursery school is under-used and operates for very short hours in school terms only. Most of the time there are no children in the building. The nursery class takes four-year-olds but makes no special provision for them, putting a strong emphasis on the acquisition of formal skills. The family centre caters for children referred by social services from a wide geographical area. It is open only four days a week; attendance is poor and the educational content minimal. The private nursery is described as 'a lively busy place' but has cramped facilities and charges fees too high to be afforded by anyone living on the estate.

There is also a play centre in the hospital next door for children with disabilities, a playgroup in the church hall, open two mornings a week, and two childminders. None of these services has contact with any other, there is no exchange of ideas, information or resources. So despite the diversity there is no provision on the estate that can offer a flexible and comprehensive service tailored to the needs of any particular child or family.

Recognising that this description would equally fit a similar area in any part of the country, the government's Childcare Strategy included two major initiatives to tackle the fragmentation of services inherited from previous administrations. These were the Early Years Development and Childcare Partnerships (EYDCPs) which bring together all the organisations in an area providing services for young children, statutory, voluntary and independent, and Sure Start, which provided funding on an unprecedented scale for local projects aimed at children aged from birth to four and

Table 8.1   Forms of early years provision in the United Kingdom

Type of provision	Eligibility	Hours
Education system		
Nursery schools	Catchment area	Sessional
Nursery classes	Referral	2+ hours
attached to primary schools	Free	
Reception classes	Payment for lunch	School day
Social services		
Day nurseries	Social need	8.00 or 8.30 a.m.
Family centres	Referral; some	to 5.30 p.m
	day care places	
Joint services		
Combined centres	Catchment area	Variable plus
Nursery education	Referral school	extended hours
Voluntary services		
Playgroups	All	Sessional
Parent and toddler groups	Usually open access	8.30 a.m. to
Community nurseries	Catchment area	4.00 or 5.00 p.m.
Family centres		
(mostly in disadvantaged areas)		
Private services		
Nursery schools	Ability to pay	School hours
Nursery classes	Availability of	(extended hours)
attached to preparatory schools	places	8.00 a.m. to 6.00 p.m.
Day nurseries	High fees	
Other		
Play centres	Parents stay	Variable
Playgrounds	Attached to classes,	
Creches	shops or leisure	
	facilities	
Sure Start		
Various facilities, including day		
care, depending on local needs.		
Children aged up to four in		
socially deprived areas		
Early Excellence Centres		
Different models attempting to		
integrate education, childcare		
and family support		

their families. Further efforts to integrate services are likely to follow from legislation under consideration (Green Paper, 2003).

Nursery education

The educational philosophy that dominated early years education throughout the second half of the twentieth century stemmed from Susan Isaac's Malting House

Nursery in Cambridge in the 1930s. Essentially it consisted of creating an environment in which children could learn through play, choosing their own activities to suit their stage of development and interests, with adult guidance rather than direction (Isaacs, 1926). It was not seen as the task of nursery workers to teach formal skills. Indeed, in many nursery schools and classes children were positively discouraged from reading and writing and parents were advised against trying to teach them before they were 'ready' – 'readiness' to be assessed by teachers not parents.

There were of course many variations, and outside the state system some with an explicit philosophy which differed in important respects from the standard model, for example Rudolf Steiner and Montessori pre-schools. However, within main-stream nursery education there was considerable complacency about a curriculum that had hardly changed since the 1930s. The debate was about quantity rather than quality and the needs of working parents continued to be ignored. There was an absence of theoretical debate about what actually went on in nursery schools and classes. Peter Moss and Helen Penn published in 1996 a penetrating critique of nursery education practice in which they argued for completely rethinking its scope and philosophy (Moss and Penn, 1996). There have been some moves in the direction they recommend. But their vision of a community-based service offering children 'a pleasurable and convivial day' still seems far off.

> There would be more emphasis on the quality of life in the here and now, conviviality, plea-surable and creative activities, fun and exercise, painting, puppetry, dance and drama, singing and music, cooking and eating, digging and building – in short what Robert Owen called 'merriment'.
>
> (Moss and Penn, 1996: 95)

If anything there is a movement in the other direction. The National Curriculum and its associated tests produced a reversion to formal teaching in primary schools with a strong emphasis on basic skills of literacy and numeracy which had a knock-on effect on nursery classes. At the same time the falling birth rate was bringing children into school at an earlier and earlier age.

The initial proposal for national standards at nursery age, *Desirable Outcomes for Children's Learning on Entry to Compulsory Schooling* (Qualifications and Curriculum Authority/Department for Education and Employment, 1999), aroused so much opposition that it had to be abandoned. It is interesting to note that the equivalent document issued by the Curriculum and Assessment Authority for Wales was very different in tone, opening with an extract from the poem *Afon* by Gerallt Lloyd Owen in which the poet remembers early childhood as a magical time of exploration and discovery (David, 2001). The Welsh guidance also stressed the importance of play, which was barely mentioned by the English version.

In May 2000 the Department for Education and Skills issued *Curriculum Guidance for the Foundation Stage* (three to six years), which applies to all early years settings in England that receive nursery grant funding, including those previously outside the education system such as childminders and playgroups. The revised guidance identifies 'stepping stones' rather than laying down rigid age-related objectives, and recognises that children learn and develop at different rates and not in a fixed sequence. However the Minister's foreword to the *Guidance* clearly envisages the 'child as project'.

The foundation stage is about developing key learning skills such as listening, speaking, concentration, persistence and learning to work together and cooperate with other children. It is also about developing early communication, literacy and numeracy skills that will prepare young children for Key Stage 1 of the National Curriculum.

(Hodge, 2000: 1)

Not much merriment there!

Services mainly for children under three

The main services for young children, previously within the welfare sector, are play-groups, family centres and childminders.

Playgroups

The playgroup movement started in response to the acute shortage of nursery places which meant that most children were at home with their mothers with limited opportunities for social interaction with other children until they started school in the term after their fifth birthday (Curtis and Sanderson, 2004). Intended as a temporary stopgap, it remained the major form of pre-school provision until schools began to admit four-year-olds and is still an important element in the patch-work of early years services. Though some playgroups attain standards comparable to nursery schools and classes, the majority have to operate in unsuitable and often shared premises, such as church halls, and staffing depends on the availability of women prepared to work for token pay or none. On the positive side this often proved a valuable opportunity for women who had been out of paid employment for several years to acquire confidence and organisational skills.

Some writers have suggested that the growth of the playgroup movement and the strength of the Preschool Playgroups Association (PPA) enabled governments to ignore the campaign for nursery education. There was well argued opposition in playgroup circles to the downward extension of the school starting age which meant that playgroups lost the older age group and were obliged to accept two-year-olds to remain viable. In Wales the Welsh-medium playgroups (Mudiad Ysgolion Meithrin) played an important role in promoting the language and were concerned that children might move into English-speaking primary schools before their speech was fully established. However, the government's strategy for extending nursery education allows playgroups to apply for education funding provided they meet Ofsted standards for the foundation stage of the National Curriculum.

Family centres

Multi-purpose centres designed to serve families with young children began to replace the old style of day nursery, providing full day care for limited numbers of children, during the 1980s. They fall into two broad types. Referral centres run by social services or voluntary organisations such as Barnardo's or NCH are designed to provide intensive support, parent education and counselling to families in difficulties, especially when there are child protection issues. Community centres, open to families with young children living in a particular area, offer a range of different services, sometimes including childcare, and provide opportunities for parents to meet and share experiences. They often run a variety of groups and activities, including health visitor sessions and further education classes. As they are usually sited in deprived areas such as large council estates they also have a compensatory or therapeutic function. They were particularly recommended in the *Guidance* to the Children Act 1989 (Department of Health, 1991a) as a service for 'children in need'. Sure Start funding has enabled some to offer full day care instead of short play sessions. In many areas they will be absorbed into Sure Start Children's Centres.

Childminding

For children under three the most common form of out-of-home care apart from playgroups and private day centres is still childminding, known as Family Day Care in most countries other than the United Kingdom. Childminding has a long history and has always been extensively used by poor working mothers, but its existence was not formally recognised in Britain until 1948 with the passing of the Nurseries and Childminders Regulation Act (amended in 1968). The Act made provision for registration of childminders and inspection of premises but was mainly concerned with physical safety.

Research by Brian and Sonia Jackson in the 1970s uncovered some shocking conditions, especially among unregistered minders – rows of carry-cots in a garage, toddlers spending long hours tied to pushchairs, overcrowding, bare and unstimulating environments and minders unable to communicate with the children they were caring for. Most other studies only included registered minders and described better physical conditions but commented on the 'distant relationship' between child and minder (Mayall and Petrie, 1977) or described many minded children as 'passive and detached' (Bryant et al., 1980).

In 1976 Brian Jackson persuaded the BBC to broadcast a series of twenty television programmes for childminders, presented by well-known television personalities. The series was accompanied by a handbook issued free to all registered minders through social services departments (Jackson and Allen, 1976). This was a breakthrough, presenting childminding as an important public service rather than a dubious back-street activity. Follow-up research showed that it did much to enhance childminders' self-esteem and status in their own communities.

The final programme in the series launched the National Childminding Association (NCMA), to which half of all registered minders belong. NCMA receives a government grant, and provides training and support, with a strong commitment to raising standards of care and improving working conditions. NCMA developed the idea of childminding networks, which has since become official policy (see below).

Childminding networks

A major problem for childminders has always been their isolation. Other countries have developed systems for linking family day care workers to provide professional and mutual support and training. For example, in France day nurseries (*crèches collectives*) often have an attached group of home-based childcare workers (*crèches familiales*). The family day care workers have access to the facilities of the centre and their own co-ordinator, sometimes the deputy head of the nursery. In other countries, such as Sweden, it is common for family day care providers to be salaried employees of the local authority (Karlsson, 2003).

The National Childcare Strategy (1997) aims to increase the supply of day care, raise standards and combat the isolation of childminders by the organisation of networks with funding channelled through the Early Years Development and Childcare Partnerships. The plan is for every EYCDP to have at least three networks with a minimum of twenty childminders per network (Owen, 2003).

A very important landmark for childminding was the belated recognition by the government that childminders are educators as well as carers. Networks can now either be approved by NCMA or accredited following inspection for nursery education funding if they look after three or four-year-olds and reach the required standards.

Childcare as a social service

Publicly funded childcare in Britain has always been seen as a welfare service, reserved for children with families under stress or who are judged incapable of caring for them well enough, a view reinforced by the Children Act 1989. The shrinking number of local authority day nurseries reserve their places for 'priority cases', resulting in a highly dysfunctional concentration of the most disadvantaged children in these settings (Goldschmied and Jackson, 2004). The Children Act 1989 did nothing to change this situation, but increasingly local authorities have seen the advantage of placing children identified as 'in need' under the Act in family day care.

Paradoxically this has resulted in still further tightening of criteria for access to subsidised childcare (Dillon and Statham, 1998). Sponsored places, in private childcare centres, in playgroups or with childminders, are short-term, usually only part-time. They are designed to help families over a crisis period and avoid the necessity of receiving a child into local authority care, not to provide ongoing day care for working parents. Often funding is withdrawn as soon as the acute crisis is over, and parents can rarely afford to continue to pay for the place (Statham, 2003).

From the viewpoint of social services professionals, who may have little appreciation of the educational needs of young children, sponsored family day care is an attractive option, low-cost and flexible. But finding and setting up a suitable placement can be extremely time-consuming. If social work time is included in the calculation the costs rise substantially. Assessed on a standardised rating scale (Harms and Clifford, 1989), few of the sponsored minders scored better than 'adequate'. Thus, as so often, children who are particularly vulnerable and most need a high-quality day care setting are least likely to receive it.

Statham contrasts child support policies in Britain with the much higher levels of publicly funded day care for all children in countries like Sweden, France and Denmark, where extra support is provided for families with additional needs but as an ongoing service, not a short-term safety net. In New Zealand over the last two decades of the twentieth century there was much increased funding for childcare, accompanied by tighter regulation. Elizabeth Everiss comments that this transformed the traditional status of family day care from that of a charitable welfare provision and positioned it within the mainstream of the formally organised Early Childhood Education sector (Everiss, 2003).

In Britain, despite the efforts of the NCMA, childminding remains a problematic service. Childminders are essentially running small businesses, and apart from the few who provide subsidised placements through social services, their income and working conditions are determined by market forces. They can only charge what the market will bear. If they live in a low-wage area the families who use their services will often be unable to afford to pay fees that cover the minder's expenses and still provide them with a reasonable income. On the positive side most childminders report high job satisfaction (Mooney, 2003), and many mothers (who are almost invariably responsible for arranging childcare) prefer the homelike atmosphere and individual care they can provide to group care for children in their first two years.

Early Excellence Centres

These build on the family centre model but incorporate high-quality nursery education, day care for children of working parents and a strong ethos of partnership with parents (Draper and Duffy, 2001; Whalley, 2000). They were intended to overcome the weaknesses of the previous combined centres where a day nursery and nursery school occupied one site but otherwise operated separately (Ferri, 1991). Only a few Early Excellence Centres (EECs) were designated when the programme was announced in 1998 but with plans to increase the number rapidly. Although many exemplify very good and innovative practice they are still limited by the differing terms and conditions of employment for teachers and those with other backgrounds and by the very low level of training and qualifications (NVQ Level 2) required of those who work directly with young children. By 2004 the EEC initiative had already been overtaken by a new Children's Centre programme, which aims to integrate all the different forms of provision in a locality into a single entity (Green Paper, 2003). There are some fears that this will simply lead to a rebadging exercise with a loss of good models of early years provision.

Learning from other countries

There is only space here to mention some of the main overseas influences on UK policy and practice. The idea of Sure Start, initiated by the Treasury mainly as a way of reducing poverty by enabling mothers, particularly those without a partner, to get back into paid employment, originated in US programmes such as Headstart, Welfare to Work and 0–3 but has grown far beyond its original conception. The widely publicised High/Scope programme, also from America, in which children are encouraged to plan and review their activities, has contributed to a much more structured approach to the early years curriculum (Sylva, 2000).

A second influence, which can be seen in the attempts, especially in Wales and Scotland, to develop an early years curriculum that escapes from the narrow economic imperative of preparing children for later schooling and the world of work comes from New Zealand. *Te Whariki* is a curriculum with its philosophical roots in Maori cultural perspectives, taking a holistic view of the child in the community. It sees the curriculum through the early years as a tapestry (the word *whariki* means 'woven mat') rather than a ladder, with a strong emphasis on play and discovery, allowing children to learn and develop at their own pace. It is explicitly bicultural and thus has particular relevance for Wales. Although there have been difficulties, due to political changes, *Te Whariki* is the officially recognised early years curriculum in New Zealand and has provided a model for other countries, including the United Kingdom (Carr and May, 2000).

A third strong influence on early years practice comes from the Italian city of Reggio Emilia, mentioned above. Inspired by the thinking of the psychologist Loris Malaguzzi and guided by him, the city designed an early childhood education system founded on the idea of the child as an active agent in his or her own learning, including the construction of the curriculum (Dahlberg, 2000). Among the many innovative ideas and practices associated with the system is that of attaching local artists, musicians and actors to pre-school facilities, an idea taken up with great effect by the Thomas Coram Early Childhood Centre in London. Lesley Abbott and Cathy Nutbrown have edited an inspiring collection reflecting on the experience of Reggio Emilia and its implications for practice in the United Kingdom (Abbott and Nutbrown, 2001).

The Nordic countries, in particular Sweden, set a 'gold standard' for early years services, integrating employment legislation, childcare services, early education, family support services, training and curriculum development into a system which is designed with the well-being of the child as the most important consideration (Moss, 2001).

Conclusion

After more than thirty years when the shape of early childhood services in Britain remained almost unchanged, 1997 marked a significant shift in government policy. For the first time the well-being of children under school age was recognised as a legitimate subject of public concern, not simply the responsibility of their own parents. The main developments have been:

1 Commitment to universally available nursery education for three and four-year-olds, albeit still on a part-time basis.
2 Transfer of responsibility for early years from the Department of Health to the Department for Education and Skills. National standards for all forms of early years provision receiving state funding.
3 Much more awareness of ethnic diversity and responsiveness to the needs of local communities.
4 Extension of after-school provision for children of working mothers.
5 Early Years Partnerships, designed to achieve better integration of all services used by families with young children.
6 Early Excellence Centres, with a strong emphasis on partnership with parents to provide a model of good practice.
7 The Sure Start programme, with substantial government funding for projects and services targeting children aged up to four and their parents in disadvantaged areas.

At the time of writing a new Children Bill is before Parliament, based on the government Green Paper *Every Child Matters* (HM government, 2003). This requires every local authority to appoint a Director of Children's Services, with the long-term aim of integrating all children's services under the umbrella of Children's Trusts. Sure Start Children's Centres are to be created in each of the 20 per cent most deprived neighbourhoods in England, combining nursery education, family support, employment advice, childcare and health promotion on one site. This may be a sign of a centralising tendency reasserting itself, in contrast to the original emphasis in Sure Start on local communities defining their own needs and designing services to meet them.

In conclusion, it seems that, despite impressive progress over a relatively short period, early childhood services in Britain will continue to be fragmented and unevenly distributed for many years to come. The United Kingdom continues to lag behind almost all other European countries in the education and care we provide for our youngest children.

Questions and exercises

1 Should childcare be a universally available service?
2 Has a focus on early literacy undermined the importance of play?
3 What do we mean by quality? What characteristics of early years services are associated with good outcomes for children?
4 How can early years policies balance the needs of parents and the well-being of young children?
5 Are there important lessons to be learnt from policy and practice in other countries?

Reading

Brannen and Moss, *Rethinking Children's Care* (2003), ranges over the whole field of child care, combining theoretical and historical perspectives with accessible accounts of empirical research. As the title suggests, it presents a highly critical view of existing policies. It includes chapters on childminding and, unusually, care within the family. Charlie Owen contributes a stimulating discussion of the gendered nature of childcare and the problems encountered by men working in nurseries and childcare centres. Boushel, Fawcett and Selwyn (eds), *Focus on Early Childhood* (2000), exemplifies the interdisciplinary ethos of the first British degree in Early Childhood Studies at the University of Bristol. All the authors have contributed to the course. Chapter 8, by Mary Fawcett, uses Bronfenbrenner's ecological framework to examine and evaluate early childhood care and education services in Britain. Other chapters discuss advances in psychology and sociology in relation to our understanding of children's needs and potential. First published in 1994, Goldschmied and Jackson, *People under Three* (2004), is one of the few texts to focus on the birth-to-three age group. It discusses management and organisation of the nursery as well as day-to-day care and curriculum. The authors draw on their experience of research and consultancy in Italy, Spain and the United Kingdom and give many illustrations from practice. Moss and Penn, *Transforming Nursery Education* (1996), came out before the 1997 watershed but provides a useful account of the range of early years services at the time and why there was such an urgent need for reform. Its critique of the standard model of nursery education is probably equally valid today and is counter-balanced by examples of innovative and imaginative practice. The discussion of early years policy is set in a wider social and political context, also drawing on the experience of other European countries. Gillian Pugh is chief executive of England's oldest childcare charity, now called Coram Family, and before that was director of the Early Childhood Unit at the National Children's Bureau. Her book, *Contemporary Issues in the Early Years* (2001), now in its third edition, has become a classic of early childhood literature. All the chapters are well worth reading. Chapter 1, by the editor, provides an excellent overview of current policy and services in the United Kingdom. Also recommended are chapter 3, by Gerrison Lansdown and Y. Penny Lancaster, on 'Promoting children's welfare by respecting their rights', and chapter 7, 'Diversity and learning in the early years', by Iram Siraj-Blatchford.

Websites

Official education/early years website   www.dfes.gov.uk
Wales   www.childreninwales.org.uk
Scotland   www.childreninscotland.org.uk
Northern Ireland   www.childrenservicesnorthernireland.com
DfES   www.childcarelink.gov.uk
Four Nations Child Policy Network   www.childpolicy.org.uk
National Childcare Campaign   www.info@daycare trust.org.uk
National Childminding Association   www.ncma.org.uk
National Children's Bureau   www.ncb.org.uk
National Day Nursery Association   www.ndna.org.uk
Effective Provision of Preschool Education Project   www.ioe.ac.uk/cdl/eppe
Pre-school Learning Alliance (playgroups)   www.pre-school.org.uk

9
Law Relating to Children
Nigel Thomas

Contents

- The development of legal provision for children
- Key principles of the Children Act 1989
- The Children Act 1989 and family disputes
- State support for children and families
- Care and supervision of children
- 'Looked after' children
- Child protection
- Regulation of day care and other child care services
- Adoption
- The UN Convention on the Rights of the Child
- The Human Rights Act 1998 and the European Convention
- Conclusion

The aim of this chapter is to introduce some key elements of the law relating to children, particularly in early childhood. The aim is not to achieve a detailed knowledge of the law, but to understand the most important provisions and some of the thinking that lies behind them. I will focus on the main legislation affecting children in the United Kingdom and the principles underlying that legislation, together with some reflection on the international and historical context, as far as space permits.

There are many laws that have an impact on children – in fact, it could be said that all laws do, directly or indirectly. Certainly, laws governing such things as health, housing and welfare benefits have a major impact on children's lives, even though they do not directly govern what children do or how their parents look after them. Education and employment law have a much more direct effect on children, because they spell out who is expected to go to school and what kind of education they are to receive, or at what age and in what circumstances children may work for payment. Criminal justice law makes specific provision for children and how they should be treated if they are thought to have committed an offence.

However, the laws that have the most profound impact on individual children's lives, and that may affect all children, including the very youngest, are the laws governing children's care and upbringing. It is these laws that will be the main focus of this chapter. The legislation of most concern to us will be the Children Act 1989, which is the main provision directly concerned with children's welfare in England and Wales. The Children Act 1989 sets out the framework for the relationship between children, parents and the state. It provides for the resolution of disputes between family members and defines the circumstances in which the state may intervene in family life. It lays down the powers and duties of local authorities to provide for children's welfare, and provides safeguards against poor care, whether it is provided by private individuals and organisations or by state agencies. The equivalent laws in other parts of the United Kingdom are the Children (Scotland) Act 1995 and the Children (Northern Ireland) Order 1995, which are based on the same guiding principles but also incorporate significant differences.

We will also consider briefly the law relating to adoption, and we will look at the effects of the UN Convention on the Rights of the Child and the Human Rights Act 1998. First, however, we will review briefly the development of law relating to children.

The development of legal provision for children

It could be said that until the nineteenth century a child was not a legal entity. No *statute law* (Acts of Parliament) referred specifically to children. The *common law* of 'wardship' was designed to provide for situations when a child of a noble or royal family – or more often his or her property – needed protection. The feudal theory was that the monarch owned all land and all allegiance, and individuals held property only by virtue of the king or queen's will. In 'wardship' the monarch took responsibility for a child and his or her inheritance, and in time the courts took on this role. A child without property or inheritance was of little interest to the legal system. Children enjoyed no special legal protection and had no right to plead a case. The only other time the law became interested in them was when they stole or robbed, when the full weight of the law – including imprisonment and capital punishment – might fall upon them.

Laws to protect children developed in the mid-nineteenth century, beginning with factory legislation designed to prevent the worst excesses of exploitation in the industrial workplace, and leading to the highly novel idea that children should not be working at all. This was followed by laws prohibiting cruelty to children (which followed on from laws prohibiting cruelty to animals). This was an important development, because it meant a breach in the principle of family privacy and parental, or paternal, authority. Laws to provide for children's welfare followed much later, beginning with the introduction of state elementary education, then of compulsory health surveillance (following alarm at the poor condition of recruits to the army in the Boer War), and finally the extension of duties under the Poor Law to provide for destitute children.

On these foundations developed the modern law relating to children, through a series of landmark Acts of Parliament during the course of the twentieth century. The Children Act 1908 extended protection from cruelty and neglect; the Adoption Act 1926 created a legal institution of adoption for the first time; the Children Act 1933 established a Juvenile Court system, introduced a 'fit person order' where children could be removed from home without an offence being proved, and established a schedule of offences against children which is still in use today; the Children Act 1948, arguably the most important single piece of child welfare legislation to date, ended the Poor Law treatment of children, required local authorities to appoint Children's Officers, introduced the provision of care as a service to children and families rather than as a punishment (by giving local authorities a duty to provide care when it was needed and to return children home as soon as possible) and improved the supervision of foster homes. The Children and Young Persons Act 1969 reformed the juvenile justice system on welfare principles (although it was never fully implemented) and established non-punitive grounds for children to be removed to local authority care. The Children Act 1975 introduced safeguards for children against abuse of parental rights, required children to be consulted about decisions in care, and modified adoption law.

Even from such a brief summary of the history of child welfare law some consistent themes can be discerned. It appears that the history of child care legislation is characterised by increasing emphasis on children's welfare and a shift away from 'cruelty' to 'care' as the key operating concept. It is also characterised by an increase in mutual accountability between families and the state; the first stage in this was the breaking of the barrier against any intrusion into family privacy or parental authority, while the second stage was bringing parents back into the picture as participants in the decision to provide 'care'.

What is missing up to this point is any real voice for children themselves, who are conceived of as *done to* rather than *doing*. Not until the Children Act 1975 does the law consider child's wishes and feelings, and then only in a very limited way. It is only with the Children Act 1989 that the law begins to take children seriously as people with the right to a say in their own lives.

Key principles of the Children Act 1989

Current legal provision in England and Wales is dominated by the Children Act 1989. Heralded by the Lord Chancellor as the greatest reform in child care law that century, it was more wide-ranging than any previous legislation because it brought together the *public law*, governing state services to children and child protection, and the *private law*, governing family life and disputes over children's upbringing, in the same statutory framework. This made it possible for courts to make decisions about children in complex cases without the confusion that had often arisen in the past between public care issues and private or matrimonial issues. It also meant that where children were placed compulsorily in state care this was done under the same rules and principles in all cases. The Act reformed the way in which courts intervened in family disputes and the kinds of decisions they could make. It also reformed the duties and powers of local authorities to children and families, and the way in which services were provided – especially when children were looked after away from home. Finally, it reformed the arrangements for regulation and inspection of all child care services.

The Children Act is divided into twelve parts and 108 sections, with the addition of fifteen 'schedules' containing additional detailed provision. Part One sets out some overarching principles for dealing with children's cases. The key principles contained in section 1 are often referred to as the 'welfare principles'. They are:

1   When a court is making a decision about the upbringing of a child it should treat the child's interests as paramount.
2   Courts should assume that delay in resolving a case is against the child's interests.
3   Courts should not make any order in respect of a child unless satisfied that to do so is better for the child than making another order, or no order at all.

It also provides that in deciding what is in a child's interests the court must have regard to a set of eight factors often referred to as the 'welfare checklist' – the first of which is 'the ascertainable wishes and feelings of the child'.

Other important principles in the Act include:

1   The concept of 'parental responsibility', which any legal parent has automatically and which others can acquire. Parental responsibility cannot be taken away from a parent except by the adoption of a child. Parents who separate or divorce are therefore expected to remain part of their child's life and share in their upbringing and in making decisions. Parents whose children go into care are also expected to remain involved in their lives.
2   The 'presumption of contact', that is, the presumption that contact is normally in the interests of children and should be positively promoted when they are separated from a parent or other significant person.

The Children Act 1989 and family disputes

Part Two of the Act provides for disputes between parents and other relatives to be settled under the above principles. The starting assumption is that children's upbringing will be a matter of agreement between those involved, without the need for court intervention. The days of automatic custody orders being made on divorce have ended – indeed, there is no longer any requirement for the court to 'be satisfied' as to the arrangements made between the parties.

The court becomes involved only if the parties cannot agree and one or more of them applies for an order to be made. The orders which can be made by the court are provided for under section 8 of the Act and are often referred to as 'section 8 orders'. These are:

1   A *residence* order. This requires the child to live with a particular person – or at different times with different people.
2   A *contact* order. This requires the person who has the care of the child to allow contact between the child and someone else at specified times and places.
3   A *prohibited steps* order. This prevents the person who has the care of the child from doing particular things which they could otherwise do in their role as a parent.
4   A *specific issue* order. This enables the court to resolve a specific issue by a targeted order without disturbing the other arrangements for the child's upbringing.

A court may make any of these orders in any family proceedings, whether or not they have expressly been applied for. (However, there is now case law which says that the court may not make a residence order in respect of someone who has not agreed to it.) Application for a section 8 order may be made by a parent or someone who has the actual care of the child; or, with the leave of the court, by a relative or the child herself. (Hence the publicity at the time the Act was passed about 'children divorcing their parents'.)

State support for children and families

There has been some state responsibility for supporting children and families in need since at least the seventeenth century. In 1908 local authorities were first given responsibilities to provide accommodation for children removed from home by the courts. In 1948 they were given the duty to receive into care any child who needed this service as a result of his or her parents being unable to provide adequate care. In 1963 there was added a duty to provide services to children and families to prevent reception into care.

The legal framework introduced in 1989 is rather different from what went before. Part Three of the Act, which governs services to children and families, starts with a definition of a child 'in need'. Section 17 (10) provides that a child is 'in need' if:

(a) he is unlikely to achieve or maintain a reasonable standard of health or development without the provision of services by a local authority under this part of the Act; or

(b) his health or development is likely to be significantly impaired or further impaired without the provision of such services; or

(c) he is disabled.

(Note that the Children Act, although modern in much of its language, still uses 'he' to stand for any child, girl or boy.) The Act provides the following definitions of terms used in section 17 (10): 'disabled' means blind, deaf or dumb, suffering from mental disorder of any kind, substantially and permanently handicapped by illness, injury or congenital deformity or such other disability as may be prescribed; 'development' means physical, intellectual, emotional, social or behavioural development; 'health' means physical or mental health.

Once it is established that a child is 'in need' within the terms of section 17 (10), other parts of section 17 give local authorities certain duties and powers in relation to the child and the family. First, there is a general duty on every local authority.

(a) to safeguard and promote the welfare of children in their area who are in need; and

(b) so far as is consistent with that duty, to promote the upbringing of such children by their families, by providing a range and level of services appropriate to those children's needs.

Schedule 2 of the Act gives the local authority a number of more specific duties:

1 To identify the extent of children to which there are children *in need* in the authority's area.
2 To maintain a register of disabled children.
3 To provide services to minimise the effect of disability on children.

4   To make assessments of children's needs.
5   To provide services to prevent abuse and neglect, and to reduce offending by children.
6   To provide a range of specific services for children living with their families, including advice and counselling, family centres and day care.

The remainder of Part Three of the Children Act relates to the provision of day care for children and of *accommodation*, which is the term that the Act introduced to replace the idea of 'voluntary' care.

Accommodation

Under section 20 (1) a local authority has a duty to provide accommodation for any child in need in the area who appears to require it if certain grounds apply; in most cases this is because the child's parents are temporarily or permanently unable to provide appropriate care. Under section 21 a local authority also has a duty to accommodate children who have been removed from home. Accommodation under section 20 normally requires the agreement of someone with parental responsibility, or of the child if over sixteen years. A child who is accommodated in this way is not 'in care' and the local authority does not have *parental responsibility*, although it does of course have a duty to look after the child properly.

Voluntary organisations may also accommodate children, in which case their duties are the same as those of a local authority. Regulations made under the Children Act provide that the arrangements for accommodating children must always be based on a plan, following an assessment of the child's needs, and that this plan must be agreed with the parents and if appropriate with the child.

Care and supervision of children

Part Four of the Children Act 1989 relates to the 'care and supervision' of children. It sets out the circumstances in which children may be removed from their families or the powers of parents restricted, and the process by which this may be done. A *care order* or a *supervision order* may be applied for under section 31 of the Act, on the application of a local authority or an 'authorised person' (normally a representative of the NSPCC). Parents and children have the right to oppose the making of an order and to be legally represented.

Before making an order the court must be satisfied that: the child is suffering or likely to suffer 'significant harm', and that the harm is attributable to the care given to the child not being what it would be reasonable to expect a parent to give to him, or to the child being beyond control. 'Harm' is defined as meaning ill treatment or the impairment of health or development, and 'ill treatment' specifically includes sexual abuse and forms of ill treatment which are not physical. Section 31 also provides that in assessing the significance of any harm, the child's health or development shall be compared with what could reasonably be expected of a similar child.

It is important to note that in establishing these criteria a *civil standard of proof* applies. Hearsay evidence may be admitted, and the court must be satisfied that 'on the balance of probabilities' the alleged circumstances exist and the grounds in section 31 are met. This is different from when criminal proceedings are taken against an abuser, and the *criminal standard of proof* applies – only direct evidence can be taken, and the court must be satisfied 'beyond reasonable doubt' that the defendant is guilty as charged.

Once the threshold criterion of 'significant harm' has been established, care proceedings become 'family proceedings' within the meaning of section 1 of the Children Act. From this point the 'welfare principles' apply, and section 8 orders are also available to the court. Prior to this point the welfare principles are not applied. This means that the child's welfare is not *paramount* when the court is deciding whether or not significant harm is likely. The law therefore creates a barrier of severity against intervention in families. It is not enough to show that a child could be better cared for; it must be shown that the child is being, or likely to be, significantly harmed without state intervention.

In all care proceedings a 'children's guardian' is appointed, independent of the local authority, to safeguard the child's interests and advise the court both on the child's interests and on the child's wishes and feelings.

Effects of care and supervision orders

A care order commits the child to the care of the local authority until the age of eighteen, unless it is discharged earlier on the application of the child, parent or local authority. Under a care order the local authority has parental responsibility, and can override the parents in the exercise of their parental responsibility. The local authority also has a duty to promote contact between the child and his or her family and friends. The court has the power to make an order enforcing contact (at the request of family members) or restricting contact (at the request of the local authority). A supervision order requires the child to be supervised, and may require the child to reside in a specified place for a specified time. A supervision order normally lasts for twelve months but may be extended. The court may also make an *education supervision order* on the application of the education authority (section 36), if a child is not being properly educated.

'Looked after' children

All children who are accommodated, as well as those who are in care following a court order, are children who are 'looked after' within the terms of the Children Act 1989. (Children who are placed for adoption are covered not by the Children Act but by the Adoption Act 1976 and the Adoption Agencies Regulations; see below.) Whether children are in care or accommodated, agencies have a duty in general to promote their welfare, and in particular to ensure that they are provided with accommodation suitable to their needs. Accommodation may be provided by the agency directly or by other people under the agency's supervision.

In particular, agencies looking after children have the following duties: to safeguard and promote the child's welfare (section 22); to consult the child, the family, and relevant others before making decisions (section 22); to take account of 'the child's religious persuasion, racial origin and cultural and linguistic background' in making decisions (section 22); to place and maintain the child in a family, in a community home or in another suitable placement (section 23); to place the child near their home and with their brothers or sisters if appropriate (section 23); to ensure that the accommodation provided is suitable for any disability (section 23); to 'advise, assist and befriend' the child to promote her/his welfare on leaving care, and to provide after-care (section 24); not to restrict the child's liberty except as authorised by a court (section 25); to review the child's case at regular intervals (section 26 and Regulations); and to hear any complaints and representations (section 26).

Child protection

Part Five of the Act deals with the protection of children. It provides a series of orders which courts may make in order to protect children from significant harm, and sets out the duties of local authorities and other agencies to investigate situations of risk.

Orders

A Child Assessment Order (section 43) provides for situations where a local authority or authorised person has reason to suspect that a child is suffering or likely to suffer significant harm, an assessment of the child's health, development or treatment is necessary to establish whether the child is suffering or likely to suffer significant harm, and the assessment cannot be carried out satisfactorily without an order. The court may order the child to attend for specified assessment (medical or other) for a period of up to seven days. A child who is of sufficient understanding has the right to refuse examination or treatment.

An Emergency Protection Order (section 44) is an order for which anyone can apply if they have good reason to believe that a child is likely to suffer significant harm unless an order is made either for them to be removed to a place of safety, or for them to remain where they are. The local authority must provide accommodation if necessary. The order lasts up to eight days, and the parents or child can challenge the order (but it may be made *ex parte*, without notifying them until afterwards).

'Police Protection' refers to the fact that under section 46 the police have the power to remove a child to place of safety in an emergency for a period of up to three days. The local authority has a duty to provide accommodation for the child.

Duty to investigate

Section 47 gives a local authority the duty to investigate suspicions of harm. It provides that where a local authority has 'reasonable cause to suspect' that a child in their area is suffering or likely to suffer significant harm, they shall make 'such enquiries as they consider necessary to enable them to decide whether they should take any action to safeguard or promote the child's welfare'; and in particular whether they 'should make any application to the court or exercise any of their powers' under the Act. Where enquiries are frustrated the authority must apply for an order unless satisfied that the child's welfare can be safeguarded without doing so. If the local authority does not apply for an order it must arrange a date to review the case if appropriate. Other agencies have a duty to assist the local authority with their enquiries – particularly housing, health and education authorities and the NSPCC. (The police are not expressly included, but they have a general duty to prevent crime.)

This provision is the basis for the 'child protection system', the whole apparatus of inter-agency work to protect children, including case conferences and child protection registers. This is a distinctively British response to the problem of how to protect children from harm. Continental approaches tend to be based more on encouraging families to seek help on their own terms – e.g. the 'confidential doctor' service in Belgium. In the United Kingdom, as in North America and Australasia, the emphasis is on investigation, often leading to legal action. In some parts of the United States there is a legal duty to report suspicions or allegations of abuse. Only in Britain, however, is there a legal requirement on agencies to work together to investigate abuse, under the leadership of social services agencies. This is supported by government regulation and guidance which requires agencies also to work together to plan a response to child abuse.

Regulation of day care and other child care services

In addition to the duty to provide day care for children in need, the Children Act gave local authorities additional duties in respect of the registration and supervision of day care, for which they had been responsible since the 1950s. Day care in this sense includes childminding, playgroups and nurseries. Local authorities also had responsibility under the Act for inspection of residential child care facilities and for private fostering arrangements. Since 2001 most of these duties have been transferred to the Care Standards Inspectorate, with the exception of private fostering. Care providers are required to be registered and to meet specified standards of provision, including the training and qualification of staff.

Adoption

Adoption has been legally recognised in England and Wales since 1926. The original law was devised in order to facilitate the adoption of babies by new families, and the assumption was that in most cases there should be a 'clean break' between birth origins and the new family. Most adoptions were arranged by voluntary adoption societies, many of them religion-based. This approach became obsolete following social changes in the 1960s and 1970s. Contraception and abortion became more readily available, 'illegitimacy' and unmarried parenthood became more acceptable, and the number of babies identified as needing adoption plummeted. At the same time adoption began to be the preferred plan for more children in care, and at the same time step-parents began to see adoption as a way to regularise their relationship with their stepchildren. These changes prompted reforms which led to the Adoption Act 1976.

The Adoption Act 1976 made all local authorities into adoption agencies, and laid on them a general responsibility to provide services, in co-operation with appropriate voluntary adoption societies. Services are to be provided for children, for parents and for adopters, and may include accommodation, assessment, placement and counselling services – including support and advice after adoption has taken place. Local authority agencies have specific duties which are not transferable to voluntary societies, to provide welfare reports to courts hearing adoption applications and to counsel adopted people seeking access to their original birth records. The latter is necessary because the new Act gave such people the right to seek their original records, even if they had been adopted under the old law.

Under United Kingdom law adoption can be arranged only by an approved adoption agency, unless the adoption is by a relative of the child. Adoption orders are made by the court only if it is satisfied that it is in the best interests of the child. Normally parental agreement is required, but this can be dispensed with if it is being withheld unreasonably. Decisions by adoption agencies to place children for adoption must first be considered by an adoption panel which includes independent members and people with experience of adoption.

Adoption law began to be reviewed with the passing of the Children Act 1989, and a series of proposals to amend the law were produced by successive governments. This culminated in what became the Adoption and Children Act 2002, implemented in 2003 and 2004. Although the Act does not alter the basic framework established in 1976, it does make substantial changes to adoption law, including the introduction of *special guardianship orders* and other measures designed to make it easier for permanent families to be found for children in care. In Scotland at the time of writing the Adoption (Scotland) Act 1978 still remains in force, amended by the Children (Scotland) Act 1995.

Why has this aspect of child care law been so difficult to resolve? In part the answer must lie in the conflicts between the wish of childless couples to adopt healthy babies, the fact that many children needing adoption do not fall into this category, and the view that adoption may not always be in the best interests of children. This is complicated by issues over 'inter-country' adoption, over the culture and ethnic background of children and adopters, over the part health issues such as obesity and smoking should play in decisions about people's suitability to adopt, and over whether gay couples can make suitable parents. Together with the developing controversies over fertility treatment, surrogacy and genetic research, this has turned the whole question of who can be a parent to a child into a political minefield.

The UN Convention on the Rights of the Child

The UN Convention on the Rights of the Child is an international treaty that was ratified by the United Kingdom in 1991. It does not have the force of law in individual cases, but the United Kingdom government is committed to implementing it and must report regularly to the UN on the progress being made. Article 3 of the convention provides that all actions concerning the child should take full account of his or her best interests, and that the state is to provide adequate care when parents or others responsible fail to do so. The following other articles of the convention are particularly relevant for our purposes here:

9   The child's right to live with his or her parents unless this is incompatible with the child's best interests; the right to maintain contact with separated parents.
12   The child's right to express an opinion, and to have that opinion taken into account, in any judicial and administrative proceedings affecting the child.
13–16   The child's right to freedom of expression, freedom of thought, freedom of association, privacy.
19   The child's right to protection from abuse and neglect.
20   The child's right to suitable care if not able to live with his or her family.
23   The disabled child's right to care and education designed to help lead a full and active life.
24   The child's right to 'the highest attainable standard of health'.
26–27   The child's right to social security and an adequate standard of living.
28–31   The child's right to a good education and to participation in recreation and culture, including his or her own minority culture.

The article that has perhaps attracted most attention is Article 12, which gives the child the right to express an opinion, and to have that opinion taken into account, in any judicial and administrative proceedings affecting them. The Children Act 1989 makes that right a reality at least for some children – those whose upbringing is being considered by a court, and those who are looked after by a local authority. It does not give the same right to children living in their own families. The Children (Scotland) Act 1995 does give parents a duty to take account of their children's wishes in making decisions affecting them, so that children in Scotland have more rights in this respect than those in England and Wales.

The Human Rights Act 1998 and the European Convention on Human Rights

The European Convention on Human Rights was signed in 1950 by the Council of Europe, an organisation formed after the Second World War which has nothing to do with the European Union, and which now includes forty states. The Convention was designed to ensure that the atrocities of the Nazi era could not be repeated. It has become the basis of much European law, under the direction of the European Commission on Human Rights and the European Court of Human Rights in Strasbourg.

The main provisions of the Convention are contained in the following articles:

2   The right to life.
3   Prohibits torture, inhuman or degrading treatment.

4   Prohibits slavery.
5   The right to liberty.
6   Rules for fair hearings.
7   The right to fair treatment at law.
8   The right to privacy and respect for family life.
9   The right to freedom of thought, conscience and religion.
10 The right to freedom of expression.
11 The right to freedom of assembly and association.
12 The right to marry and found a family.
14 Prohibits discrimination in enjoyment of these rights.

The Human Rights Act 1998 incorporates the European Convention into national law. It says that a court or tribunal determining any question in connection with a convention right must take into account any judgement or decision of the European Court or Commission, and that as far as possible national law must be interpreted in a way which is compatible with the convention. If national law is incompatible with the convention, the court may make a declaration of incompatibility, and the government then has the power to amend the legislation by making an order.

The Human Rights Act also says that it is unlawful for a public authority to act in a way which is incompatible with a convention right. A person may bring proceedings against a public authority which has acted unlawfully in this way; the court can order the authority to act differently, and may also award damages.

Although the Human Rights Act and the European Convention do not mention children directly, they are clearly included. Article 14 prohibits discrimination 'on any ground such as sex, race, colour, language, religion, political or other opinion, national or social origin, association with a national minority, property, birth or other status'. It does not specifically mention age, but there is nothing in the convention to suggest that all rights do not apply equally to children.

In addition, several of the provisions have particular implications for children. Article 3 (protection against degrading treatment) arguably applies to corporal punishment, and also to immigration procedures. Article 5 (the right to liberty) is likely to restrict the use of secure accommodation orders. Article 6 (the right to a fair hearing) applies to family proceedings and may apply to local authority complaints procedures and to *ex parte* emergency protection orders. Article 8 (the right to privacy and respect for family life) has many potential implications for children.

Conclusion

We have considered the main provisions of the law relating to children, in particular the law governing children's welfare. We have done so through concentrating on the Children Act 1989, and I hope that in learning about some of its most important provisions for children we have also learned something about the way in which the law frames child care policy. Space has not permitted us to look in similar depth at other areas of law, or at the detailed provisions in Scotland and Northern Ireland, which in some respects are different. However, I hope this chapter will have served as an introduction to the field, and that the suggestions for further reading below will help those who wish to take the subject further. I have also included a few case examples which readers may like to use in further study.

Questions and exercises

1   John's parents are separated and he lives with his mother. He wants to see his father but his mother is unwilling. She has been insulted and verbally abused by John's father in the past, he does not pay regular maintenance, and she does not see why he should visit John and take him out for treats when she is struggling to bring him up on a limited income. What are the options for the parties in this case, and how could it be resolved using the Children Act 1989?

2   Helen is aged sixteen. She met a man of thirty when she was on holiday in Greece, and she wants to marry him. Her mother supports her plan, but her father is opposed. What are the important issues in this case, and how could it be resolved using the Children Act 1989?

3   Paul is eight years old. He lives with his mother and his two-year-old sister in a council flat, and he attends the local school. The school has complained that Paul's behaviour makes it increasingly impossible to manage him. He does not concentrate in lessons and he occasionally attacks other children. Paul's mother says that she cannot manage him at home, either; she has recently seen her doctor for depression. Is Paul a child in need? What, if any, are the local authority's duties to him and his family?

4   Maria is thirteen years old. She lives with her parents and three younger brothers in a rented house. Recently she has often seemed distressed at school and a friend has told her teacher that Maria's father beats her and will not let her go out at evenings or weekends. The school have little contact with Maria's parents. What powers and duties does the local authority have in this situation? Who else may have a role to play in providing services? What rights does the family have?

Reading

Bainham, *Children: the Modern Law* (1998), Barton and Douglas, *Law and Parenthood* (1998), and Fortin, *Children's Rights and the Developing Law* (1995), are excellent guides to the law and the thinking behind it. Hershman and McFarlane, *Children Act Handbook* (2002), Lowe (ed.), *White, Carr and Lowe: the Children Act in Perspective* (2002), and Masson and Morris, *Children Act Manual* (1992), are authoritative sources for the Children Act 1989, includng the full text of the Act as amended together with a commentary. Allen, *Making Sense of the Children Act* (1998), and Ryan, *The Children Act 1989: Putting it into Practice* (1999), both offer good practical guides to the Children Act, aimed mainly at social workers. Stainton-Rogers and Roche, *Children's Welfare and Children's Rights* (1994), is good on the policy issues. The most authoritative source for adoption law in England and Wales is now Bridge and Swindells, *Adoption: the Modern Law* (2003).

Websites

Stationery Office   www.hmso.gov.uk/acts/
Department of Health   www.doh.gov.uk/adoption/
Children's Legal Centre   www.childrenslegalcentre.com

10
Early Childhood Education
Branwen Llewelyn Jones

Contents

- Why the current emphasis on early childhood education?
- What is childhood?
- What is early childhood education?
- What are the characteristics of early childhood education?
- The influence of researchers
- What provision exists for early childhood education?
- Early childhood education in practice
- What is the approach of other countries?
- Different pedagogical models in early childhood education
- Defining quality
- 'Developmentally appropriate practice'
- The early childhood practitioner
- The way forward
- Conclusion

This chapter will examine the current position of early childhood education, the research which has contributed to its increasing status and prominence and the approach of other countries. Different pedagogical models will be considered, together with the role of the early childhood practitioner. It will look closely at the social construction of childhood and the resulting implications for both policy and practice. The concept of quality will be explored and the chapter will conclude by identifying those issues which need to be addressed in order to determine the way forward.

Why the current emphasis on early childhood education?

Early childhood education has historically had two main thrusts: the compensatory education of underprivileged children and the pursuit of knowledge about how young children learn. The field of early childhood education has become an increasing focus of worldwide attention in recent years. Interest in it has developed to encompass perspectives derived from national studies, from the different views of childhood held by other societies and from analysing global trends.

One of the principal reasons for this interest is the increasing information provided by recent brain research (Catherwood, 1999; Nash, 1997; Bell and Fox, 1994). A young child's brain experiences enormous changes in the first years of life. Unless it is nourished by a stimulating and nurturing environment a child's brain is damaged. Research (Nash, 1997) suggests that children who engage very little in play and/or are rarely cuddled, develop brains which are 20–30 per cent smaller than they should be. Nash argues that such evidence informs us that remedial education is too late after the age of seven and that appropriate childcare of high quality is essential: 'If policymakers don't pay attention to the conditions under which this delicate process (brain development) takes place, we will all suffer the consequences starting around the year 2010' (1997: 8).

The survey undertaken by the Organisation for Economic Co-operation and Development (OECD) of Early Childhood Education and Care (ECEC), *Starting Strong* (2001), which was conducted in twelve of the OECD's member states, argues that knowledge of current brain research should be used to inform children's education in an holistic way, that is, by integrating services and giving children properly funded education and care by highly trained professionals.

Another factor which is driving countries to increase the provision for young children is the growing number of women who wish to work. David (2002) points out that in addition to this trend, many governments, including that of the United Kingdom, have a policy of encouraging women to return to the work force. In the United Kingdom, the New Labour government has made considerable financial investment in children's education and care. Numerous policies have been implemented to increase the provision of places in early childhood settings and their hours of opening. This development has made it possible for more women to return to the work force whilst also raising the profile of early childhood education.

What is childhood?

An understanding of early childhood education necessitates an understanding of childhood itself. The term 'child-centred' is often applied to early childhood pedagogical approaches. The imputation is that the child is at the epicentre not only of the system, but also of the world. In reality this is often far from the truth. The term connotes a separation of the child from his/her context and relationships, a situation which would be quite undesirable. Defining what childhood actually is requires a deep examination of old truths, received wisdom and terms which trip off educators' tongues but which they perhaps have not examined critically. 'Children's lives are lived through childhoods constructed for them by adult understandings of childhood and what children are and should be' (Mayall, 1996: 1).

When considering childhood from a global perspective, and in particular in the Third World, it is apparent that childhood means very different things to different children. There is no one childhood; rather there are many different ones according to the constructs of adults, which, in turn, are influenced by their perception of what childhood should be. Adults' constructs of childhood influence the sorts of places we create for our young children, how and what we teach and what they learn, and also our expectations of them. This is a heavy weight for young children to bear, yet it is the reality. As David (in Abbott and Pugh, 1998) observes:

> Once we become aware of the ways in which childhood itself is constructed in different societies at different times, we also begin to ask ourselves why children are treated in certain ways, what is considered an appropriate education for children at different stages in their lives and what does all this tell us about that society.

> (1998: 19)

For too long in the United Kingdom childhood has been viewed as preparation for adulthood and the workplace. The current government emphasis on literacy and numeracy reflects a commonly held perception of children as blank sheets to be written on with all the 'right' things. Little, if any, acknowledgement has been made of what children know or the desirability of co-constructing their learning from this starting point. The content of the National Curriculum, the Foundation Stage in England and the Desirable Outcomes in Wales, demonstrates an underlying assumption: that young children are viewed as needing to possess certain knowledge and acquire specific skills by a certain stage in their development. We know from our observations of how these curricula are put into practice that, more often than not, a transmission model characterised by adult domination is used in order to prepare children for more schooling.

It is very telling that senior economists are entering the debate about childhood for the first time. Research by de Gaay Fortman (2003) and Hertz (2003), for example, suggests that policy makers should pay more attention to the effects of poverty and the way in which children are cared and provided for. There is a growing consensus in the fields of economics and social studies that happiness and consistency in childhood are the best preventatives of a dysfunctional society. It is increasingly acknowledged that happiness and stability are established in the early years, and there is a growing perception of childhood as the foundation of long-term societal and economic success.

Child care provision has, as a result, increased both in availability and quality, and there is a shift in perception from children being viewed as their parents' responsibility to the shared responsibility of parents and the government. This is reflected in all the early childhood initiatives instigated over recent years in the Uinted Kingdom such as the Children Act 1989 and the introduction by the government of Early Years Development and Childcare Partnerships (EYDCP). The rights of children have been addressed, together with children's status and their recognition as members of a social group in its own right. This shift has emphasised the need for the child to be a co-constructor not merely of his or her learning, but of his or her identity.

What is early childhood education?

Put simply, early childhood education is about studying the holistic development of the young child. This can be problematic, as childhood will be perceived, and therefore defined, differently in different countries. There will also be significant cultural variations within countries themselves which are determined by such things as tradition, socio-economic factors, an increased divorce rate, increased employment of women and the effects of deprivation. Young children need to be nurtured (in every sense) if they are to develop desirable dispositions for life. They also need to enjoy emotional stability and intensely lived learning experiences in appropriate settings if they are to become fulfilled adults who can make their contribution to a cohesive society. In order for this to happen there needs to be far greater understanding of all aspects of children's development as well as the differing social and cultural contexts of their lives. Early childhood education must, therefore, involve the study of young children's cognitive, emotional and social development together with their physical and mental health, within the particular culture of their lives.

In recent years politicians worldwide have placed greater emphasis on investment in children, resulting in much media interest and political attention. The proliferation of early childhood publications and consistent media attention reflect growing public awareness of and interest in both childhood and children as individuals in their own right rather than as miniature adults. This has culminated in such significant landmarks as the Children Act 1989 in the United Kingdom and the Convention on the Rights of the Child and Young Children (1989), which contains fifty-nine articles setting out the basic human rights of children. Perhaps the most significant consequence of such legislation is that for the first time children's rights, needs and education are increasingly accepted as being holistic and that a 'wrap-around' approach involving education, health and social services is widely acknowledged as desirable, if not essential.

What are the characteristics of early childhood education?

Foremost among the characteristics of early childhood education is that children are viewed respectfully and, as the vast majority of children's learning takes place within the first five years of life, their education and care, which are indivisible, should be very carefully thought through. It is also during this critical period that the young child's self-esteem is established. If children receive education which does not meet their individual and socio-cultural needs they will undoubtedly develop a poor self-image; this situation is very difficult to redeem as the child grows older. Early childhood education, therefore, is concerned with laying a sound foundation for children's all-round development not only for later life, but in order that they may 'be as well as become' (Gammage, 2003).

The principle of holistic development underpins everything that comprises early childhood education. In order to properly educate and care for young children, much knowledge is required by all those involved. In recent years there has been an increase in research into early childhood throughout both the developed and the Third World. Bodies such as the OECD and the Bernard van Leer Foundation undertake regular research and evaluation of early childhood provision. Without such systematic investigation of childhood, education systems, the development of young children, educational policies and their outcomes, there would not exist the essential information which is required to understand young children within their differing social, economic and cultural contexts. David (1998) argues that 'If we wish to generate debate about what early childhood is, what it means to be a young child in a particular society and what educational services should be provided as a result, we, the researchers, need to make our debate more accessible to a wider audience' (1998: 5).

The influence of researchers

Research in early childhood education in the United Kingdom has focused in the past on psychology. The emphasis on the young child of Piaget's research in particular was enormously influential in the 1950s. Later research by Donaldson (1978) demonstrated that Piaget's research had underestimated young children's abilities, thus causing under-expectation. The role of the adult in children's learning development was well documented by Bruner (1986) and Vygotsky (1978a), who highlighted the essential role of the adult in supporting and extending children's learning and social development.

David (1998) traces the more recent development of research into early childhood. She points out that the nature of research changed to the observation of young children within their specific social and familial contexts. The general perception of the academic world at the time was that this newer form of research was less rigorous than earlier models such as Piaget's. David notes that by 1974 research undertaken by Tizard had diverted from the field of psychology to include educationists. Research into early childhood increasingly took the form of large-scale studies of children's lives in context. Popular foci were the effects of poverty and maternal deprivation, reiterating the increasing emphasis on the need for holistic education and the integration of education and care.

The 1970s and 1980s brought a plethora of early childhood research projects. More funding became available for research projects and the focus moved from the purist empirical approach to that based on observation and, in particular, action research. The Tizard and Hughes research (1984) was ground-breaking inasmuch as it was conducted in participants' homes, indicating how far research had moved from the days of Piaget's clinical model. This increase in accessibility was significant and paved the way for research which is far more meaningful to those working with young children. Further research projects in the 1990s used both quantitative and qualitative data, with a stronger emphasis on the latter. The projects of Athey (1990), Cleave and Brown (1991), Pascal et al. (1995), Pollard with Filer (1996), Tymms (1997), Bennett et al. (1997) and Blenkin and Kelly (1998) demonstrated that early childhood education was assuming ever-increasing importance. Practitioners began to embrace action research models, deriving theory from their own practice. Athey's research project (1990) was the first major project to involve practitioners other than teachers. It also sought the views of parents whose involvement was significant. Developmental psychology continues to dominate early childhood research, though multidisciplinary research is increasing. All these factors indicate that early childhood education has become not only a subject which commands respect, but also a field of serious study attracting significant funding.

What provision exists for early childhood education?

Early childhood is internationally defined as the period from birth to eight years of age. This, however, differs between countries. In the United Kingdom the early years are generally accepted in education as the years between the ages of three and five. After leaving the reception class, children follow the National Curriculum. In England, children of three to five follow the Foundation Stage (QCA, 2000) and in Wales at the time of writing these children follow the Desirable Outcomes (ACCAC, 1996). This is to change to a Foundation Phase in Wales if the proposals set out in the consultative document *The Learning Country: Foundation Phase 3–7 years* (Welsh Assembly Government, 2003) are adopted. The new Foundation Phase proposes a continuum of learning from three to seven years with an emphasis on learning through play.

There are, at present, great regional variations in provision within the United Kingdom which include day nurseries, pre-schools, private nurseries, childminders, early excellence centres and state schools. As a result of this disparity of provision, many of the young children of today will have experienced a variety of disjointed settings and a high number of adult caregivers. It is significant to note that children from socio-economically deprived backgrounds are least likely to be able to access high-quality early childhood education. Accessibility is, as a result, a major issue.

The defining point in raising the profile of early childhood education and the need for a cohesive system of early childhood education and care was the publication by the DES of *Starting with Quality* (1990). Following the 1989 Children Act, which stressed the need to provide more co-ordinated children's services, this report also highlighted the need to provide appropriate services which meet young children's needs. With the government's introduction of Early Years Development and Childcare Partnerships (EYDCP) into every local authority, responsibility for policy making and provision was devolved. This necessitated the co-ordination of the numerous separate groups of providers who had previously operated in an essentially competitive way. This devolvement thus had significant implications for the quality of services provided.

Early childhood education in practice

Variations exist not only in the nature of provision, but also in practice. There is growing unease about the over-formality of the education that young children receive in school settings. The consultative document (Welsh Assembly Government, 2003) points out that 'teachers introduce formal learning too soon, before some pupils are ready' and that 'children are given too many tasks to do while sitting at tables, rather than learning through well-structured play, practical activity and investigation' (2003: 7). Large-scale research by Bennett et al. (1997) has also found that children's play, for example, receives scant attention and is frequently used to allow practitioners to get on with their tasks, thus signalling clearly to the children its unimportance and implicit low status. The increase in the formalisation of learning that has spiralled downwards into some nursery classes and the majority of reception classes appears to be a direct consequence of the introduction of a National Curriculum. Formal learning has increased in inverse proportion to the diminution of learning through play in early childhood education. The situation has deteriorated further in England with the inception of such initiatives as the Literacy Hour and the Numeracy Strategy, with the result that many practitioners feel compelled to adopt approaches which are inappropriate for young children.

As David (2002) argues, the different perceptions of what constitutes quality in early childhood will differ markedly according to personal philosophies, experiences and training. Whatever else early childhood may be widely perceived to be, there is consensual agreement that all those involved in early childhood education and care need not only to explore and reflect on their provision but to engage in ongoing reflection on their practice.

What is the approach of other countries?

In recent years it is perhaps the approach to early childhood education in Reggio Emilia in Italy which has attracted most attention. Educators in Italy have been engaged in debate about what type of education their young children (defined as under six years) should have. It is important to bear in mind that the practice in Reggio Emilia is embedded in the context of an area which has sought to provide a coherent education system. Underpinning the values of that system are its people's social and cultural values, which are exemplified by participation of shared meanings and the mission to ensure that everyone feels 'a sense of belonging' and 'part of a larger endeavour' (Rinaldi, 1998: 114).

The schools in Reggio Emilia not only share a philosophy about how children best grow in every sense, namely cognitively, socially and emotionally, but they also have a shared sense of mission in terms of perceptions of children, their families and their communities. This sense of mission is explicitly communicated to parents and, most important, to new teachers. Continuing professional development of practitioners is given a high profile and, significantly, it takes place within the school. Moss and Pence (1994) claim that it is perhaps the role of the teacher as researcher which marks the greatest difference between their early years education practice and that of practitioners in the United Kingdom. It is unlikely that practitioners in Reggio Emilia fail to grow professionally. The constant quest to know more is reflected in discussion between teachers and other teachers, teachers and pedagogista and with children.

New Zealand undertook a major reform of its early childhood provision in the late 1980s. The reform was underpinned by the accommodation of the diversity of philosophies and cultures within New Zealand. It was achieved by a process of chartering in which all the stakeholders – parents, practitioners, families and community – were given the opportunity to define quality in conjunction with a government agency. The result was an agreed programme of services which reflects the policy makers' (that is, the government's) uncompromised characteristics of quality together with the values and philosophies of the other stakeholders. The debate in New Zealand led to the publication of the *Te Whaariki* document, which sets out Early Childhood Curriculum Guidelines (Carr and May, 1992) and the Meade report (1992). Smith and Farquhar (in Moss and Pence, 1994) observe that the process of collaboration achieved, to some extent, a positive impact on the quality of education in early childhood centres. Most significantly of all, 'Staff have been forced to clarify and codify their practices and they have had to think through their philosophy and values' (Smith and Farquhar, in Moss and Pence, 1994: 136).

Te Whaariki reflects Bronfenbrenner's work (1979) in that it takes into account children in their familial, community and national context, thus reflecting the social construction of childhood. Settings are characterised by dialogue and interaction between children and their peers as well as adults. Children explore and interact with their environments, learning to meet challenges and to cope with change. Individual needs are met and children develop a growing sense of responsibility. *Te Whaariki* encompasses the years from birth to school entry which takes place at six years and takes account of the differences between children, so that the focus of the curriculum and the direction and pace of learning will vary from day to day according to children's needs and interests.

The OECD Thematic Review of Early Childhood Education and Care Policy (Gammage, 2002) describes the Finnish position of the right of every child to supported growth and learning in the family and/or public day care. Finland perceives educare as 'a concept where care and education are carefully blended and where play is understood as the central tool of both pedagogy and learning' (Gammage, 2002: 18). Pre-school education in Finland refers to the year prior to compulsory schooling in which the curriculum is more structured; children begin formal schooling at six.

Different pedagogical models in early childhood education

The increase in the use of the term 'pedagogy' reflects the growing interest in young children and how their education shapes society when they reach adulthood. Pedagogy is frequently described as the craft of teaching. This definition, however, makes no reference to learning, thus a more precise definition might be 'the art of teaching and learning'. It embraces not only what, but also how, children are taught. Weikart (1972) investigates and identifies three pedagogies which he refers to as 'curriculum models': (1) child-centred; (2) programmed; (3) open-framework or constructivist. Child-centred pedagogy is characterised by holistic development with the emphasis on child-initiated learning, autonomy, creativity, self-regulation and the social interaction of children with their peers as well as adults to promote learning through discovery.

Programmed pedagogy is, at its core, the antithesis of child-centred pedagogy and is characterised by the teacher determining what will be taught and the child learning it. Such curricula are highly structured and the teacher dominates. Although the National Curriculum is matched to perceived notions of what is developmentally appropriate, it is more akin to a programmed pedagogy than any other.

A constructivist pedagogy is one in which the practitioner works within an open framework to provide a context for children in which they can play an active part in their own learning. Practitioners adopting a constructivist pedagogy place great emphasis on what the child already knows and is interested in. It reflects the research of Vygotsky (1978a) and Bruner (1986) inasmuch as the adult supports the child's learning. Latterly, the constructivist pedagogy includes children learning from other children in a social environment which is structured by the teacher according to the children's interests, thereby reflecting Bronfenbrenner's influence (1979). As a result, the term 'socio-constructivist' pedagogy is being increasingly used.

Defining quality

The examination of different pedagogical models poses the question of what is meant by 'quality' in terms of early childhood provision. Moss and Pence (1994) stress that quality in early childhood education 'requires the adoption of an essentially holistic approach'. Moss and Pence go on to say that 'It is about the dynamics which characterise a particular setting and it is about the mindset of the practitioners within a setting or service' (1994: 2). It is also, they argue, a means by which the success of a setting or service in meeting its objectives can be judged. Moss and Pence point out that quality is subjective and will mean different things to different practitioners. They advocate the rejection of the definition of quality as being historically in the possession of an exclusive number of stakeholders dominated by a powerful few, a model which they describe as 'exclusionary in nature' (1994: 172). Moss and Pence favour a definition of quality arrived at by a much broader range of stakeholders bringing their equally valid values, philosophies and experiences to underpin the definition. They call this model the 'inclusionary paradigm' (1994: 173). They acknowledge that working with a new inclusionary paradigm will be difficult and that there is much that is innovative and creative to be done, pointing out that existing examples will be difficult to find. Quality in early childhood education is a quest, and Moss and Pence view it as an evolutionary journey.

The debate about quality has been an historical one characterised by sharp differences between the views of practitioners and those of policy makers. Athey (1990) highlights the problem of defining quality, particularly in interactive pedagogical models. Athey's research into children's schema demonstrates that children's emotional growth and cognitive growth are interwoven. Athey's Froebel Early Education Project, which examined children's schema in order to help practitioners to develop thinking in young children, was extremely innovative. It was one of ten major research projects undertaken at the time which involved young children, their families and professionals. This signalled the new direction in which early childhood education was moving in the 1990s.

'Developmentally appropriate practice'

When defining quality it is necessary to examine the concept of developmentally appropriate practice which continues to preoccupy educationists and, in particular, policy makers. Bredekamp (1987), who is probably the most influential writer on the subject, argues that a developmentally appropriate curriculum is based on two factors. The first of these is that children develop according to universal, predictable stages of growth during the first nine years of life. Second, that within this universal pattern 'each child is a unique person with an individual pattern and uniting of growth, as well as individual personality, learning style and family background' (1987: 2). This indicates how complex and idiosyncratic a developmentally appropriate curriculum can be. There are, however, certain widely accepted conditions which are consistent with such a curriculum. These include such tenets as: children learn best through self-motivated experiences; different types of experiences and materials are appropriate for children of different ages; young children learn through play; and children's learning can be supported and enhanced by the sensitive verbal interaction of practitioners.

These principles are common to early childhood education but this commonality can lead to dangerous generalisations. It is too often assumed that all children learn and develop in the same way and at the same rate. This assumption is challenged by the fact that children's development is influenced by the cultural values and adult patterns of socialisation which enable them to assimilate the socio-cultural and economic conditions in which they live and grow. There is widespread disagreement within the discipline of developmental psychology on a number of issues. Ingleby (1986, cited by Lubeck in Mallory and New, 1994) and Dahlberg et al. (1999) argue that the concept of development in relation to children as a predictable continuum which all children everywhere follow is being increasingly questioned. They stress the need to adopt a postmodern perspective which places children's development in context and acknowledges diversity in all its forms. Indeed, universalist perspectives have been increasingly challenged since the mid-1990s. Growing numbers of educationists have become ever more uneasy about the notion of a universal recipe for child development which could be prised from one context and made to fit, with a few concessionary adjustments, different customs and cultures anywhere.

The context for early childhood education is becoming increasingly complex, and diversity and context are challenging the assumption that there is a universal, 'all fit' model for early childhood education which is underpinned by a developmentally appropriate curriculum: 'The dream to create foundations that could support the weight of universal truths and certainties – in understanding children's development, in knowing the ingredients of quality care, in evaluating environments, in predicting child outcomes and more – never was more than a dream' (Dahlberg et al., 1999: 186). This crystallises the current state of affairs in early childhood education. There are different models and perceptions to learn from throughout the world and in order to improve early childhood education and better our children's lives: 'Development cannot be studied in isolation from its social and historical context' (Lubeck, in Mallory and New, 1994: 33).

The concept of a developmentally appropriate curriculum brings with it an attendant and potentially dangerous assumption, that those people who know about it are believed, as a result, to know more about, and be better at, bringing up children. This displaces a large proportion of practitioners, parents and others who hold different beliefs about the developmental needs of young children. It is interesting to note, however, that in a later article Bredekamp and Rosegrant (1992) play down the term 'development' and emphasise child-centred learning in the context of democratic values.

The early childhood practitioner

The concept of the early years professional is still developing. Part of the way forward is to arrive at an explicit consensual definition of the role of an early childhood practitioner. Certain qualifications have developed haphazardly over the past decade or so, but quality early childhood education will not be universally achieved until the importance of an integrated service is reflected in a clear, unified policy which gives direction to the training, education and continuing professional development of all who work with young children. Pugh (in Abbott and Pugh, 1998) describes the complex and unco-ordinated variety of early years provision in the United Kingdom. She observes that 'Given the strength of the research evidence, it is extraordinary that the gradual increase in the amount of provision over recent years, and in recent legislation … have ignored the need to provide a qualified and well-trained work force' (1998: 9).

The OECD identifies the need for appropriate training for early childhood practitioners and highlights the paucity of male representation in the field. 'There is a critical need to recruit and retain a qualified and diverse mixed-gender work force' (2001: 126). Perhaps the way forward is for practitioners to be respectful educators who view children as capable learners. Nutbrown (1996) examines Article 29 of the UN Convention from the perspective of children's rights, which, she says 'are the responsibility of everyone' (1996: 101). In order to ensure that our children receive a respectful curriculum in whatever setting, all those involved must not only know what they are doing, but be able to articulate why they are doing it.

The way forward

The education imperative is changing, albeit not quickly enough for some. It is widely acknowledged that the pattern of childhood which has been fairly constant for generations is now 'being transformed within a generation, and, for many children, even within the span of their own childhood' (Woodhead, 1996: 12). What happens to children in all early childhood settings is the principal means, besides the family, of socialisation and a major determinant of how children will fare in life. As such, the education and care young children receive are major contributory factors to the quality of their lives, not only in the present, but as adults. Early childhood education, therefore, matters very much. Sadly, there has been a lack of vision of coherent integrated early childhood education and this is reflected in the too often sterile environments and activities young children experience. Yet:

> Vision inspires and motivates. It expresses belief in the long-term value of an enterprise and commitment to progress. It offers the prospect of a better tomorrow, which today's hard work and effort will contribute to achieving. The development of good early childhood services depends on the long-term, co-operative and committed relationships between all the parties involved: shared and sustained vision is at the heart of such a partnership.
>
> (Moss and Penn, 1996: 2)

Politicians are beginning to take heed of what is happening and a vast increase in spending on young children has been evidenced in the United Kingdom since New Labour took power. Gammage (2002) considers the present position of early childhood education in a worldwide context. He points out the contrast between attitudes and, as a result, provision in Western countries and observes that childhood is socially constructed far more than those who are at the very heart of it realise. The stark reality is that OECD and UNESCO data indicate that the minority of the world's children, fewer than 10 per cent, who are born in the richest countries of the world, are those who inform statistics and knowledge about early childhood provision. Gammage shares the international concern of professionals about the nature of early childhood education, notably the increasing emphasis on product, particularly in the United Kingdom. There has been an historical tension between process and product in education. This tension is particularly marked in early childhood education, for context is critical and 'socially constructed dispositions and habits of mind are learned and built upon early in the child's life' (2002: 187). This has important implications for process, both in the short and in the long term, as the dispositions developed in the early years will influence behaviour and, thus, the nature of society when children become adults.

There still remains a large gap between public demand for early childhood education and provision in the United Kingdom. It is a sobering fact that children in other European countries fare much better. Surely it is time to invest money in the early years so that we can make a real difference to children's lives.

Conclusion

There is now a general consensus (Moss and Pence, 1994; Blenkin and Kelly, 1994; Dahlberg et al., 1999; Blenkin and Kelly, 2000; OECD, 2001; Gammage, 2002), that a wider perspective of young children, their special way of learning and their needs should be reflected in early childhood education. Research indicates that emphasis on education alone will not suffice. Appropriate care and fostering of children's health and social development must be combined to provide educare. Moss and Penn (1996) articulate their vision of early childhood services which will meet the needs and demands of a changing world, one which is based on the achievement of social cohesion, which recognises the right of all children to the same opportunities, which is inclusive, respectful and which acknowledges the importance of appropriate parenting and gives young children access to high-quality education.

The way forward is best indicated by the policy lessons derived from the OECD Education Committee's thematic review of early childhood education and care. The eight key elements of successful ECEC policy which it identifies (2001: 126) are:

1　A systematic and integrated approach to policy development and implementation.
2　A strong and equal partnership with the education system.
3　A universal approach to access, with particular attention to children in need of special support.
4　Substantial public investment in services and the infrastructure.
5　A participatory approach to quality improvement and assurance.
6　Appropriate training and working conditions for staff in all forms of provision.
7　Systematic attention to monitoring and data collection.
8　A stable framework and long-term agenda for research and evaluation.

This chapter has argued that the way forward should be underpinned by these key elements, a robust examination of what childhood is and a rigorous assessment of the quality of provision for children – not merely in terms of rhetoric, but in reality.

Given the nature and speed of socio-cultural change, the key question now is 'Who socialises the child?' If early childhood education is to meet the needs of the children of the twenty-first century it must address this question as a matter of urgency.

Questions and exercises

1 Why has early childhood education become a focus of attention in recent years?
2 How do different cultural perceptions of childhood influence the nature and amount of early childhood education worldwide?
3 What contribution has research made to the status and nature of early childhood education?
4 What range of provision exists for early childhood education in the United Kingdom?
5 Which factors determine quality in early childhood education?
6 Which pedagogical models have exerted most influence on practice in early childhood education and on the role of the practitioner?

Reading

Brazelton and Greenspan are the United States' most distinguished paediatrician and most influential child psychiatrist. What they identify as the unmet needs of children are robustly explored in *The Irreducible Needs of Children* (2000). They examine the fundamental requirements of children in their contemporary socio-cultural context, setting out the seven irreducible needs of every child. Among the issues explored are the need for nurturing relationships, the effect of full-time day care on young children and the need for developmentally appropriate experiences. David, *Teaching Young Children* (1999), examines what childhood is and what the purpose and nature of early childhood education should be. Current thinking and practice in young children's learning are considered in ways which will enable readers to reflect on their own practice and consider ways of developing their pedagogy. It arises from the contributors' evidence-based practice and explores effective pedagogy in the context of the ever-changing socio-cultural constructions of childhood. In *From Neurons to Neighborhoods* (2000) the National Research Council Institute of Medicine uses the latest findings in neurobiology together with those in the behavioural and social sciences to consider how the well-being of children can best be addressed in society. It is explored in the context of the dramatic transformations of the socio-economic circumstances in which families with young children live today. The impact of childcare on children's development and the effects of family stress on young children are examined, together with the most significant influences on early brain development and the benefits of appropriate early intervention. The text offers specific conclusions and recommendations which are derived from an extensive research base.

11
Inclusion and Special Educational Needs
Kate Wall

Contents

- Definitions and terminology
- Historical context and recent developments
- Human rights
- Models of disability
- Development of inclusive practice
- Integration or inclusion?
- Inclusion within early years settings and within curricula
- Requirements on early years providers
- Identification of difficulties and appropriate provision
- Case study
- Current issues
- Conclusion

If we are working towards a society that accepts all its members, then the educational system should celebrate and accommodate difference and diversity. The system should provide the right opportunities for every child to achieve her or his maximum potential – both academically and personally. It should embrace the challenge of educating all children in local provision that offers effective and developmentally appropriate opportunities for each individual child, with no barriers to full participation. Resources, training and policies – both local and national – should support the work of professionals working within an inter-agency system that gives access to all the resources needed to support continued progress and development. If this is the system of education we want, what are the barriers to achieving it within our existing education system?

This chapter aims to identify and discuss key issues in the field of special educational needs (SEN). We will situate the development of philosophy, legislation and provision historically, and consider its changing impact on the current provision for the youngest children. Throughout there will be strong emphasis on children's right to inclusion.

Definitions and terminology

For the purposes of this chapter the definition of 'special educational needs' will be that used in the revised Code of Practice for Special Educational Needs (Department for Education and Skills, 2001a) and in the draft SEN Code of Practice for Wales, since this is the definition that practitioners work with in England and Wales: 'Children have special educational needs if they have a *learning difficulty* which calls for *special educational provision* to be made for them' (Department for Education and Skills, 2001a: section 1:3). 'Practitioners' will refer to all those working in early years settings. 'Early years setting' will refer to pre-school and primary providers, including:

> maintained mainstream and special schools, maintained nursery schools, independent schools, non-maintained special schools, local authority daycare providers such as day nurseries and family centres, other registered daycare providers such as preschools, playgroups and private day nurseries, local authority Portage schemes and accredited childminders ...

> (Department for Education and Skills, 2001a: section 4:2)

Definitions of 'inclusion' are plentiful – in this chapter that offered by Thomas et al. (1998) will be used:

> The notion of inclusion, therefore, does not set parameters (as the notion of integration did) around particular kinds of putative disability. Rather, it is about providing a framework within which all children – regardless of ability, gender, language, ethnic or cultural origin – can be valued equally, treated with respect and provided with equal opportunities at school.

> (Thomas et al., 1998: 15)

Historical context and recent developments

Legislation and guidance in relation to special needs have developed gradually over the last sixty years, but the speed of change has increased over the last twenty years, as can be seen from the following brief chronology:

1945   Handicapped Pupils and School Health Regulations.
1970   Education (Handicapped Children) Act.
1978   Warnock Report.
1981   Education Act.
1989   Children Act.
1993   Education Act.
1994   Special Educational Needs Code of Practice.
2001   Special Educational Needs and Disability Act.
2001–2   SEN Codes of Practice (revised).

This progression has seen major changes in policies and practices, for instance the move away from a 'medical model' of diagnosis and the adoption of a graduated response to special needs that begins with early identification and culminates in a formal statement. During the same period there has also been a steady devolution of policy making to Wales and Scotland. Although most of the references to recent law and policy in this chapter relate to England, readers should note that in most cases Scotland and Wales will have their own equivalents, which in some instances will be different.

In England and Wales provision is now dominated by the Special Educational Needs and Disability Act 2001 (SENDA) and by the Special Educational Needs Codes of Practice (Department for Education and Skills, 2001a; National Assembly for Wales, 2002). The codes of practice have been revised to take account of the rights contained in the new Act, which 'makes it unlawful for schools, colleges and other education providers to discriminate against disabled people' (Disability Rights Commission, 2003). The Scottish equivalent is the Education (Disability Strategies and Pupils' Educational Records) (Scotland) Act 2002.

For the first time a whole chapter is dedicated to identification, assessment and provision in the early years. The five-stage approach to assessment, as laid down in the 1994 Code of Practice, has now become a 'graduated response' incorporating *Early Years Action* and *Early Years Action Plus* (equivalent to *School Action* and *School Action Plus* in later years). The code identifies triggers for intervention at each stage, together with the responsibilities of Special Educational Needs Co-ordinators (SENCO). The expectation is that agencies will work together to provide a 'seamless service', and parental involvement throughout the process will be seen as crucial. The code recommends that children should be provided for within their local mainstream setting, in the current philosophy of increased inclusion and as required by section 1 of the Special Educational Needs and Disability Act.

Following implementation of SENDA the government published additional guidance documents for practitioners, including *Inclusive Schooling: Children with Special Educational Needs* (Department for Education and Skills, 2001b), *Providing for Children with Medical Needs* (Department for Education and Skills, 2001c) and *Promoting Children's Mental Health within Early Years and School Settings* (Department for Education and Skills, 2001d).

In Wales the code of practice, with its clear aim of raising the attainment of children with special needs, varies little from the English version. Perhaps most obvious are the references to Welsh-language education, but definitions with regard to identification, assessment and provision in early education settings follow the same graduated stages as *Early Years Action* and *Early Years Action Plus*. One of the key differences relates to development of the early years curriculum – in England 'desirable learning outcomes' have been replaced with 'early learning goals', whilst in Wales the 'desirable outcomes' are contained within the newly developed foundation phase (ACCAC, 1996). The Welsh Advisory Group on SEN (WAGSEN) first met in 1998 and has supported developments for children with special needs in Wales. The consultation on the Green Paper, the BEST for Special Education (1997) has also supported such developments which echo the key features of the Code of Practice (Department for Education and Skills, 2001a).

Scotland has also been developing SEN provision over recent years. The 1998 discussion paper on special educational needs, and the 1999 Riddell Advisory Committee (on educational provision for children with severe low incidence disabilities) were followed in 1999 by the announcement of an inclusion programme and the setting up of an SEN helpline, and in 2000 by the SEN Programme of Action and the establishment of a National SEN Advisory Forum. In 2003 the Early Years Strategy was declared.

The progression of legislation and guidance on SEN provision continues, at a speed which practitioners have sometimes found overwhelming. With heavy work loads it can be difficult to read and assimilate new information with all the consequent changes in policy, planning and provision. This speed of implementation does not always allow thorough and detailed planning, training or the allocation of appropriate resources.

Human rights

Human rights apply to every individual, but have a particular application to children with special needs and to the issue of inclusion in the early years. The Universal Declaration of Human Rights, the European Convention on Human Rights and the UN Convention on the Rights of the Child are all relevant here. The Universal Declaration includes a right to education, as does the European Convention, which now has the force of law under the Human Rights Act 1998. (For more detailed information refer to Chapter 9.)

Article 23 of the UN Convention gives 'mentally or physically disabled' children the right to appropriate care and education to allow them to lead 'full and decent' lives. Children should have access to appropriate resources to education, which should be free of charge whenever possible and designed to enable the child to achieve 'the fullest possible social integration and individual development'.

Article 29 of the UN Convention declares that education should support:

> the development of the child's personality, talents and mental and physical abilities to their fullest potential; the development of respect for the child's parents, his or her own cultural identity, language and values ... ; and the preparation of the child for responsible life in a free society, in the spirit of understanding, peace, tolerance, equality of sexes, and friendship amongst all people ...

Also relevant is the Salamanca Statement and Framework for Action on Special Needs Education which followed a world conference on Special Needs Education: Access and Quality in 1994. Ninety-two governments were represented along with twenty-five international organisations at this conference confirming the rights of children with special needs. The fundamental principles underpinning the document include:

> Every child has unique characteristics, interests, abilities and learning needs.
> Provision should take into account the wide diversity of these characteristics and needs.
> Those with special educational needs must have access to regular schools which should accommodate them within a child-centred pedagogy capable of meeting these needs.

(UNESCO, 1994)

The progress regarding children's rights in general and then the focus on children with special educational needs has been gradual but consistent, indicating a commitment to effective and inclusive provision for all children from the United Kingdom and internationally.

Models of disability

A number of different ways of understanding disability have been identified, including the magical model, moral model, social competence model and medical model (see Sandow, 1994, for a useful summary). However, research that takes the perspective of people with disabilities suggests that the central contrast is between the 'medical' and 'social' models (Oliver, 1990).

The *medical* model tends to label and segregate, as an individual is given a diagnosis of a condition or disability and 'treatment' is prescribed. (In the case of young children this might mean removal from the family to special provision some distance away.) The child is perceived in terms of the condition, rather than as an individual. The *social* model sees disability in terms of obstacles put in the way of an individual's participation in society. It places individuals within their social community and is therefore more inclusive by philosophy. The model 'acknowledges that barriers should be removed to enable access for all members of the community in all aspects of their chosen life' (Wall, 2003).

Development of inclusive practice

The continued move towards inclusive education throughout the United Kingdom has gathered pace from the first steps in the 1970s. Wolger (2003: 190) summarises these changes:

> In the 1970s, for example, children with severe mental handicaps who were previously considered to be 'ineducable' were brought into the educational framework for the first time and, from the 1990s onwards, a whole raft of government documents and legislation has set out an educational vision in which the inclusion of children with special educational needs is seen as a major part of the future development of educational provision in this country, and the rights of children to that provision have been legally established.

Through the history of SEN provision can be discerned a steady move from a segregated approach based firmly in a deficit philosophy, through the development of 'integration' to the more recent emphasis on 'inclusive practice'. Up to the 1970s SEN provision was located in special schools, often outside the child's local community. Specialist SEN teachers were appointed to provide appropriate educational opportunities to support the development of the children, and many of these teachers had further qualifications in SEN. SEN teachers were often regarded as the 'experts' by mainstream educators. With the child's problems and difficulties clearly defined and situated firmly within the child, educators would work to remedy the perceived deficits. Educators were therefore responding specifically to identified learning difficulties, and training aimed to offer skills and strategies to provide for individual learning difficulties. At this stage educators were still attempting to reduce or eliminate the effects of the child's difficulties to enable the child if possible to 'fit' into mainstream education. The Warnock report (Department of Education and Science, 1978) began a change in educational thinking and practices through its discussion of integrated approaches to SEN.

During the later 1980s and the 1990s this philosophy was further developed in line with increasing debates surrounding equal opportunities, human rights and increased inclusivity within wider society. At the beginning of the twenty-first century, we are working towards an inclusive education system in which all children should be able to participate, irrespective of issues relating to SEN, gender, race and/or culture. This system will celebrate diversity and accommodate the learning needs of all children. If we believe that all children have the right to appropriate learning experiences, then in an inclusive system all settings will be able to provide effective and individualised learning and there will no longer be a need for separate legislation and guidance relating to children with special needs, which in itself produces contradiction and confusion. As long as the government produces guidance on SEN provision suggesting that inclusion is not appropriate for all children, practitioners in schools or pre-school settings will lack a clear lead.

Within the early years sector much has been written concerning the inclusive nature of existing early years practices. After summarising such evidence Lloyd (1997: 177) concludes that:

> These principles are totally compatible with the model of education proposed ... as offering opportunities for genuine inclusion ... Indeed, as the starting point is what the child *can* do rather that what she or he *cannot* do, there are inevitably more possibilities to include a wider range of difference and diversity from the onset.

At the same time it is important to recognise the pressures on early years practitioners to deliver the curriculum and to provide for increasing numbers of children with SEN as a part of an increasingly inclusive system. Many pre-school providers do not have formal qualifications, and in many pre-schools the turnover of staff can be high, as pay and conditions are poor. Once their own children have passed the pre-school phase, many pre-school practitioners will want to progress with their own careers, either within or outside early years provision. Although many early years providers are highly skilled, some will have undergone little training relating to special needs provision and this is a concern. Ashdown (2003: 159) concludes that: 'what many early years practitioners need is quality training and opportunities to view models of good practice and to get practical advice about specialist equipment, teaching materials and appropriate teaching methods from experienced SEN specialists'.

The Index for Inclusion (Booth and Ainscow, 2002) was developed during the late 1990s as a collaborative work to promote the development of inclusive practices in schools. The index supports practitioners through a process of evaluating current practices and developing them towards more inclusive practices, which in turn should support pupil attainment. It offers three 'interconnected dimensions of school life' – creating inclusive cultures, producing inclusive policies and evolving inclusive practices – which can be included in a school development plan. These three dimensions, combined with the phases of the index process, should promote the progressive development of the school, using everyone's skills and expertise.

Integration or inclusion?

The notion of integration contained in the Warnock Report (Department of Education and Science, 1978) proposed three distinct types of integration: *locational, social* and *functional*. Within a system that incorporated special schools as fundamental, there were concerns about issues relating to the segregation of children and young people echoing the medical model. Children identified as experiencing difficulties, and therefore deemed unable to cope in mainstream settings, were removed to segregated special school provision. This created an invisible barrier between mainstream and special providers, as the special school staff were perceived by many as 'experts'. Many schools developed policies whereby children were 'integrated' within the mainstream setting, but in reality varying forms of 'integration' were in operation, from Warnock's 'locational' integration, whereby a special unit was situated on a school site but there was little or no interaction between the two, to the functional integration whereby children fully shared educational experiences. At the time there existed a spectrum of specialist provision available from 'remedial' help in a mainstream school through to full-time attendance within a special school. Thomas et al. succinctly express the view at the time as 'received opinion that special schools provided a sensible way of meeting the needs of a minority of children, at the same time as safeguarding the efficient education of the majority in the mainstream' (Thomas et al., 1998: 4).

As research highlighting the limitations and inappropriateness of segregated special educational provision combined with the civil rights agenda, which was increasingly demanding equality for disabled people, changes began to emerge with increasing speed. Resistance to continued segregation and the demand for access to mainstream services, including education, were forcing change. Such changes are supported by initiatives such as the Index for Inclusion, which focus on changes within the processes of education to accommodate all children, as opposed to the 'integration' model, which is pupil-focused and responds to perceived deficits or problems within the child. The underpinning philosophy of special provision is therefore changing. (Inclusive practice is further explored in Chapter 17.)

Inclusion within early years settings and within curricula

The process of developing inclusive practices within schools should necessarily incorporate moves to ensure inclusion within curricula. Appropriate curricula in early years settings for all children will place demands on individual practitioners. Advanced specialist skills should not in principle be needed, since the existing responsibilities of practitioners include providing appropriate learning experiences for each child, taking into account his or her strengths and current levels of ability.

At the same time, however, some support and training in differentiating the curriculum to accommodate the needs of *all* children may be needed. While many practitioners are already providing effectively for children with special needs, it may be important to consider a comprehensive training programme to ensure that all pre-school providers are adequately prepared for continued inclusive developments. In such a programme, tools such as an Index for Inclusion for early years would be particularly useful.

Within early years we have now moved from a curriculum-led approach to recognition of the importance and value of a play-based curriculum (see Chapter 8). Taking a more holistic view of children, we are expanding our provision to accommodate children's affective development as well as cognitive development, which can only be viewed as positive. The roles and responsibilities of early years practitioners have also changed considerably, and guidance documents now clearly identify observation, assessment, intervention and evaluation as crucial elements of working practice.

Requirements on early years providers

The demands and expectations placed upon early years providers are now considerable and are exacerbated by the speed of change. It is important to consolidate existing progress and practices before undertaking further development. In England the Foundation Stage requirements (Qualifications and Curriculum Authority, 2000), relating to children from age three to the end of reception year, encompass the notion of inclusive practice and identify clear expectations:

> An awareness and understanding of the requirements of equal opportunities that cover race, gender and disability and of the code of practice on the identification and assessment of special educational needs is essential. Practitioners should plan to meet the needs of both boys and girls, children with special educational needs, children who are more able, children with disabilities, children from all social, cultural and religious backgrounds, children of different ethnic groups including Travellers, refugees and asylum seekers, and children from diverse linguistic backgrounds.
>
> (Qualifications and Curriculum Authority, 2000: 17)

The Foundation Stage supports individualised learning through the use of 'stepping stones' within the Early Learning Goals, with clear examples given within the guidance (QCA, 2000). Such a system supports the identification of *individual differences* in learning (as opposed to 'special needs') and will therefore dovetail with the identification processes highlighted within the Special Educational Needs Code of Practice (Department for Education and Skills, 2001a). A similar system exists in Wales, with the 'desirable outcomes' being fundamental to the new Foundation phase. Through the processes of *Early Years Action* and *Early Years Action Plus*, a graduated approach to providing for children experiencing difficulties, clearly outlined within the Code of Practice, should help practitioners to work towards effective provision for all children. This process has also been adopted in Wales. The purpose and place of Individual Education Plans are indicated, as are the support and guidance of the Special Educational Needs Co-ordinator (SENCO) who will oversee all special needs provision within the setting. The guidance suggests:

> Early education settings should adopt a graduated response so as to be able to provide specific help to individual young children. This approach recognises that there is a continuum of special educational needs and, where necessary, brings increasing specialist expertise to bear on the difficulties a child may be experiencing.

> (Department for Education and Skills, 2001a: section 4: 10)

Access to a range of outside professionals will be necessary to ensure that difficulties such as speech and language disorders, physiotherapy and providing for children with autism are understood and supported appropriately with specialist knowledge. Perhaps the use of specialist support teachers, attached to a group of early years providers, would support developments in this area and enable staff who may previously have worked in special schools and units to continue developing and sharing their knowledge and expertise.

Overall, early years practitioners have the skills to deliver an inclusive education system provided that appropriate levels of training and support are made readily available to *all* settings. Current differences and difficulties must be addressed, such as access to outside professionals for all providers. Private day nurseries and schools, for example, would have varying degrees of access to outside professionals, and funding issues would exist. Within the school the SENCO will have ready access to a range of professionals via the local authority, but for private settings such access is not readily available. Equity for all providers must, therefore, be a priority if we are aiming to support increasing numbers of children with special needs in mainstream provision.

Identification of difficulties and appropriate provision

Some children will enter pre-school settings having already had their difficulties identified, and reports may offer a diagnosis. This diagnosis, however, should not prohibit practitioners from considering other areas of possible difficulty, or affect our expectations of the child. It could be easy to perceive a child as dyspraxic but then overlook a possible hearing problem.

As part of effective early years practice, practitioners are required to include regular ongoing observations and assessments of all children. This will be part of a cyclical provision process (Figure 11.1). Through this process potential difficulties can be highlighted, plans made to provide for children's particular needs, intervention put in place and its effects monitored. If the child's needs are such that ongoing individual planning is required, it may be appropriate to develop an Individual Education Plan (IEP) with parental and SENCO approval. At this point the child would be recorded as on *Early Years Action* in the Code of Practice.

Observations should be well planned to ensure their effectiveness; practitioners therefore need a thorough understanding of the range of observational methods

Figure 11.1   Cyclical provision process

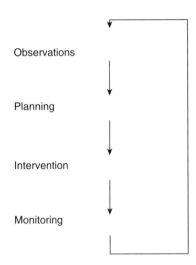

Observations

Planning

Intervention

Monitoring

available. (See Chapter 16 for a more in-depth discussion of child observations.) Observations should consider the child in a holistic way, whereby the child is viewed within all his/her environments and every possible influencing factor is reflected on to inform decisions. To do this practitioners should reflect on the child, the home, the setting and the practitioners involved.

If observations support the professional's view that external support is required, then an appropriate referral should be made. Unfortunately, the availability of appropriate services for a child may well depend on issues relating to local funding and geographical variations. For example, in the case of a young child with autistic-spectrum difficulties, the professional responsible for the diagnosis may vary from county to county, and the availability of local provision to accommodate the child's needs may also vary. In one county there will be mainstream early years educators who have undergone autism-specific training, in another a child may have to attend a local authority special unit or school, whilst in a third county the child may have access to a school specifically for children with autism. This raises issues of equity for all children and their families, and also an issue of which is the most appropriate setting for a young child with autism.

Wall (2003: 131) suggests that the key issues for programmes of intervention include:

1   Any interventions should begin at the child's current stage of development and progress in small steps, reflecting individual needs and taking into account any contributing factors.
2   Regular evaluations and monitoring are needed.
3   IEPs comprising 'SMART' targets are needed.
4   Parental partnerships and interagency working are essential for effective intervention.

Case study

Paul is three years old and has been registered since a few months old to begin attendance at his local mainstream pre-school group. Shortly before the start date his mother contacted the supervisor to request a meeting. At the meeting she presents for discussion a file of reports and medical evidence concerning her son. He has a rare medical condition that has necessitated frequent invasive surgery since birth. He will need further surgery and is likely to be away frequently. Paul cannot eat everyday foodstuffs and wears a feeding backpack all day, being fed by intravenous tube through the night. In addition he has a colostomy bag which will require changing during the pre-school session. Owing to his prolonged and regular hospitalisations he has missed his routine progress assessments with the Health Visitor, but it is assumed that his development may be delayed.

This scenario raises questions and issues for discussion by staff, such as:

1   Can the pre-school cater for Paul's needs?
2   Are there health and safety issues to address?
3   Are the staff trained to provide for his medical needs?
4   If not, can this be achieved?
5   If one-to-one support is needed who will fund it?
6   Which professionals are already involved with Paul and how can liaison be managed?
7   What effects would the difficulties have on Paul's development across all developmental areas?
8   What effects would Paul's illness and hospitalisations have on his parents and siblings?

This situation is simply an example to highlight the impact on the family, practitioners and early years settings, but underlying the difficulties there is a clear need to support this little boy appropriately and effectively to ensure that he achieves his maximum potential. The responsibility is considerable but should be met.

Current issues

Current issues in relation to special needs in the early years may be summarised as follows:

1   Policies are necessary, at local and national level that support inter-agency working systems.
2   Equity of training opportunities for all early years practitioners.
3   Equity in pay, terms and conditions.
4   A continuation of research and developments acknowledging the importance and value of the early years.
5   A continuation of research and developments in early years special needs provision.
6   Further developments to raise the profile of early years workers.

7   Access to resources for all practitioners.
8   Equity of access to 'needs-led' provision, as opposed to 'budget-led provision'.
9   Resolution of funding issues.
10 Clarification of the 'qualifications' framework.

In addition, the commitment of parents and early years practitioners will be key motivators for future developments in achieving greater inclusion.

Conclusion

Early years practitioners deliver in many cases a highly skilled service for children with special needs, and will continue to provide for an increasing diversity of needs. However, it should be acknowledged that for some self-funding groups additional issues arise that compromise their abilities. These issues do not reflect on the abilities of the staff, but on wider issues which are generally outside their direct control. The success of inclusive practices will depend on both the recognition of potential barriers and the motivation and support to address and overcome them.

An ongoing commitment to inclusive practices must be made, with the needs of parents, children and practitioners being heard and responded to. Clear commitment and direction are needed at national level to encourage effective multidisciplinary working systems, without which early years special provision will be severely compromised. The NfER report undertaken by Atkinson et al. (2002) identified key difficulties with current multidisciplinary working and highlighted issues for further development. This indicates the need for ongoing research and development to examine current practices and identify best practice, which can then be shared with the wider audience. Issues connected with physical access are also beginning to emerge as current government requirements call for Action Plans to identify where physical adaptations and improvements are required within schools and early years settings, and how the setting is working towards this goal for future inclusion.

Inclusive practices already exist within many early years settings. With positive and practical encouragement and support, inclusion can evolve from an ideal to a reality. In the future it is hoped that all children will be provided for appropriately within their mainstream settings and the wider society, with the wider society welcoming the diversity presented and enabling and empowering each individual to achieve their maximum potential. We should never forget that this is every child's right.

Questions and exercises

1   What is the difference between an educational system that *accommodates* difference and diversity and one that *celebrates* it?
2   Are there any difficulties with the idea that 'every child has a right to achieve her or his maximum potential'?

3 How relevant are the various conventions and declarations of human rights to the needs of disabled pre-school children?

4 Try to find out more about the 'medical' and 'social' models of disability.

5 How and why has thinking on special education moved from a segregated approach based on a deficit philosophy, through the idea of 'integration' to that of 'inclusive practice'?

6 What are the distinctions between *locational*, *social* and *functional* integration?

7 What are the advantages of a graduated response to special needs that begins with early identification and culminates in a formal statement, as modelled in the code of practice?

8 What special skills or training do early years practitioners require in order to work with children with special needs?

9 What are the most challenging current issues in providing appropriate pre-school experiences for children with special needs?

Reading

The current DfES guidance document *Special Educational Needs Code of Practice* (DfES, 2001a) (can be downloaded or ordered online: www.dfes.gov.uk) is sent to all schools in England to support, develop and inform practice. All students and practitioners working in England should be familiar with this guidance. Wales and Scotland have their own versions. Mortimer, *Special Needs and Early Years Provision* (2001), is a general text covering a range of issues relating to effective special needs provision in early years settings. Sandow (ed.), *Whose Special Need?* (1994) A useful text exploring a range of differing perspectives on special needs issues including legal aspects, foci on therapeutic approaches, sociological considerations and parents' perspectives. Wall, *Special Needs and Early Years* (2003), is another essential early years special needs text covering standard areas such as legislation and intervention strategies but also exploring the affective needs of children, families issues and current issues in the field. Case studies, further reading and discussion suggestions, combined with the accessibility of the text, make this an excellent reference for student and practitioners alike.

Websites

Department for Education and Skills (England)   www.dfes.gov.uk/sen
National Assembly for Wales   www.wales.gov.uk
Scottish Executive Education Department   www.scotland.gov.uk
Disability Rights Commission   www.drc-gb.org
National Association of SEN   www.nasen.org.uk
Centre for Studies on Inclusive Education   www.inclusion.uwe.ac.uk

12
Child Welfare and Child Protection
Bob Sanders
with additional material by Nigel Thomas

Contents

- Family support services for children in need
- Disabled children
- Children 'looked after' by the local authority
- Adoption
- Protecting children from abuse and neglect
- Conclusion

This chapter considers the role of social services agencies in providing and co-ordinating welfare services for children. These principally include: (1) family support services for children in need, including disabled children; (2) services for children who, because they are unable to be with their families, are looked after by local authorities or voluntary organisations; (3) adoption services; and (4) services to protect children from abuse and neglect. Although the delivery of these services may be differently organised in different parts of the country – social services may be autonomous or may be combined with education services, with housing services or with other services, and the organisation of teams and the types of specialisations within teams may vary – they will invariably be provided locally in one way or another.

Although this chapter is based mainly on law and policy in England and Wales, it has relevance to other parts of the United Kingdom, and indeed more widely.

Family support services for children in need

In general, families who require support ought to be able to receive it without stigma; however, there is a threshold for entitlement to local authority support. In England and Wales this threshold is in section 17 of the Children Act 1989, where certain children are defined as 'in need' (see Chapter 9, p. 112). The vast majority of children in the community will not be 'in need' as defined in the Act. Being a child in need is not necessarily a permanent state of affairs, and not all children who need services in the ordinary way will be considered as 'in need' for the purposes of the Act. Even many children who have special education needs may not be defined as children 'in need' of local authority social services. The intention in defining 'need' in this way is to provide a means to target limited resources at those children who *most* need services.

This concept of 'in need' is both restrictive and expansive at the same time. It is restrictive in the sense that the definition, whilst fairly vague and open to interpretation, is intended to specify a small group of children from the wider population of children, who are *entitled* to help from local authority social services departments. The concept is expansive, however, in that at both the individual level and at the level of services for all children who are in need there is a range of specified duties in relation to those children. Previously, this entitlement to services applied only to children who were looked after by the local authority.

In general terms local authorities are *required* to 'to safeguard and promote the welfare of children within their area who are in need', and to 'promote the upbringing of such children by their families, by providing a range and level of services appropriate to those children's needs'. These services may be provided to the child directly or to the child's family. There are a number of specific services (see Chapter 11) which local authorities are expected to make available to children in need, but not necessarily all of them to every child in need.

Under the Act local authorities are expected to be *proactive* in their provision of services – to take reasonable steps to identify which children in their area are in need, to publish information about services provided locally for children in need (both by the authority and by other providers) and ensure that those who could benefit from this information receive it. In providing day care and foster care, they are also expected to take account of the racial groups to which children in need in their area belong. In practice the extent to which these things are done is highly variable. However, local authorities are expected to produce Children's Services Plans, comprehensive plans for responding to the needs of children and families in their area which are drawn up by local authorities in collaboration with other statutory and voluntary agencies, and these plans are produced in most areas on a regular basis.

In practice, the principal services provided for children in need and their families are the services of social workers, access to support groups of various kinds, day care and family centres, and foster care and residential care for those who need it. The provision of foster and residential care is discussed later in the chapter; in this section we will focus on social work services and on family centres.

The Children Act for the first time introduced an expectation on local authorities to provide *family centres* as appropriate for children in their communities. Some areas already provided family centres before the Children Act, but since 1991 there has been growth in their provision. To begin with many centres were little more than enhanced day nurseries, although they were at least seeking to involve parents more positively in the care of their children. Since then many new purpose-built family centres have been developed, frequently in partnership between the statutory and voluntary sectors, providing valuable support to families in many different ways. The Children Act Guidance on family support (Department of Health, 1991a) describes three types of family centres: therapeutic, community and self-help.

There are a number of ways that *social workers* can assist children in need and their families. They may provide advice, guidance and counselling. They may provide advocacy on behalf of clients with Income Support, Housing, Health, Education and other agencies. They may in exceptional circumstances provide direct financial assistance to families. Much of the work of social workers with children and families is focused on assessment of need, now increasingly carried out in ways prescribed by national standards and frameworks such as the *Framework for the Assessment of Children in Need and their Families* (Department of Health et al., 2000; National Assembly for Wales, 2000a). The subsequent provision of services may be directly undertaken by the local authority, or arranged indirectly through the independent (private or voluntary) sector.

During the 1990s direct service provision by local authorities became less common. In keeping with the Act's emphasis on working in partnership with the voluntary sector, local authorities increasingly used the services of voluntary organisations through 'service contracts'. In Wales, for instance, there is great reliance on the voluntary sector for service provision, especially in childcare; for example, Barnardo's and NCH Action for Children have many projects operating in Wales. In addition there is the private sector, including private children's homes, private foster care agencies and private day care facilities. The links between local authorities and the independent sector take a number of forms: referring families to services, providing financial support for families to use services, and funding services directly (mainly in the voluntary sector). In the past local authorities were also responsible for registering and inspecting services provided by the independent sector, but this is now the responsibility of a separate Care Standards Inspectorate.

A number of studies in the 1990s looked at the effectiveness of the delivery of services for children in need, for instance the *Children Act Report 1992* (Department of Health, 1993), the Audit Commission report *Seen but not Heard* (Audit Commission, 1994), the research of Colton for the former Welsh Office (Colton et al., 1995) and the report by the Social Services Inspectorate of the Department of Health (Social Services Inspectorate, 1996). All these reports commented on the nature of inter-agency working (see Chapter 16). In addition they all found a strong tendency to concentrate on children for whom the local authority already had responsibility, for example looked after children and abused or neglected children. Colton et al. looked at the 'operational definitions of need developed by local authority SSDs ... identification and prioritisation of children in need; partnership with parents and children; interagency co-operation; cultural issues; publication of information about services; and complaints procedures' (1995: 3). They found that whilst 81 per cent of parents interviewed were comfortable to approach social services for help, only 63 per cent of parents were satisfied with the help they had received. The rest were dissatisfied. The SSI report (1996) noted that because routine services were generally so underdeveloped, cases other than those in crisis were rarely afforded priority. Formal assessments were rarely being undertaken and care plans arising from assessments were consequently rare.

Disabled children

Disabled children are defined as children 'in need' for the purposes of local authority services. As noted in the Introduction to Part III and in Chapter 11, there is more than one model of thinking about disability. Increasingly in social work the *social model* is the one used to understand and respond to the significance of disability in the lives of children and their families.

It is worth starting by looking back to the principles underlying the All-Wales Strategy for Mental Handicap. This was a Welsh Office initiative that ran for ten years from 1983 and was designed to transform services for people with learning disabilities. The strategy rested on three simple principles:

1 People with a learning disability have a right to ordinary patterns of life within the community.
2 People with a learning disability have a right to be treated as individuals.
3 People with a learning disability have a right to additional help from the community in which they live and from professional services, in order to enable them to develop their maximum potential as individuals.

It is argued here that these principles should apply to all children with disabilities, including physical and sensory disabilities.

A view frequently expressed in connection with disabled children is that they are children first and disabled second. The significance of this is clear when we face situations in which the child's needs arising from a disability are in conflict with the ordinary needs that all children have. An example was the former practice of placing children with severe learning difficulties in long-stay hospitals. It was believed that the need which all children have, for experience of a family life, with opportunities for attachment and bonding, was less important than the need for highly trained specialist care arising from the child's special needs. The All-Wales Strategy, with its clear principles, enabled many children with severe learning difficulties to be moved from long-stay hospitals into foster and adoptive families.

Disabled children are required to receive specific consideration in Children's Services Plans, and guidance under the Children Act specifies a range of services which ought to be available. Social services departments should be providing social work and counselling, family centres, day care and childminding services, both respite care and longer-term accommodation. They should also provide occupational therapy, holiday play schemes, toy libraries, home care and home help services, rehabilitation services and loans of equipment. In addition they should offer help with transport costs, information on services available, welfare benefit advice, interpreters and other services for people from minority ethnic groups, advocacy and representation for children and parents, after-care and a transition to adult services.

Alongside these services are those provided by local education authorities, which in addition to school and related services may include the services of home-school liaison teachers and Portage services for children with learning disabilities. In this scheme a home visitor visits a family each week to assess children and help them to achieve complex tasks by breaking them down into simple units which can then be combined. There are different views on the benefits of Portage, but some families find it extremely helpful (Mittler, 1990).

According to Russell (1992) *respite care* is a 'key service for families with disabled children', although only a small proportion of families with disabled children have access to it. The service is normally provided either directly by the local authority or by a voluntary agency, usually under a service agreement. As the name implies, respite care aims to provide parents with a break from the demands of looking after a disabled child. Respite care was once provided in residential settings, but since the 1970s successful efforts have been made to find families willing to care for disabled children, and the main type of care now is in families. Names given to schemes such as 'Family Link' and 'Contact a Family' reflect this new pattern of service delivery. Respite is usually offered for a specified short period such as a weekend, or for longer periods to enable families to have holidays.

Three reports in the 1990s focused on evaluating services for disabled children: the *Children Act Report 1992* (Department of Health, 1993), the Social Services Inspectorate report (1995) and that by Weston et al. (1995). The main themes arising from the *Children Act Report* were about partnership with parents, consultation with children (or lack of it), low take-up of services by minority ethnic communities, insufficient information to parents, the work needed to integrate services into mainstream, the lack of assessments and the lack of effective multi-agency registers. The SSI report developed twelve standards against which to measure the provision of services for children with disabilities and inspected four authorities against those standards. Some of the themes that arose were: the need for more policy work; wide disparities in the skill levels of workers; work needed to develop racially and culturally sensitive services; a lack of clarity in some authorities about which agency had the lead responsibility for service provision; too many respite care arrangements still in residential establishments; lack of assessments; lack of effective registers; the impact of service reorganisation; and the lack of increased involvement of the voluntary sector following the Children Act. Weston et al. (1995) evaluated six day care services for under-fives chosen to include a range in type of provision, geographical location and demography. They reported on the following eight areas: isolation, diversity of provision, quality of care, integration, cultural sensitivity, partnership with parents, publicity and information and relations between agencies. There were three areas they considered needed particular attention: the role of services to disabled children and how they fit into the pattern of services for other children, the importance of retaining specialist knowledge and expertise in disability during local authority reorganisation, and the 'continuing need for better collaboration between agencies providing for disabled children' (Weston et al., 1995: 65).

Children 'looked after' by the local authority

As we saw in Chapter 9, the Children Act 1989 and the Children (Scotland) Act 1995 brought significant changes in the way we think about children in the care system. Among these was the concept of 'looked after', which includes children who are 'accommodated' under voluntary arrangements and children who are 'in care' under compulsory provisions ('under supervision' in Scotland).

Children may be looked after in a variety of settings and by a variety of different agencies. These include foster family placements provided by the local authority or by private or voluntary agencies, foster placement with relatives of the child, residential care of various kinds, and sometimes supported lodgings for older children.

In addition many children formally in care are supported in living at home with their own families.

Whether a child is looked after on a voluntary or compulsory basis, there are legal requirements concerning the arrangements to be made, as we saw in Chapter 9. The agency has a duty to safeguard and promote the child's welfare and a responsibility to accommodate and maintain the child. The agency must find out and give 'due consideration' to the wishes and feelings of the child and the family. It should arrange for the child to be looked after near his or her home, and for siblings to be accommodated together, whenever appropriate. The particular needs of disabled children should be catered for, and the agency must give consideration to the child's religious persuasion, racial origin, and cultural and linguistic background when arranging a placement.

Regulations require that written plans for the child should be made in advance – or, in an emergency, as soon as possible afterwards. These plans should include the immediate and long-term plans for the child; the expected duration of the placement; the arrangements for contact; the child's state of health and health care needs; arrangements for the child's education; and whether an independent visitor should be appointed. The child should be medically examined (unless this has been done within the previous three months). There are also requirements for the child's plans and progress to be reviewed at regular intervals. In these reviews there should be consultation and participation by the child and family, and the child's rights should be explained to her or him.

Contact with family and friends is very important when a child is living apart from family, home and community. Research shows that regular contact is associated with a successful placement and successful return home, and legislation strongly emphasises the importance of family contact. Planning for the child's eventual return home, or if necessary for a move to a permanent substitute family, should be a part of every review.

The Looking After Children materials

Perhaps the most significant development in looking after children in recent years has been the development of standardised means of monitoring the progress of children who are looked after through the Assessment and Action Records (Department of Health, 1995a). These forms and the associated planning and review documents are often referred to as the 'LAC' forms. The Assessment and Action Records are intended to be completed at regular intervals for all children who are looked after and linked with periodic reviews. The records are designed differently for each age group, but all are organised under the same seven 'developmental dimensions':

1   Health.
2   Education.
3   Identity.
4   Family and social relations.
5   Social presentation.
6   Emotional and behavioural development.
7   Self-care skills.

The records address most of the important issues when a child is being looked after away from his or her parents, and have often been found helpful in focusing attention on the whole child. However, there have been objections to the view of parenting embodied in the LAC system (e.g. Knight and Caveney, 1998).

Adoption

Children who have been adopted are not 'looked after' by the local authority. But, given the trends in adoption over the last three decades, most children will have been looked after for a period prior to being adopted.

Over the last thirty years, the overall number of children being adopted has declined from over 20,000 to around 7,000 per year. Within that decreasing number the proportion of adoptions which are of children under one year has also been declining, and fewer than 1,000 babies per year are being adopted in the United Kingdom. This is far fewer than the number of couples unable to have children of their own who would like to adopt.

There are three main reasons for the declining number of babies available for adoption. First, there is the greater availability and use of contraception which result in fewer unwanted pregnancies. Second is the greater social acceptability of single parenthood. Although it is difficult to raise a child on one's own, and considerable societal disapproval and stigma are attached to single parenthood, these difficulties are not nearly so marked as in previous decades. A third reason is the increased use of abortion as a means of ending an unwanted pregnancy.

Under the Adoption and Children Act 2002 (see Chapter 11) local authorities are expected to provide adoption services for:

1   Children who may be adopted, their parents and guardians.
2   Persons wishing to adopt a child.
3   Adopted persons, their parents, natural parents and former guardians.

This includes making arrangements for the adoption of children and providing adoption support services. Agencies other than local authorities can also provide adoption services, and local authorities are expected to work in partnership with such agencies.

Under adoption regulations, which may change following the 2002 Act, the major decisions of an adoption agency in relation to the adoption of a child are based on the recommendations of an adoption panel. The panel has three primary functions: to consider the needs of children and recommend whether adoption is the best plan; to consider the circumstances of prospective adopters and recommend whether they should be allowed to adopt a child; and to make recommendations concerning the 'match' between a particular child and particular adopters.

Adoption is a controversial topic about which many people have strong views (sometimes related to lack of knowledge of the complexities involved). Issues such as transracial adoptions, inter-country adoptions, openness in adoption, post-adoption services, applicants being overweight or smokers, upper age limits of applicants, have at different times all been the focus of considerable media attention – often concluding that social workers and adoption agencies are being unfair or 'politically correct'. However, the standards applied to adoption in the United Kingdom are second to none in the world, and it is only through keeping a clear focus on adoption as a service designed to meet the needs of the child, and not the needs of adults wishing to have children (important as those may be), that such standards have been able to be maintained.

Protecting children from abuse and neglect

This section will consider the social services function in working with other agencies to provide a comprehensive and co-ordinated local service to protect children from neglect and abuse in their various forms. Like adoption, child protection is another extremely controversial area of practice, and practice has been repeatedly scrutinised and changed as a result of high-profile cases and intense media and political interest. This has led to considerable anxiety within practice, and concern about whether practice in this area is truly developing or simply reacting to temporary concern at different times. Here we will briefly consider some of the dilemmas in child protection.

Processes and structures in child protection

Local authorities have a legal duty to investigate abuse and neglect (see Chapter 9). Understanding that may help to avoid confusion over why social workers sometimes get involved in less serious cases. We discuss the balance between under-intervention and over-intrusion later in this section, but it is important to understand this duty to investigate as an overarching legal context of practice.

The fundamental premise of child protection work in the United Kingdom, apart from the obvious need to keep the child's welfare in the forefront, is that children are best protected when the various agencies involved work well together. It follows that children are less well protected where there is disharmony, poor communication or even hostility between agencies. In the wake of a series of child tragedies in which children have been killed by their parents or carers, since the 1970s an elaborate system has been developed enabling agencies and departments to work together at each level: the national level, the local level, and the level of the individual case.

At the *national* level, it is important to note that although public agencies such as the police, social services and health services are ultimately accountable to Parliament, this is achieved via different departmental routes. Prior to political devolution and greater autonomy for Scotland and Wales, a single document of uniform government guidance on child protection (Home Office et al., 1991) was produced by four governmental bodies working in unison to enable harmonious working between public bodies with different professional backgrounds and different political accountabilities (see Sanders, 1999). The four Ministries involved at the time were the Home Office, responsible for police and probation, the Department of Health for social work, nursing and medicine, the then Department for Education and Science for teachers and other education staff, and the Welsh Office, which was responsible for health and education services in Wales. These four departments had first to agree between themselves how they wanted professionals to work together in child protection. This entailed a process of negotiation whose ultimate objective was to remove the barriers to working together which might arise from different understandings and objectives on the part of different departments. The result was *Working Together under the Children Act 1989* (Home Office et al., 1991). That guidance has since been revised and reissued to reflect devolution and reorganisation as well as changes in practice (Department of Health et al., 1999; National Assembly for Wales, 2000b).

At the local level the key institution is the Area Child Protection Committee (ACPC). This is the successor body to the Area Review Committees established following the inquiry into the death of Maria Colwell in 1974. It is a local 'forum for agreeing how the different services and professional groups should co-operate to safeguard children in that area, and for making sure that arrangements work effectively to bring about good outcomes for children' (Department of Health et al., 1999: 33; National Assembly for Wales, 2000b: 34). The membership of the Area Child Protection Committee, although variable, includes senior managers from those agencies which have a significant role in the health and welfare of children.

At the level of the individual case the key institution is the *child protection conference*. It is here that the individual circumstances of particular children are considered, usually at an initial child protection conference, followed if necessary by review conferences. Whenever a case involves suspected harm in relation to a child or children, a decision will be made as to whether to convene a child protection conference. The conference aims to bring together information concerning the child and carers, to assess the future likelihood of significant harm, and to make a plan to promote the child's welfare. Someone independent of the management of the case chairs the conference. A range of professionals are invited to attend: social worker, health visitor, teacher, police, paediatrician, and so on. Parents are normally invited, although in rare circumstances they may be excluded from part or all of the meeting. Depending upon age and understanding children may be invited to attend, although this is still quite rare; other ways may be found to convey the child's views to the conference by an advocate or professional speaking on their behalf, or *via* video-tape, audio-tape or letter. The conference decides whether to add the child(ren)'s name to the *child protection register*. If it does so then a *key worker* is appointed, a *child protection plan* developed, and a core group nominated to implement and monitor the plan between review conferences. Parents are normally part of the core group, and occasionally children may be included. In these ways the conference is responsible for co-ordinating inter-agency work to reduce the risk to the child. However, the conference cannot override individual agencies in their particular responsibilities for children. Thus the decision as to whether or not to initiate care proceedings remains with social services, and the decision whether to prosecute remains with the police and Crown Prosecution Service.

Proposals to change the child protection system were made by Laming (2003) in the report on the death of Victoria Climbié and in the subsequent Green Paper (HM Government, 2003), in the context of an extensive review of childcare and child protection services. Key recommendations of the Green Paper include:

1   An independent Children's Commissioner for England (like those already introduced in Wales and planned for Scotland and Northern Ireland).
2   A clear statement of a child's right to expect: staying safe; being healthy; experiencing enjoyment and achievement at school; making a positive contribution to society; economic well-being.
3   The establishment of children's trusts uniting local health, education and social services.

4   The appointment of a local children's director to take the place of education and social services directors.
5   ACPCs to be replaced by local children's safeguarding boards.
6   Every child to be given a unique identifying number.
7   Joint training and protocols for childcare professionals to promote inter-professional working.

After a long series of child death inquiries since Maria Colwell (Department of Health and Social Security, 1974) with varied impact on law and policy, the Laming report appears to be spearheading a major transformation of children's services, perhaps the most radical since the establishment of children's departments in 1948 following the Curtis report (1946) into the death of Dennis O'Neill, or the establishment of 'generic' social services departments in 1971 following the Seebohm Committee report (1968).

Issues and dilemmas in child protection

Since the publication of *Child Protection: Messages from Research* (Department of Health, 1995b) child protection in the United Kingdom has been engaged in a so-called 'refocusing debate'. The publication summarised the findings of twenty research studies into child protection commissioned after the events in Cleveland in summer 1987 and the subsequent report in 1988. Summarised here are some of the main themes to emerge from *Messages from Research*.

1   Definitions of abuse are important, and can influence thresholds of intervention. As quoted in one study (Gibbons et al., 1995: 12), 'child maltreatment is more like pornography than whooping cough. It is a socially constructed phenomenon which reflects values and opinions of a particular culture at a particular time.'
2   It was found that families overwhelmed and depressed by social problems formed the greatest proportion of those assessed and supported by child protection agencies. However, these are not the families perhaps where children are most in need of protection. Whereas child protection appears to work well with the most severe cases, it seems to work less well with needy families, who resent being brought into the 'abuse' system. Therefore, many of the families being scrutinised by the child protection system are families in need of help. However, in a majority of cases, families received no services as the result of professional concerns. It was suggested therefore, that a more effective approach in many situations where abuse is relatively minor would be to tackle the causes of maltreatment by means of inquiry followed by family assessment, followed, where appropriate, by support services, rather than with heavy-handed investigations which leave the family unassisted.
3   Achieving partnership with parents, whilst always an objective when working with families in need of support, is nonetheless a goal in child protection. In initial discussions with parents the provision of information is helpful. At a protection meeting, preparation, understanding of procedures, physical layout and styles of interaction are important. Protection issues are best viewed in the context of the children's wider needs. It was found that social workers wanted to work with families because they believed it would make their practice more

effective. But achieving partnership is difficult; there are many barriers to overcome. However, when family support is being offered, parents find questions about abuse less traumatic, and they are more likely to co-operate with professionals. But failure to follow interventions through with much-needed family support prevented professionals from meeting the needs of children and families. An important conclusion was that the general family context is more important than any abusive event within it.

4   The overall conclusion was that there should be a reconsideration of the balance of services to alter the way in which professionals are perceived by those parents accused of abusing or neglecting their offspring. Five specific themes were developed. First, practitioners should aim for sensitive and informed professional/client relations. Second, it should be an objective to achieve an appropriate balance of power between the key parties. Third, a broad perspective is needed on child abuse. Fourth, there needs to be effective supervision and training of social workers. Finally, there needs to be determination to enhance the quality of children's lives.

(Department of Health, 1995b: 52)

How has government reacted to these findings? Initially the government adopted a 'hands off' approach. Local authorities were left to reconcile the conflicting agendas of 'defensive child protection' based on sensitivity to media criticism following child deaths and a 'lighter touch' based on understanding of the harm that can be done to families by the wrong intervention. However, the government eventually indicated that it would revise guidance to integrate the new themes. It has done this in the revised versions of *Working Together*, which have been implemented in conjunction with the *Framework for the Assessment of Children in Need and their Families* (Department of Health et al., 2000; National Assembly for Wales, 2000a). The reasoning is that if the same assessment framework is applied to all children in need and to the smaller subgroup of children in need of protection, it should be easier to deal with a family as being in need of family support rather than needing the heavier end of child protection. However, because the assessment framework is being applied to the wider group of children in need, there are significant resource implications. Many families will be required to have the kind of assessment which, although previously recognised as good practice to provide, was not in fact undertaken because of lack of resources such as staff time. It remains to be seen how these conflicting demands will be resolved.

Conclusion

This chapter has summarised the main roles of social services in providing welfare services for children. It has considered the family support services that are provided to families who are attempting to overcome adversity in raising their children. To do this, and to rationalise and make efficient use of scarce resources, social services have had to rely on the Children Act definition of a child being 'in need'. One group of vulnerable children are those with disabilities, and the chapter has given particular consideration to how social services help them and their families.

Social services are frequently called upon to look after children when, for one reason or another, they cannot live at home. There has been considerable development in this area with the increasing use of the Looking After Children (LAC) materials, which have brought a higher degree of consistency to caring for children away from their family, and raised the standards of practice in this area. Social services (and others) also have responsibility for other children who cannot live with their family, those who go on to be adopted. The trends in adoption were noted, as well as the controversy frequently surrounding adoption issues. Another area of controversy addressed in this chapter is child protection. Here the ongoing challenge of finding the right balance between over-intervention and under-intervention, as well as the dramatic consequences of getting it wrong, are considered. The chapter ends with a brief consideration of the most recent (at the time of writing) government proposals to provide a more integrated service for children.

Questions and exercises

Arrange to interview a child care social worker in a child and family team, or a project worker in a voluntary organisation family support project (for example a family centre). Ask the social worker/project worker about: (1) what the worker is trying to achieve in work undertaken with children and families, (2) what are the obstacles to achieving the agency's objectives, and how are the agency and worker addressing those obstacles?

Reading

There are good overviews of child welfare services in Hill and Aldgate (eds), *Child Welfare Services* (1996), and Stevenson, *Child Welfare in the UK* (1999). Hill and Tisdall, *Children and Society* (1997), is a good general introduction to this and other areas. Colton, Sanders and Williams, *An Introduction to Working with Children* (2001), Butler and Roberts, *Social Work with Children and Families* (2003), and Brandon, Schofield and Trinder, *Social Work with Children* (1998), are all useful texts guiding social workers in their practice with children and families; Hill (ed.), *Effective Ways of Working with Children and their Families* (1999), is also useful on ways of working with children and families in practice. Parton, *Child Protection and Family Support* (1997), offers a stimulating discussion of some of the more contested issues in child welfare. The government Green Paper *Every Child Matters* (HM Government 2003) is also recommended reading; it is likely to lay the foundation for child welfare services for many years to come.

13
Child Health
Anne Kelly

Contents

- Defining health
- Models of health and health care
- 'Nature versus nurture'
- Child health and social factors
- The state, family responsibility and child health
- Programmes to improve children's health
- Conclusion

Over fifty years ago the World Health Organisation described health as a 'state of complete physical, mental and social well-being, not merely the absence of disease and infirmity' (World Health Organisation, 1948). The purpose of this chapter is to explore the concept of child health and identify the means by which it can be achieved. Recognising that the concept of health is usually viewed in a more negative way, Downie et al. (1991) suggest that often it merely conveys the notion of an absence of ill health. Thus, a child who has no tangible symptoms of ill health, such as 'spots' or pain, may be regarded as healthy. This kind of reasoning prevents us from recognising that health should entail a positive feeling of well-being. It also disguises the fact that there are many determinants of health other than physiological malfunction. Hall and Elliman (2003) argue that many factors which have the potential to 'seriously harm' a child's health may at best be ignored, and at worst remain unrecognised, if we fail to accept that social, economic and environmental factors are as important as biological disorders as causes of poor health in children.

In the light of these considerations, this chapter will take account of all those factors which may affect child health, and consider how they are addressed. Over the past three decades there has been growing acceptance of ecological theories of child health (Hall and Elliman, 2003; Beckman Murray and Proctor Zentner, 1985). These theories alert us to the fact that throughout life health may be more dependent upon a balance of factors that influence interactions between the child, the family and the environment than on the presence of disease or malfunction. This view helps us to understand that although the family is primarily responsible for nurturing children and promoting their health, the family in turn is dependent on community resources for its survival (Daniel and Ivatts, 1998). Thus, it appears that the concept of child health cannot be divorced from environmental and social conditions within a country, neighbourhood, community or family. All these factors may adversely affect children's health and development throughout their lifetime (Power, 1995; Barker, 1992). This raises the question of where the responsibility for child health lies – with the family or with the state – and to what extent can policy affect children's health and life chances? Consequently, this chapter will also review current policy interventions intended to improve child health.

Defining health

The most commonly quoted definition of health is that of the World Health Organisation, quoted at the beginning of this chapter. More recently, however, health has been defined as 'a positive concept emphasising social and personal resources as well as physical capacities' (World Health Organisation, 1984).

In day-to-day work with children, this positive notion of child health may be neglected in favour of a 'sickness service' rather than a service to promote, sustain or improve child health (Hall and Elliman, 2003; McIntyre, 1997; Oakley, 1992). It is important to distinguish between 'negative' and 'positive' views of health, but this is not easy, as although negative views of health concentrate only on ill health, the concept of ill health is not straightforward (Downie et al., 1991). Whereas one child may feel and be seen to be ill because of a diagnosed disease, another may have a disease without feeling ill; for example, a pre-symptomatic disease such as child-hood cancer may exhibit no immediate symptoms. On the other hand, a child with no diagnosed disease may feel ill as a result of situational factors – for instance, family or school tensions such as bullying (Smith and Sharp, 1994). The complications of defining illness incorporate both subjective and objective views of illness; children may be aware of distinctions between *feeling ill* and *being ill*, and that they may not receive attention for 'subjective' accounts.

A child who is labelled as ill must suffer from a medically defined condition, which can be identified by a set of predetermined symptoms, often recognised only by health care professionals (see Hill and Tisdall, 1997). Although such symptoms may cause recognisable and predictable changes in the way body systems work (for example, a child who complains of tiredness, shortness of breath and fails to thrive may have heart disease), taken to extremes this perspective fails to recognise sub-jective feeling of illness. As a result discomfort caused by social or environmental factors may be dismissed as unimportant although it may cause extreme distur-bance in physical or mental health (Coppock, 1996). A parallel may be drawn with regard to disability or deformity. Whilst severe forms of these conditions may attract various forms of medical intervention, minor defects may not be judged to warrant intervention although they cause suffering to the child.

More positive views of health, such as that quoted from the World Health Organisation, embrace more complex notions of fitness and well-being. Fitness is viewed as the ability to carry out routine activity, whilst well-being is described as being a 'foundation for achievement' (Seedhouse, 1990: 12); both help the individual to achieve maximum potential. In contrast to a negative view of health, this positive perspective suggests that health is soundness of body and mind and a state of 'wholeness' (Hall and Elliman, 2003: 6).

Downie et al. (1991) suggest that such a level of health can be achieved only if a child is nurtured, has friends and the confidence that material needs will be satisfied. According to this view, fitness and well-being go hand in hand to constitute a state of positive health, with health best regarded in terms of a continuum from fitness and well-being at one end to ill health and disease at the other. Although health is a product of many components, and precise quantification is almost impossible, it is suggested that improving health may depend on moving from negative to positive views of health which emphasise the importance of fitness and well-being.

This means that a new value system may be required to increase the emphasis on social rather than medical care (Macdonald, 1998). Such a value system would recognise the importance of differentiating between disease, ill health and well-being. It would also appreciate that good child health is dependent on the ability to distinguish the differences between medical and social models of health care, and on the recognition that to achieve high standards of child health both medical and social interventions are necessary, provided by a number of agencies other than those solely concerned with health care. Hall and Elliman (2003) suggest that since the Human Rights Act 2000 and the UN Convention on the Rights of the Child there has been a strong government commitment to reducing inequalities in the health of children, and to developing fiscal policies that address social issues which impinge on health. Such policies require cross-departmental collaboration or 'joined-up thinking' on the part of social and health care professions.

Models of health and health care

Medical and social models

Medical models of care are focused on aspects of negative health, disease and disability. They tend to view the human being as a machine which can be repaired when specific faults arise (Macdonald, 1998). Those who adopt this model are concerned with interventions to relieve symptoms rather than the achievement of a complete state of health.

Social models of health, on the other hand, adopt the view that disease and illness are not necessarily caused by dysfunction of the body. According to this view, a variety of ecological and social factors can all cause ill health. Acheson (1998), the government's official adviser, has asserted that health will continue to decline as long as many families are socially excluded. According to this view, fulfilling engagement with family, community and society is an essential prerequisite of health.

Between the two extremes of medical and social models of health care lie a number of perspectives which Beckman Murray and Proctor Zentner (1985) suggest are helpful in formulating a framework for assessing health status. These models will be addressed briefly in order to provide a broad overview of the frameworks in which the concept of health may be defined in our multi-ethnic contemporary society.

Other models

Philosophical models of health care are often underpinned by religious doctrines which suggest that a certain degree of discomfort, pain or disease are an inevitable part of life. Such conditions are seen as opportunities for empathising with less fortunate others, so growing in self-understanding, moral strength and wisdom. Meaning is thought to evolve from such experiences and as a result a positive state of health or well-being may emerge. This model shows how the concept of health may be socially constructed according to prevalent cultural beliefs or values.

Psychoanalytical models of health care are based on the assumption that emotional or physical trauma in childhood may affect health. It is assumed that identification of such experiences will allow professionals to recognise the cause of traumatised personalities. This model recognises the importance of the quality of the nurturing process in children's lives, and emphasises the importance of good parenting.

Behavioural models of health believe in the necessity to change health behaviours through processes of stimulus and reward. This model is frequently applied to the medical management of child health problems such as obesity, antisocial behaviour and daily living skills so that children can be socialised to conform with acceptable patterns of behaviour (Hill and Tisdall, 1997). However, reviews of the literature on health (Hall and Elliman, 2003; Bartley et al., 1998) show that there is a shift away from models of health and health care which focus on individual defects and behavioural deficits, and towards holistic models of health in which the wholeness of an individual is paramount and each element capable of contributing to the creation of well-being is valued. Thus a model is currently favoured which recognises the value of the nurturing process in developing the 'natural' tendencies of a child and the importance of a child's social environment.

'Nature versus nurture'

The consideration of medical and social models of health and health care clearly illustrates the spectrum of thinking that informs decisions on child health interventions. Those who are largely influenced by medical models of care may favour the view that child health is more likely to be the product of heredity, whereas those influenced by social models of health may be more inclined to recognise that a child's environment is influential in determining health status.

Mendelian laws of inheritance (see Hull and Johnson, 1987, for an account) do not explain diseases or illnesses caused by environmental factors which have an effect on a child's genetic potential from the moment of conception (Barker, 1992; Power, 1995). It is the view of Beckman Murray and Proctor Zentner (1985) that, whereas in the past negative views of health may have contributed to the belief that child health and development were dependent on nature, realisation of more positive interpretations of the concept of health have shown that nurture, or the presence of certain social conditions, has a more profound effect on child health. Aside from hereditary factors, it has been shown that maternal age, maternal nutrition and teratogens such as radiation, food additives, smoking, drugs and alcohol can all have an adverse effect on the developing foetus. From the moment of birth a child's health may be influenced by culture, race, ethnicity, child-rearing practices and family factors such as family structure, stresses and status, as well as the family's access to work, leisure, travel, material comforts, habits of daily living and environmental surroundings. All these factors appear to be able to affect the child's self-concept, learning capacity, physical well-being and health throughout the life span (Hall and Elliman, 2003).

Whereas in the past mothers and fathers tended to be held responsible for many of these processes (Lynn, 1974; Morgan, 1995), it is now agreed by many commentators that a positive environment may overcome negative perinatal or hereditary influences, but a negative environment may have lasting effects (Morgan, 1995). This means that the advantages of inheriting good health can be lost if a child does not have the right environment in which to develop. For example, many studies show that social disadvantage and lack of opportunities can 'seriously damage health' (Davies, 1993: 48; see also Hall and Elliman, 2003; Children and Young People's Unit, 2000). Hall and Elliman conclude that achieving child health depends on recognising that the health of children is the product of both nature and nurture; a holistic approach is therefore required to promote child health. Traditional 'medical models' of health based on assumptions about parental deficits in knowledge, skills, insight or motivation are flawed, as the reality is that parental preoccupation with life and environmental circumstances may prevent them benefiting from professional advice on child health. The majority of parents expect their children to have good health, but life and environmental circumstances may interfere with their expectation. This means that for some families the acceptance of total responsibility for their child's health is not a realistic option.

Child health and social factors

Even the best standards of health care provision can ensure good health only if a child's circumstances provide him or her with an environment that is conducive to good health. As has already been discussed, health is only partially dependent on the presence or absence of disease; it is often dependent on factors outside the scope of doctors or institutions of health care. Daniel and Ivatts (1998) comment that whereas few people would deny a child's right to health or health care, this right is mediated by a child's parents, their social situation and environment. It is also the case that although there have been tremendous improvements in child health during the twentieth century, differences in standards of health between different sectors of the population have increased, so that there are significant variations in child health which can be attributed to social, geographical, ethnic and occupational factors.

The social support of parents and their children is therefore a critical factor in child health. Hall and Elliman (2003: 31) define support as 'information leading the subject to believe that s/he is cared for, loved, esteemed and a member of a network of mutual obligations'. To ensure child health parents themselves require a sense of belonging to a wider community. Putnam (2000) suggests that a sense of social cohesion is essential to health; the development of social networks reduces the stresses of disadvantage, isolation and hopelessness, improves health and provides a form of 'social capital' which ensures long-term health gains.

Social class and child health

Marked class differences are still apparent in measures of child health. Whereas infant mortality rates have improved steadily in all social classes, there are still marked class differences for children who belong to social classes IV and V (Hall and Elliman, 2003). In fact, infant mortality rates for children of semi-skilled and unskilled workers are respectively 40 per cent and 60 per cent higher than for children of professional (social class I) parents (Woodroffe et al., 1993). This inequality exists throughout childhood and persists into adulthood (Benzeval et al., 1995). Boys appear to be at greater risk than girls, but the differential in child mortality by social class affects both sexes, so that children from social class V are nearly four times more likely to die from injury – especially road accidents, fires or poisoning – than children in social classes I, II and III. Whitehead (1992) has shown that if all infants and children up to the age of fifteen enjoyed the same survival chances as children from classes I and II, then over 3,000 deaths a year might be prevented. Although class differences are less pronounced for childhood illness, Woodroffe et al. suggest that 'a higher proportion of children from manual groups [are] ... suffering from a long-standing illness limiting their activities' (1993: 92). Numerous studies have shown that childhood circumstances have long term sequelae for adult health and socio-economic circumstances (see Strachan, 1997). Probably the most powerful research method for detecting such information is birth cohort studies, such as the ongoing British study commenced in 1946 (Graham, 2000) and the cohort study undertaken by Berney et al. (2000), which show how childhood and lifetime exposure to combined hazards of a social nature affect both health and social status.

Poverty, unemployment and child health

Links between unemployment, poverty and health status have long been recognised (see Whitehead, 1992: 253). The children of families in which one or both parents are unemployed may therefore be doubly disadvantaged in that not only do they suffer the deprivations of low income, but they may have parents whose health is impaired. Fagin (1981) showed that unemployment affected families in many ways. Financial worry caused family tension, depression, headaches, asthmatic attacks and loss of appetite. Since the 1980s recession in the United Kingdom, there has been a polarisation in the distribution of work between 'work-rich' two-earner households and 'work-poor' no-earner households. Particular areas of the country have born the brunt of this situation, resulting in many families experiencing a form of social exclusion. Curtis and Rees Jones (1998) show how health data for geographical areas can be used to demonstrate health inequality. Blaxter's (1990) 'health and lifestyle study' showed that, for individuals of similar social class, health status varied according to their residential area. People living in deprived districts showed a greater prevalence of illness than those with a similar social profile in more privileged areas (see Congdon et al.,1997). Conditions in local labour markets and the effects of industrial restructuring may therefore have relevance for health variation. Phillimore and Morris (1991), for example, showed the environmental impact upon health of industries in Middlesbrough and Sunderland, whilst Haynes et al. (1997) demonstrated that in areas of high unemployment more people were likely to report long-term illness. Similarly, Senior (1998) confirmed that high levels of illness in Wales and the north-east of England are associated with decline in coal mining.

Other studies of the association between health and deprivation show that that there is more ill health in urban than rural areas (Phillimore and Reading, 1992). However, Bentham (1984) showed that whilst suburban and semi-rural areas have a more favourable health status than inner cities, populations in remote rural areas may also be disadvantaged. There are also clear north–south gradients in health status. Congdon et al. (1997) showed significant differences in both mortality and self-reported illness between the north and the south, after allowing for socio-economic differences between the two areas. Thus it appears that health disadvantage may be exacerbated in socially and economically deprived areas, particularly in declining industrial areas.

It may be concluded that changes in the labour market in various parts of the country have contributed to many families having to live on a low income. A growth in the number of people losing their jobs, coupled with an increase in the length of time taken to find another one, has resulted in high levels of unemployment, and long-term unemployment in particular. At the same time here has been a shift from full-time permanent jobs to part-time, temporary or casual work.

The effects of these trends are devastating for many families; Kempson (1996) showed that a little money can make all the difference between a life devoid of 'luxuries' and one in which there is insufficient money for food and heating. Although actual experiences of poverty may therefore differ according to people's circumstances, potentially children suffer the worst effects of being poor. A poverty and nutrition survey by NCH Action for Children (1991) found that in a sample of 354 families on low income one in five parents and one in ten children had gone without food in the previous month because there was insufficient money. Children may also suffer the stigma of poverty; Kempson (1996) showed how children may be teased and bullied when they are dressed differently from their peer group.

Poverty which results from unemployment may therefore filter into every aspect of family life. Oppenheim and Harker (1996) emphasise that poverty is not merely about doing without things, but is about being denied the expectation of decent health education, shelter, social life and a sense of self-esteem, which the rest of society take for granted. Poverty can therefore be said to be a condition of partial citizenship. Cohen (1992) showed how many people in poverty experienced a sense of isolation and exclusion, and most had little money for social activities which might promote health. It can be seen, then, that poverty has both an immediate effect and a long-term impact on children's lives. Despite the efforts of parents, children inevitably suffer from the hardships that accompany living on little money. Many have few play facilities and there are no 'luxuries' like school trips or holidays which others may take for granted.

Aside from immediate experiences of poverty, there is evidence to show that deprivation has a long-term effect on children's lives and life chances. Holterman (1994) showed that children from poorer homes have a lower life expectancy, are more likely to die in infancy or childhood, have a greater likelihood of infections and poor health, a lower chance of educational attainment, a greater risk of unemployment, a higher probability of involvement in crime and homelessness, and a higher risk of teenage pregnancy. Parental unemployment and consequent poverty therefore mould children's futures and diminish parents' capacity and resources for good parenting. Rutter suggests that good parenting requires permitting circumstances, life opportunities and facilities (quoted in Utting, 1995). When these are lacking, even the best parents may find it difficult to exercise their skills.

Housing and child health

Housing is a critical element in child health, and the younger the child the more important is the quality of physical shelter. According to Daniel and Ivatts (1998), proper growth and development depend on satisfactory housing. Housing conditions appear to affect a child indirectly, as housing has a powerful effect on parental well-being. Security, comfort, warmth and ease of management facilitate effective parenting; overcrowding, poor conditions or homelessness may reduce the ability of parents to care for their children. The loss of public sector housing since 1980 means that in many instances poorer families have a more restricted choice in housing. Gill (1992) found that many poorer children are brought up in flats without gardens, whilst others have to endure the problems of substandard housing. Such conditions may affect their physical and mental development. The 1991 English House Condition Survey showed that, although in general housing conditions have improved, there are still 1.5 million unfit dwellings in Britain. Twenty per cent of houses have dampness problems, and 6 per cent of households live at a density of one or more people per room.

Certain groups of children appear to be particularly affected by continuing housing deficiencies and shortages. For example, the 1991 census revealed that children of lone parents were the ones who experienced the greatest deterioration in their housing situation (Dorling, 1995). Children from minority groups also experience some of the worst housing privations in Britain. Specifically, most ethnic minority communities are concentrated in inner cities which contain the poorest housing, and a continuing history of racial prejudice and discrimination prevents access to better-quality housing. The London Housing Survey in 1995 found that a third of all children residing in social housing in London live in overcrowded conditions, but that Asian and Afro-Caribbean children are twice as likely as white European children to be overcrowded. Nationally children from Bangladeshi and Pakistani communities are particularly badly affected, with 31 per cent of all households below 'the bedroom standard' as opposed to 12 per cent for other minority groups and 3 per cent for white households (Central Statistical Office, 1995).

Daniel and Ivatts (1998) show that poor housing can affect a child's health and development. Poor housing may result in serious accidents to children such as falls, burns and scalds, whilst poor cooking facilities are a major cause of poor diet. Respiratory illness is aggravated by cold and dampness – especially condensation. In addition, poor housing may have psychological effects on children: stresses caused by unsatisfactory conditions may lead to depression, disturbed sleep, poor eating, over-activity, bedwetting and soiling, temper tantrums and aggression. This is particularly the case in accommodation for homeless families (Health Visitors' Association and General Medical Services Committee, 1989: 12).

Perhaps even more of a hazard is the fact that poor housing may cause developmental delay in children. Over prolonged periods, housing deprivation can damage a child's innate intellectual potential, speech patterns, physical development, the acquisition of physical skills and emotional development. As Daniel and Ivatts (1998: 139) remark, 'we simply do not know what human potential continues to be lost day in, day out by our inability to ensure a better housing environment for all of our children'.

Diet and child health

Poverty and poor housing may also have an effect on the nature and quality of a child's diet. Although there is evidence to show that the British diet has improved in nutritional quality (Department of Health, 1991b: 108), the content of many children's diets remains unsatisfactory, and poorer children are more seriously affected (Dowler and Calvert, 1995). Evidence from the Nutrition Task Force shows that more people are obese, and the available evidence on children's diet shows that for many the main sources of energy intake are bread, chips, milk, biscuits, meat products, cake and puddings (Power, 1995). An official survey of the diet of children aged eighteen months to four and a half years showed that they had a high content of 'junk foods, too much fat and sugar' (Department of Health and Ministry of Agriculture Fisheries and Food, 1995). This situation bodes ill for future health standards, as poor eating habits in childhood will shape future eating patterns, poor diet in childhood has a deleterious effect on adult health. It is predicted that as a result of current eating patterns in children heart disease is likely to soar in the twenty-first century (Hall and Elliman, 2003; see also *The Guardian*, 3 November 1995). Daniel and Ivatts (1998) comment that, whereas in previous generations physical symptoms of food deprivation were immediately apparent, harm resulting from poor diet will not become apparent until adulthood; long-term health risks faced by children may be masked by physical appearances and the apparent abundant choice of foods available on the market.

Child health in minority ethnic groups

Child mortality and morbidity are higher among children in ethnic minorities and 'Travellers'. According to Daniel and Ivatts (1998) these groups share many of the lifestyle attributes associated with economic and social deprivation, therefore their life chances are related to the social class hierarchy. Specifically, statistics show that children whose mothers were born outside the United Kingdom, in New Commonwealth countries and Pakistan, have higher mortality throughout infancy (Raleigh and Balarajan, 1995: 85–6). It is also the case that certain illnesses are more common in ethnic minority children. These illness include rickets and tuberculosis among Asian children, and sickle cell anaemia among African-Caribbean children (Whitehead, 1992: 257). Daniel and Ivatts suggest that in the case of Traveller children health needs are not being met. Despite the Caravan Sites Act of 1968, which obliges local authorities to provide adequate sites for Travellers, Pahl and Vaile's (1986) study of Kent Gypsies showed that, in a sample of 263 families,

14 per cent had no mains water, 21 per cent had no electricity and 33 per cent had no lavatories. In addition the infant mortality rate was 17.5 per cent, 50 per cent higher than the national average.

Although many refugee children are using health services in the United Kingdom, at the time of writing asylum seekers are not eligible for welfare food and vitamins, a situation which can have serious consequences for children's nutrition. Although these children are entitled to routine health surveillance, health promotion and immunisation, they lack the degree of medical and social support required to fulfil their needs (Hall and Elliman, 2003: 324).

Parenting and child health

In a pre-election paper the Labour Party (1996) recognised that the parents' role is critical if a difference is to be made in the well-being of children. The Department of Health (1998) similarly recognised that the future of the United Kingdom depends on parents' success in bringing up their children. It was argued that the interests of children must be paramount, that they need stability and security, and that the government should support parents to exercise their parental responsibilities in the face of family stress caused by rising divorce rates, single-parent households, child poverty and family breakdown.

Morgan (1995) comments that between 1971 and 1991 the number of lone-parent households more than doubled (from 570,000 to 1.3 million), as did the number of children living in such households (from 1 million to 2.2 million). Britain's proportion of lone-parent families has now reached one in four of all families. Whilst the largest proportion of lone-parent households are still those produced by separation or divorce, lone parenthood is increasingly the result of a growth in the number of mothers who have never married. Whereas only one baby in ten was born to an unmarried mother in the 1970s, by 1992 31 per cent of children were in this position, and the figure has continued to rise by 2 per cent per year. Currently 84 per cent of births in women under twenty are to unmarried mothers. Morgan comments that although three-quarters of these births are registered by both parents, data from the 1988 and 1989 General Household Survey showed that seven out of ten mothers were never married. According to Morgan these mothers were frequently without a stable partner, and informal relationships appeared to break up at a higher rate than marriages.

Many commentators, however, hold the view that lone parenthood provides a satisfactory environment for child rearing. An extensive review of literature on family well-being (McKeown and Sweeney, 2001) shows that although there is a strong association between children's well-being and family structure, other factors such as a lack of family support, economic factors, low income, poverty and social exclusion are often ignored or played down, and their effects on child health are therefore unrecognised. Although Morgan argues that the infant mortality rate for babies born outside marriage and registered by the mother alone is 80 per cent higher than that of babies born within marriage, McKeown and Sweeney point out that 29 per cent of lone parents live in poverty, and their children are therefore susceptible to poorer levels of health associated with low income, disadvantage and poor housing.

McKeown and Sweeney argue that that public policies and services should be more accommodating of the growing diversity of family types and partnership arrangements which characterise Western societies. Such accommodation might ensure that lone parents have access to childcare services so that they can take employment on more equal terms to other households. The European Commission Network on Childcare has also argued that public policies in such areas as income, social support, health services, employment policies and education need to be flexible and acknowledge that a 'single size fits all' approach is likely to discriminate against newer family forms.

Child health and family diversity

However benign one's perspective on the greater diversity of family types and partnerships, there is accumulating empirical evidence about some of the consequences for child and family health, and specific concerns about health problems associated with failed relationships and loneliness. In the United Kingdom divorce rates are around 40 per cent of all marriages. McKeown and Sweeney (2001) point out the costs to children of parents' divorce or separation in poorer health, behavioural and educational outcomes, while recognising that where there is conflict between parents children may actually benefit from separation. There is strong evidence to suggest that family dysfunction can cause retarded physical development (Wilkinson, 1996), emotional disturbance (Najman et al., 1997), vulnerability to neglect or abuse (Case, 2000) and poor mental health (Corlyon, 1999). In adolescence problems may escalate, increasing the costs to public services, which have to deal with outcomes such as underperformance at school, juvenile crime, teenage parenthood and substance abuse. However, concerns over these effects should not lead to family diversity being identified as a surrogate cause of poor child health when the underlying causes are more directly related to social and economic circumstances.

The state, family responsibility and child health

Traditionally, British social policy has viewed the family as a distinct and separate realm from the state, a 'private' institution immune from state interference. Daniel and Ivatts (1998) suggest that there has been some reluctance on the part of the state to intervene actively in matters related to children's health and well-being, even though support for children's health and welfare has been seen as a public investment in the nation's future. The Commission on Social Justice (1994: 311) stated that 'the best indicator of the capacity of our economy tomorrow is the quality of our children today'. Allied to the concept of the privacy of the family is the concept of its responsibility for dependent members. Feminist critiques, such as that of Williams (1989), suggest that legislation and policy frameworks have played a significant part in shaping family obligations. Certainly, since 1945 British social policy has shown concern with the need to 'support' families in the discharge of their responsibilities, a theme which has become more dominant during the 1980s and 1990s (Pascall, 1986). However, this author makes the distinction that 'the real meaning of supporting the family is supporting family responsibility, as distinct from state responsibility' (Pascall, 1986: 38). This might suggest that responsibility for child health lies ultimately with the family, regardless of their social and environmental situation.

In the United Kingdom 'New Labour' puts much emphasis on family responsibility but accepts that there is now a diversity of family types. Government appears to believe that social policy can be used to enable families to fulfil their responsibilities more effectively (Daniel and Ivatts, 1998). Hall and Elliman (2003) argue that the UN Convention on the Rights of the Child and the Human Rights Act have had a marked impact on political attitudes to child health. There is now a strong policy commitment to reducing inequalities in child health and inequities in access to healthcare provision, and to developing health and fiscal policies that address these concerns. It appears that government is taking a more prominent role in ensuring that improved child health becomes a reality, adopting a social model of health and a series of cross-cutting policies to achieve its aims for improved child health. These policies are focused on a variety of public health issues and are aimed at supporting families through pre-school support schemes and social inclusion programmes, to improve their children's health and well-being. Hall and Elliman (2003) also argue that these policies represent a shift from a 'defect' notion of health to a proactive health promotion model of intervention, and from an individualist to a public health model of health care. There is now growing interest in how the health of communities impinges on the health of people, particularly the health of children. This would suggest that the state is taking a more active stance in supporting parents to improve child health, rather than relying on medical models of health and health care, which often blame parents for poor standards of child health (see Hall and Elliman, 2003).

Programmes to improve children's health

Baggott (2000) showed how the World Health Organisation has emphasised the importance of reducing inequalities in health. Targets for health improvement are focused on the necessity for reducing socio-economic inequalities and improving housing, social environments, and family skills. A number of countries, including Finland, Sweden, Spain and the United Kingdom have carried out independent inquiries into inequalities in health status. As a result policies and programmes have been implemented that aim to improve health, reduce inequality (including gender and ethnic inequalities) and improve living standards, including the quality of housing, education, work opportunities and public transport.

In the United Kingdom the Blair government declared its aim of tackling the underlying causes of poor health by improving children's health and meeting social needs, particularly in deprived areas. £3.6 billion was allocated to local authorities to renovate housing stock, and a programme of 'New Deals' was introduced for the unemployed, lone parents and disabled people (Department of Social Security, 1998). Baggott comments that although these programmes are to be applauded for providing greater opportunity, they may be cynically viewed as a means of limiting the welfare budget. However, the Blair government has also attempted to redress broader structural factors underlying health inequality and social problems by establishing a Social Exclusion Unit to formulate policies to tackle multiple deprivation in England. (Other parts of the United Kingdom are expected to draw on the work of this unit, whilst accepting responsibility for their own strategies.) Work has been organised under five themes: getting people to work, improving community support systems, building a future for young people, improving access to services and tackling social exclusion. All these programmes have the potential to improve child health through their influence on family, community and environmental status.

Hall and Elliman (2003) argue that such programmes are the key to improving the lives and health of children. They recommend universal programmes of child health which provide parents with access to health professionals, early diagnosis and intervention, screening programmes, prevention and health promotion strategies, social support, parent education and health-promoting schools. In addition, comprehensive multi-agency intervention strategies on a community-wide basis, such as Sure Start programmes (Graham, 2000), are recommended to combine prevention, problem recognition and intervention. Vulnerable children are perceived to require priority, including those with disabilities and children whose safety or emotional, cognitive and language development is adversely affected by their environmental circumstances.

Although government has shown obvious concern with family and parenting issues, as Roberts and MacDonald (1999) point out, the primary responsibility for the welfare and care of the majority of children is still perceived as resting with parents. The key policy document placing children's interests at the heart of modern family policy was the Green Paper *Supporting Families*, which set out the government's proposals for 'strengthening family life' and improving child health and welfare. The government also set up a National Family and Parenting Institute to raise awareness of parenting issues, develop parenting support programmes, support research, advise government on family policy and disseminate information. A national parenting helpline, 'Parentline Plus', was also established to provide a first point of contact for parents with concerns and problems that can then be directed to more specialised services. Health visitors were envisaged as having an enhanced role in pre-school and the later stages of child development. A system of parental leave (unpaid) has been implemented since 1999. These developments are evidence of government commitment to improve the support available to parents, but at the same time it has made much of the responsibility of parents for children's health, welfare and behaviour, as is evidenced by 'home–school agreements' under the School Standards and Framework Act 1998, and parenting orders under the Crime and Disorder Act 1998.

Throughout the United Kingdom a number of units and partnerships have been developed to address the structural causes of ill health and child deprivation (see Boxes 13.1–2). The aims of these partnerships are to (1) improve health and well-being, (2) improve economic prosperity, (3) reduce crime and disorder, (4) encourage education and lifelong learning, (5) improve the environment and (6) build confident communities. All local authorities are required to produce a comprehensive children and youth strategy to meet these aims and the ultimate goal of social inclusion for all children and their families. The aim of the Sure Start programme is described by one local authority as 'to work with parents-to-be, parents, and children to promote

---

Box 13.1: Relevant Policy

Home Office (1998) *Supporting Families: A Consultation Document*. London: The Stationery Office.

Child Support Agency (1998) *Children First – A New Approach to Child Support*. London:

The Social Exclusion Unit (1999) *Truancy and School Exclusion*. London: The Stationery Office.

Department of Health (2002) *Connexions Strategy – Teenage Pregnancy*. London: Department of Health.

Department of Health (2002) *Protecting Children Supporting Parents*. London: Department of Health.

Box 13.2: Relevant Health Policy

Department of Health (1998) *Our Healthier Nation: A Contract for Health*. Cmnd 3852. London: The Stationery Office.

Health Act 1999. London: The Stationery Office.

Health and Social Care Act 2001. London: The Stationery Office.

Department of Health (2003) *National Service Framework for Children [England]*. London: Department of Health.

---

the physical intellectual and social development of babies and young children under the age of four years, particularly those who are disadvantaged, to ensure they are given the best possible start in life', whilst the aims for older children are 'for them to fully participate in the lives of the community [and] to maximise their opportunities to be educated, trained, find work, have access to warm, safe and affordable housing and sufficient income to meet the basic necessities of life' (Neath and Port Talbot Borough Council, 2002: 11–12).

According to the Children and Young People's Unit (2000), Sure Start programmes are creating local solutions for local problems, and 'Connexions' services are reducing school truancy and exclusions for older children. The Children's Fund is helping to reduce social exclusion for fifteen-to-thirteen year-olds, whilst the programme 'Excellence in Cities' is focused on raising standards in urban schools. New funding of £60 million has been earmarked for services for children with disabilities and their families, and extra funding of £15 million has been put into improving mental health services for children and young people. Health inequalities are being addressed through 'healthy schools' programmes, national healthy school standards, a personal health and social education (PHSE) framework, the 'national fruit scheme', a welfare foods scheme, a health visitor and school nurse development programme and the establishment of Health Action Zones. If such schemes result in healthier diets and lifestyle choices for children, they will undoubtedly help to combat the growing problem of childhood obesity (Hall and Elliman, 2003). Similarly, school breakfast schemes help to ensure that young children are adequately prepared to cope with their school day (Hall and Elliman, 2003). Finally, the Home Efficiency Scheme provides funds to insulate and warm houses for families on benefit. Early evaluation of such schemes suggests that they are creating better health outcomes, with the potential for savings in long-term expenditure on health care, education and crime control programmes (Lynn et al., 2002).

Conclusion

This chapter has shown that the concept of child health is much more complicated than it appears at first glance. It has been shown that the true concept of health incorporates much more than the absence of disease and illness. Whereas traditional medical definitions of health convey a negative view that physical health is all that matters, a more positive social view of child health shows that many factors contribute to an absolute state of health and well-being. Thus it has been argued that a knowledge of the factors which affect the nurture of children, such as parenting, family structure, social class, social exclusion, unemployment, poverty, housing and diet, is as important as a knowledge of 'natural' causes of disease or illness. This suggests that child health is not the sole concern of the health care professions, but the responsibility of all who contribute to children's development. Greater social advantage may enable children to shrug off early health problems. Children who experience a combination of health and social disadvantage, on the other hand, may find themselves drawn into a downward spiral of ill health from which it is difficult to escape. In the light of current evidence of the social conditions of poor health in children, policy appears to be taking a firmer stand in supporting the responsibility of parents. Specifically, it appears that a more holistic view of child and family health is prevalent in current policy. This has resulted in the proliferation of health and social policies and programmes aimed at prevention and health promotion as well as care and treatment. In particular, programmes are concerned with tackling inequalities, supporting families and children, involving parents and children in choices about care, and integration and partnership between statutory and voluntary bodies to improve health. Current evaluation appears to suggest that social intervention of this kind will improve child health and children's life opportunities.

Questions and exercises

1   What are the ways of defining child health, and which model of health is most appropriate?
2   What are the social and environmental factors that determine child health status?
3   How are current government policies influencing child health?
4   Should parents or the state take responsibility for child health?

Reading

Baggott, *Public Health: Policy and Politics* (2000), is of interest to all professionals in health and social care, particularly in relation to issues of public health, with a detailed description of current policies and an analysis of broader issues and political dilemmas. Foley, Roche and Tucker, *Children in Society* (2001), provides a critical and comprehensive account of theoretical and practical issues raised in working with children and their families, and engages in debate about how services should be organised and delivered. Graham, *Understanding Health Inequalities* (2000), turns the spotlight on questions at the heart of health and social care policy and makes excellent use of the results of current research studies to illustrate the links between poor health and social inequalities. Hall and Elliman, *Health for all Children* (2003), is essential reading for all health professionals who work with children, but will also prove valuable to other professionals in education, social care and service planning concerned with child health. It considers in detail the health and developmental needs of children, and gives a comprehensive account of government attempts to improve children's services through collaboration. Hill and Tisdall, *Children and Society* (1997), adopts a multidisciplinary approach and offers a sound introduction to critical analysis of key issues affecting children. The authors also present vivid accounts of children's first hand experiences of health and health care.

Part IV
Developing Effective Practice

This final part of the book looks at some of the ways in which we can put our understanding of early childhood into practice, and at some of the practical issues that arise in working with young children. The chapters that follow address these themes in different ways and on different levels. Although the focus is on practice, theory still features very strongly. We referred in the Introduction to Schön (1983) and the 'reflective practitioner'. The reflective practitioner develops his or her theories in practice, by thinking and reflecting on work in progress, and by testing different approaches to see how they work in particular situations. However, s/he does this on the basis of the theories and knowledge that have been developed by others – both other practitioners and academic researchers. The final chapters in their several ways all deal with this relationship between theoretical knowledge and what makes for effective and ethical practice.

We have seen in previous chapters how important it is to have good collaboration between services if we are to provide for children in a holistic way. In Chapter 14 Bob Sanders introduces some models of inter-agency and multidisciplinary working, and shows how they can help to promote effective collaboration in practice with children and families. Sanders looks closely at the advantages and the disadvantages of working together, and at some of the organisational and other barriers to good interprofessional working.

In Chapter 15 Branwen Llewellyn Jones focuses on the role of play in practice with young children. After reviewing the history of ideas about the role of play, she notes that despite being recognised in theory as central to children's learning and development, play is still underutilised in educational practice. She argues that this is because practitioners lack knowledge of *why* play is important and skills in *how* to support teaching and learning through play. She suggests that there may need to be a societal mind-shift, from concern with future targets to appreciation of the *here and now*, if play is to regain its rightful place in children's lives.

Listening to children is vital, as we have noted – but, especially with very young children, knowing how to observe them is equally important. In Chapter 16 Bob Sanders presents a model of child observation for students and practitioners. He gives advice on practical arrangements and draws attention to important ethical issues, such as consent. Sanders goes on to explain how the material from their child observation can be used by students and practitioners to extend their understanding of child development.

Finally, in Chapter 17 Sharon Airey looks at what is meant by 'inclusive practice', and at how early years practitioners can work with all children and their families in ways that are empowering, non-discriminatory and inclusive. She shows us how wide a range of children may be vulnerable to exclusion, demonstrates the often pernicious effects of discrimination on children's lives, and looks at some of the benefits of inclusive practice. She tackles directly the issue of language and the words we use when talking about people or working with them, asks what are the barriers to inclusive practice and how can we tackle them, and considers some of the legislation that is relevant to inclusive practice.

Some of the issues addressed by Airey's chapter are similar to those addressed earlier by Kate Wall in relation specifically to disabled children, and by some of our other contributors. By widening her scope to consider all young children, and by speaking directly to the early years practitioner, Sharon Airey reminds us that the point of studying early childhood is to provide good quality settings for young children – services, or 'spaces' (Moss and Petrie, 2002), that will enable them to flourish.

14
Inter-agency and Multidisciplinary Working
Bob Sanders

Contents

- Definitions and terminology
- Antecedents of inter-agency and multidisciplinary working
- Advantages and disadvantages of working together collaboratively
- Barriers to inter-agency and multidisciplinary working
- Dimensions of multidisciplinary teams
- Working together in children's services
- Evaluation of working together in children's services
- Conclusion

This chapter looks at theoretical concepts underpinning interprofessional working, and considers how they relate to provision for joint working in services for children and families. It concludes with an evaluation of inter-agency working in children's services. But first let us consider the justification for collaborative working. At first, it may seem self-evident, in light of the more obvious benefits and the very strong emphasis in government policy on agencies crossing organisational and professional boundaries to communicate more effectively and develop joint working arrangements. However, it is useful to remember that there is a cost to collaboration. In this chapter the advantages and disadvantages of collaborative working are discussed. One might think it strange to think of disadvantages to collaboration, and yet it is important, because workers may have a sense of having given up something (for example, autonomy of action, independence of thinking, in some cases professional status, the relative comfort of working exclusively with likeminded people, etc), in order to work effectively across agencies, or as different disciplines within multidisciplinary teams. It is important the worker understands that what is given up is worth what is gained.

Definitions and terminology

What exactly do we mean by words such as 'inter-agency' and 'multidisciplinary'? There is potential for confusion. Rawson (1994) describes terms associated with three aspects

Table 14.1   Terminology

Problematic association	Grouping	Focus of operations
inter	professional	work
multi	occupational	teamwork
trans	disciplinary	collaboration
	sectoral	co-operation
	agency	integration

Source: from Rawson (1994)

of these interrelated concepts: the problematic associations (how individuals are connected), the grouping (the nature of the groups to which the individuals belong), and the focus of operations (the nature of the collaborative work in which the people are engaged). Each of these has various terms linked with it (Table 14.1). According to Rawson, 'Any permutation from the list is possible and has indeed been used in the literature.' Using just the examples in Table 14.1, there are seventy-five different ways, derivable from the table, to describe the process of different people working together, formed by combining one term from each of the three columns, for example: interprofessional work, transdisciplinary collaboration, multi-agency teamwork, etc.

This suggests the question: are there at least seventy-five different variants of working together, or are we talking about the same mechanism underlying collaborative processes? To what extent are these seventy-five combinations the same or different? Let us consider these components. What is inter/multi/trans? These word parts have different meanings. 'Inter-' means between, implying the link between two entities; 'multi-' means many, and 'trans-' means across. Although some people prefer 'multi' to 'inter-' because the latter implies only two, both are commonly used.

Likewise, if we look at the groupings, professional, occupational, disciplinary, sectoral, and agency, we find differences in meanings. Not all occupations that may be involved in delivering services to young children are professions; indeed, even within the 'professions' there are different statuses, with some being regarded as 'semi-professions' rather than full professions. 'Interoccupational' would therefore be a more inclusive term (although it is rarely, if ever used). Likewise, 'disciplinary' is a broader concept than 'professional', but in a different way from 'occupational'. 'Disciplinary' refers to the underlying academic base of the work. We might, for example, talk in terms of 'health' (perhaps subdivided into 'nursing' and 'medical'), 'legal' and 'psychology' as being 'disciplines'. The final two terms in the list, however, do not have to do with the occupation of the individual worker, but rather with the location of the person's employment. 'Agency' is clearly less problematical; for all intents and purposes it can be seen as the employing body (even if that 'employment' is in a voluntary capacity). 'Sectoral' can again be seen as a more inclusive and broader category than 'agency'. A good example here would be comparing the 'statutory' sector, the 'voluntary' sector and the 'independent' sector. These terms are not mutually exclusive, however, and the 'independent' sector can be seen to comprise the 'voluntary' (not for profit) sector and the 'private' (profit-making) sectors.

Finally, when considering the terms 'work', 'teamwork', 'collaboration', 'co-operation' and 'integration', we find that there are shades of meaning, which may relate in part to the extent to which the individuals have a sense of collective agency (that is, a sense of 'we-ness') in their joint working. This will be discussed in more detail below, when the work of Øvretveit et al. (1997) is considered. 'Teamwork' implies a greater sense of 'we-ness' than 'work'. Likewise, 'integration' implies a greater degree than either 'collaboration' or 'co-operation'. Arguably, 'collaboration' implies a greater degree of 'we-ness' than 'co-operation'.

From these etymological considerations, it would appear that we are discussing a number of very different concepts (even if not so many as seventy-five), and not simply different aspects of the same concept. Nevertheless, Rawson (1994) concludes, 'As Leathard (1990, p. 1776) aptly discerns: 'What everyone is really talking about is simply learning and working together.' Interprofessional work is arguably the phrasing with greatest utility.' Likewise, Øvretveit et al. (1997) adopt the terminology 'interprofessional working', defining it as 'how two or more people from different professions communicate and co-operate to achieve a common goal'.

Antecedents of inter-agency and multidisciplinary working

A powerful driving force behind collaboration has been the continued emphasis in the last thirty years on working together in child protection. However, it is important to remember that other areas of public services (and even other areas of work with children) have placed considerable emphasis on collaboration. Leathard (1994) in her consideration of the history of interprofessional working describes six areas in which government policy appears to be based upon, and to promote the importance of, interprofessional working. As she notes, 'the pressure to go inter-professional has speeded up under the impact of government policy, since the mid-1980s, and noticeably in the 1990s' (1994: 9). The main focus of her consideration is on the links within the health services and *between* the health services and other services. Some of the areas that she discusses are teamwork in hospitals, health prevention strategies, child protection, primary health care teams, and health and community care provisions.

The development of inter-agency working in child protection can be seen as a watershed of inter-agency working on different levels. Government guidance issued in April 1974 following the inquiry and subsequent report into the death of Maria Colwell (Department of Health and Social Security, 1974) led to the setting up of Area Review Committees (predecessors of the current Area Child Protection Committees described in Chapter 9). However, the background to such committees goes back thirty years earlier to the Co-ordinating Committees set up in the early 1950s, whose role was to secure co-operation within the statutory sector, and between the statutory and voluntary sectors, in relation to issues of the welfare of children including child abuse and neglect. The 1974 guidance also introduced the notion of child protection registers and case conferences, later termed 'child protection conferences', in respect of maltreated children. By 1976 all areas in England and Wales had established Area Review Committees, child protection registers and case conference systems.

Nevertheless, failures of agencies to co-ordinate their efforts continued to be seen as a significant contributing factor in the death of children through abuse (see Sanders et al., 1999). In relation to the inquiry into the circumstances surrounding the death of Jasmine Beckford, Leathard (1994:11) notes that there were 'thirty-seven different individuals and agencies who, not for want of trying, failed to co-ordinate their work on child protection'. Therefore, working collaboratively continued to be a child protection theme, both in terms of government guidance and in primary legislation.

Advantages and disadvantages of working together collaboratively

> A lesson to be learned from the 1980s is that inter-agency working is not easy, and not self-evidently useful.
>
> (Department of Health, 1989: 41)

Professionally, we now operate in context in which working together collaboratively has become a principle so firmly entrenched in government philosophy ('joined-up thinking') that it is sometimes difficult to acknowledge that there can be disadvantages in working together collaboratively. And yet, in order to engender commitment to interprofessional working, one must be aware of the down side. An 'eyes wide open' approach is always to be preferred to an approach in which one adopts the dictates of government rhetoric in an undigested and unanalysed manner.

Let us first consider the *advantages* of working together. Many of the arguments in favour stem from cost–benefit considerations, and in this sense the reasons for its adoption by government concerned to deliver the best service at the lowest cost will be obvious. Working together is seen, for example, as entailing a more efficient use of staff, more effective service provision, and enabling professional and lay people to achieve their objectives more fully and economically. From the perspective of the worker, if they can get a full picture of a situation (assessment) by drawing on the contributions of different workers to form an overall assessment, this will save effort and, depending upon the nature of the information, may also be more reliable. For example, consider an assessment of a child with learning and physical disabilities being undertaken by a social worker. The worker is likely to need information on the child's educational and medical needs. This information is best obtained from those with specialist knowledge in such areas, rather than by the worker, without the benefit of specialist knowledge, attempting to gain such information from the family.

From the point of view of the agency, there are a number of dangers to be avoided if workers from different agencies are operating jointly. The main two in terms of service delivery are *service gaps* and *duplication of service*. People who need services may fall between the activities of different agencies because the agencies either do not know of their existence or are not aware that other agencies are not providing the services. Failure of agencies to communicate with other agencies about families they are working with may lead to the family not receiving much-needed services from those agencies. This is variously described as 'falling through the net', 'slipping through the cracks' or other metaphors.

On the other hand different agencies, despite their generally different remits, may be providing a similar or even identical service to the same family. In that case failure to communicate between agencies contributes to waste of resources. One family may be being provided with the same or a similar service twice, whilst another family is not receiving a service at all or is experiencing long delays before a service can be provided. This is clearly not cost-effective from the point of view of the agency, which will be intent on delivering the most efficient service.

We have discussed how effective working together may help the worker and the agency, but how will it help the service user? Clearly it will be of benefit to the service user to be on the receiving end of a service that is effectively delivered, avoiding both service gaps and duplication of services. They are more likely, within resource constraints, to get the service needed. And of course more effective use of existing resources should mean more resources available for service delivery. On a more pragmatic level, however, many service users become bewildered by the host of professionals involved in their lives (sometimes with reasonable justification because of the different services required), and find it particularly taxing when they are required to provide the same answers to the same questions from different agencies.

Finally, there is the *jigsaw* metaphor which has become established within child protection. Fatality inquiries have revealed that in many cases, whilst many of the agencies involved had a piece of the puzzle, no single agency had the sort of overview that might have resulted from better sharing of information. This is why the child protection conference and the role of the key worker in child protection are so important (although clearly still not foolproof – hence the continuation of child abuse fatalities). The child protection conference provides an opportunity for all those involved with the child and the family to come together to share the information that they have. The agencies are contributing their pieces of the puzzle to the overall picture. The role of the key worker is to act as a focal point for all the agencies involved to provide information, and to disseminate that information when it is received. Ideally, depending upon the nature of the information received, the key worker is the individual who should have the overall picture in mind.

It is possible, however, to overemphasise the significance of omissions in interprofessional communications to child abuse fatalities. In networks as large as those surrounding children at risk of abuse (for example, the previously noted thirty-seven individuals and agencies involved in the case of Jasmine Beckford), it is almost inevitable that there will be gaps. To date there have been no fatality inquiries that have compared the pattern of inter-agency communication surrounding the fatally abused child with those patterns surrounding another child, or other children, in the same child protection system who have not been fatally abused. If, as suggested here, gaps in communication may be an inevitable feature of communication in networks so large and complex as those surrounding abused children, then it may be unjustified to conclude that gaps in communication are significant factors contributing to the child's death. They may always be present, and yet their significance may seem magnified when examined retrospectively. That being said, there is clearly a benefit to maximising the effectiveness of interagency communication surrounding children who are at risk of abuse; indeed, the Green Paper *Every Child Matters* (HM Government, 2003) sets out proposals for removing some of the current constraints on interprofessional communications concerning children who are, or may possibly be, at risk of abuse.

Now let us consider some of the disadvantages of working together. First, it is not necessarily easy. As we observed in Chapter 9 in relation to social workers working in partnership with parents, wanting it is one thing but achieving it may be another. There are barriers to inter-agency and multidisciplinary working, and, whilst they are not necessarily insurmountable obstacles, some of the barriers do present very real challenges. Some of these will be discussed more fully in the next section.

Although we have acknowledged that interprofessional working can be cost-effective, there are costs associated with it. It takes time to liaise, consult, co-ordinate and collaborate. If a busy worker has to get on the phone to a number of different agencies to find out what they know about a child's situation, or to provide information about the latest developments in a particular child's case, this uses the worker's time – time taken away from direct contact with service users. Administrative and communication costs may also be high. Consider, for example, the cost of a child protection conference which may have fifteen or so professionals in attendance for at least one and a half hours, some of whom may have travelled a considerable distance to attend. The cost in terms of staff time and expenses can be considerable.

Finally, collaborative working, and in particular collective decision making, can make workers feel deskilled. The reduction in autonomy consequent on inter-agency working – even if actual decision making continues to be devolved to agencies, as it is in child protection conferences – can lead workers to feel unable to make decisions without involving other agencies. For many, this may be perceived as undermining professional judgement and autonomy, which is not conducive to good interprofessional working.

Barriers to inter-agency and multidisciplinary working

In his work on primary health care teams Øvretveit (1990) describes 'barriers to effectiveness and efficiency: 'lack of time owing to pressure of work; large team numbers; different patient populations; unclear roles; and different policies between practitioners and different management structures' (cited in Leathard, 1994: 13). Øvretveit et al. (1997) consider the inherent problems in multidisciplinary working: understanding the purpose of interprofessional practice, understanding the roles of others, professional rivalry, exclusion of significant others (non-professionals), ownership of resources, discrimination and racism, and making sure that assessment is effective. Thompson (2002) describes 'helps' and 'hindrances' to the process of working together. Under hindrances he includes stereotypes, hidden agendas, differences in values, lack of trust, inappropriate use of language (jargon), lack of understanding of roles, and blurring of roles. Sanders et al. (1997) described two factors that influence the ability of different agencies to work together on Area Child Protection Committees: first the extent of match between the child protection agenda of the agency and the agenda of the Area Child Protection Committee, and second, the extent of devolution of decision making within the agency. They found that barriers to joint working were created by the interests of the agency being remote from the child protection agenda, and by agencies being relatively autonomous to the extent that they could (or were seen to be able to) decide for themselves how far they would go along with locally agreed procedures.

What other obstacles may arise when agencies, and workers within agencies, attempt to work together? For one thing, the professions they come from are frequently unalike in many ways. There may be different leadership styles, a factor encountered by Sanders et al. (1996) when comparing police involvement in child protection with that of other agencies. The professional groups may have different language and values; the use of 'jargon' facilitates communication within a professional or occupational group, but is likely to have the opposite effect on communication outside the group. The professional groups may have profoundly different training backgrounds. The positivist model of knowledge serving as a foundation within the medical model, which places a great emphasis on objectivity, contrasts strongly with a postmodern understanding of knowledge, in which power is seen as an important influence on the subjective experience of knowledge, which may be found in a more socially-oriented knowledge base. Inequalities in status and pay between different professional groups may also be a barrier to effective working, and these may be related to levels of management support and accountability. Higher-status professions are able to function more autonomously – a factor which caused considerable concern amongst those interviewed by Sanders et al. (1997).

These factors may also relate to lack of clarity about *roles*. Successive volumes of *Working Together* in child protection (Department of Health and Social Security, 1988; Home Office et al., 1991; Department of Health et al., 1999; National Assembly for Wales, 2000b) have stressed the importance of clarity of roles in child protection. A further factor may be negative perceptions about other roles. In the 1970s, at the time of the Maria Colwell inquiry (Department of Health and Social Security, 1974) there was considerable mutual distrust between the police and social workers. Over the twenty-five years since, although there are still some frictions between the two, the situation has so vastly improved as to be almost unrecognisable. As Sanders et al. (1996) note, both services have had to go through changes, not only in relation to child protection, that have enabled this process of coming together. During the same period of time, when police were having a greater involvement in social issues as part of their everyday practice, social workers were taking on more of a policing role in their approach to child welfare. Whilst this may contain internal issues for both occupations, the greater degree of likemindedness is no doubt a major contributing factor to the increased ability to co-operate between the two groups.

Finally, there are always individual differences. Within any professional grouping there are likely to be some individuals who are amiable, adaptable, accommodating and a pleasure to work with – and there are others. Generally, one has to simply grin and bear it and make the most of a bad deal when one is unlucky enough to be working with one of the 'others'. It is important, however, not to over-generalise, and to conclude therefore that abrasiveness in working relationships is a characteristic of a particular professional group, when it may in fact simply be a characteristic of an individual who coincidentally happens to be a member of that professional group. A general abundance of skill in diplomacy frequently helps to smooth working relationships in such situations.

Dimensions of multidisciplinary teams

Øvretveit et al. (1997) offer a framework for understanding multidisciplinary teams (a concept which we can for our purposes take to include those 'teams' that might be formed by separate agencies working together). They propose four significant dimensions of how such teams might differ from each other: degree of integration, membership of a permanent work group, process (the client 'pathway' through the team) and management (how the team is led and how practitioners are managed). We shall consider each of these in turn.

Degree of integration

If we define integration as the extent to which the team influences the decisions of its members, there is a continuum along which teams can be located. At one end is the 'loose-knit' team in which the membership changes and is voluntary. At the other end is the 'closely integrated' team, in which the work of the team is governed by team policy and team decisions, and the group is jointly accountable for its service to the service users. A distinction can also be made between the 'co-ordinated profession team' (CPT) and the 'collective responsibility team' (CRT). In the former the professional services are separately organised and accountable, although there are joint meetings to take on work and for other liaison purposes. In the latter there is collective accountability on the part of the members of the group, to use collective resources to meet the needs of service users. Using these two models for understanding teams, the concept of 'inter-agency working' can be seen as a form of multidisciplinary teamworking in which the 'team' is on the one hand very loose-knit and on the other organised as a 'co-ordinated profession team'.

Membership of a permanent work group

There are four aspects of membership which Øvretveit et al. (1997) consider to be significant influences on the nature of the work group: whether members are *core* or *associate* members, the *professional mix* within the team, the *personal mix* within the team and the *roles* of the members. Being a *core* member of a team can mean being full-time, governed by team policy, managed by a single team leader and having voting rights within the team. In contrast, being an *associate* member can mean being part-time, not being governed by team policy, managed by individuals outside the team and not having voting rights on team decisions. The *professional mix* of the team refers to which professions and staff are included in the team and how many of each there should be. *Personal mix* refers to the personal attributes that individuals bring to the team. Membership *roles* refers to the work that members do and the autonomy they have within those roles. It may also relate to the types of informal roles that people take up when working within organisations.

Process – client 'pathway' through the team

This is one of the more difficult concepts of Øvretveit et al.'s framework, and one which benefits from the use of visual aids which they provide. They describe ten stages in the client pathway, which in general, all clients will pass through:

1 Referral sources.
2 Reception.
3 Acceptance for assessment.
4 Allocation for assessment.
5 Assessment.
6 Acceptance for longer-term care.
7 Allocation for longer-term care.
8 Intervention and/or monitoring.
9 Review.
10 Closure.

Using this model, they describe six common types of team process, on a continuum which reflects more and more of the decision making being done by the team at different stages in the process. In the *parallel pathway* team, groups operate largely independently of each other, but members of the different groups meet to refer to each other. The *postbox* team is similar, but there are meetings for professionals to pick up referrals and take those referrals back to their separate professional pathways. In the *reception and allocation* team there may be some work done on a short-term basis at the reception stage, as preparation for or an alternative to longer-term work. In the *reception–assessment–allocation* team there are two points of coming together: one for assessment and another, when assessment is completed, for allocation to longer-term work. The worker who takes on the assessment is not necessarily the same as the worker who takes on the longer-term work. The *reception–assessment–allocation–review* team includes as a fourth stage a review of the work being undertaken. Finally the *hybrid parallel pathway* team is an amalgam of the two or more of the previously described teams. To complicate things, some professionals may operate within the team on the basis of one model whilst others may operate on a different basis.

Management – how the team is led and how practitioners are managed

A very important aspect of how any team operates is its management. Øvretveit et al. suggest that there are two particular challenges to creating management structures in multidisciplinary teams. First, there is the task of establishing management which allows members from different professions appropriate autonomy.

Second, there is a need to establish responsibility for managing the total resources of the team. This includes assessing needs and making sure that members' time is efficiently used. Øvretveit et al. describe the key management tasks as drafting job descriptions, appointing staff, introducing the person to the job, assigning work, reviewing work, performance appraisal and objective setting, ensuring practice quality, training and professional development, and disciplinary action.

In order to fulfil the role of management within the team, supervision is required, but there are different meanings attached to the concept. Supervision can mean *clinical advice* from a more experienced colleague. In this case the practitioner remains accountable, and the adviser has no accountability for the quality of the work done. *Clinical supervision* is undertaken by a senior staff member who is accountable for the quality of the supervisee's work. With *management monitoring* the role is to ensure that the worker adheres to agency procedures, but the manager is not normally accountable for clinical decisions. Finally, in *full management* the manager assumes responsibility for both the clinical and the organisational components of the role. They note that someone from a different profession could in principle undertake any of these four types of supervision.

Following these considerations of management and supervision, Øvretveit et al. describe five types of management structure for teams. In the *profession-managed* structure practitioners are managed within their professions by line managers who undertake all the key management tasks described above. In the *single manager* structure all practitioners, regardless of the professional discipline from which they come, are managed by a single manager who undertakes all eight key tasks in relation to all team members. This model is more common in the United States, Australia and the rest of Europe than it is in the United Kingdom. The *joint management* structure is a mixture of the previous two models: there is a central team co-ordinator and professional supervisors; the two types of supervisor have to clarify who is responsible for which key tasks, but all team members are employees. In the *team manager-contracted* structure the team is co-ordinated by a manager who has a budget and who contracts-in the services of different professionals to the team. Finally, there is a *hybrid management* structure based on characteristics of the other four models.

Working together in children's services

Joint working in children's services is achieved primarily through what Hallett and Birchall (1992) describe, in relation to child protection, as 'mandated co-ordination'. This entails agencies being 'directed or required to co-ordinate their activities by those in superordinate positions' (p. 32). At the most superordinate level this requirement is contained within legislation. For example, in relation to children in need, section 27 of the Children Act 1989 provides that a local authority may request help from the local education authority, Housing, the health authority, and indeed from any other local authority, when exercising any of its functions in relation to such children and their families, and that the authority whose help is requested is under an obligation to assist unless compliance is not compatible with its other duties and functions. Likewise, section 47 of the Children Act, discussed in Chapter 9, places a duty on the same agencies to help a local authority with its enquiries in cases involving child protection. Also, we have seen that both education and health authorities are involved in the process of looking after children, by contributing to the plans that are made for such children, and the periodic reviews of those plans. This has broadened the conception of responsibility for vulnerable children, and it is common now to hear people talking of 'corporate parenting', a concept indicating that the responsibility for vulnerable children in the community is no longer the sole concern of the social services department. 'Local authority' is no longer tantamount to the social services department, but includes the local education authority and Housing as well.

A further vehicle for promoting inter-agency and interprofessional working in children's services in England and Wales has been the advent of *Children's Services Plans*. These are required to be developed by local authorities to ensure that local services for children are co-ordinated and comprehensive. Plans should identify the need for services locally and the services provided or planned to meet them. This should include family support services for children in need, child protection, and adoption services, and should encompass services provided both by the independent (private and voluntary) sector and by the statutory sector. Plans should address the needs of children in particular circumstances, for example children under eight, children with disabilities or with mental health problems, young carers, looked after children, young runaways, young people leaving care and young people in conflict with the law.

Inter-agency and interdisciplinary work in assessment is at the heart of the *Framework for the Assessment of Children in Need and their Families* (Department of Health et al., 2000; National Assembly for Wales, 2000a). The *Framework* applies both to children who are in need generally, and to children who may be in need because of risk of abuse or neglect. It is based upon a number of underpinning principles. Assessments should be child-centred, rooted in child development and ecological in their approach. They should ensure equality of opportunity, be based on working in partnership with children and families, and build on strengths as well as identifying difficulties. They should be multi-agency in their approach to assessment and service provision. The *Framework* prescribes three dimensions of the assessment: the child's developmental needs, parents' or caregivers' capacity to meet those needs, and wider family and environmental factors. Each of these is subdivided into component categories of the assessment.

In relation to inter-agency working, the *Framework* advises that it is essential to be clear about the purpose and anticipated outputs from the assessment, the legislative basis for the assessment and the protocols and procedures to be followed. There should be no confusion about which agency, team or professional has lead responsibility for collecting information, analysing the results, constructing a plan and taking it forward. This means that it is vital to be clear about the respective roles of the different professionals involved. Consideration must be given to the way in which information will be shared across professional boundaries and within agencies, and be recorded. In a time of increasing awareness of the need to be exceedingly vigilant in the security of the data held by public bodies, this can present considerable challenges. Finally, consideration should be given to how the child and members of the child's family will be involved in the assessment.

Evaluation of working together in children's services

There are four significant reports that have considered the effectiveness of inter-agency working in children's services, which we will briefly consider here: the *Children Act Report 1992* (Department of Health, 1993), the Audit Commission report *Seen but not Heard* (Audit Commission, 1994) and two studies of family support services for children in need (Colton et al., 1995; Social Services Inspectorate, 1996).

The *Children Act Report 1992* reported that development of inter-agency approaches had been 'patchy'. A number of issues were associated with this conclusion: there were discussions between the statutory and voluntary sectors but no mechanisms for strategic development; there were positive links between social services and Health, Housing and Education but links with the police were variable, and with Probation less than might be expected; on the other hand, there was a trend towards a more pragmatic use of a 'mixed economy of care'.

Seen but not Heard (Audit Commission, 1994) looked at the provision of services for children in need across health and social services boundaries. The report identified three key themes in achieving the most cost-effective support for children in need: (1) *need* should form the focus of services, (2) services should be offered only where there is a reasonable expectation of a beneficial outcome, (3) inter-agency working and partnership with parents should underpin provision.

The study of Welsh local authorities by Colton et al. (1995) reported positive findings in relation to inter-agency working, although concern emerged about the predominance of child protection within services for children in need: 'the present study has confirmed the often-expressed fear that child protection will absorb a major share of available resources, leaving an inadequate amount for effective prevention work' (1995: 196). The Social Services Inspectorate (1996) described inter-agency working in a favourable light, and noted that local authorities were beginning to adopt a corporate approach to children in need, rather than simply leaving it to social services.

Conclusion

This chapter began by examining the vexed question of the terminology used to describe the process of workers in different disciplines and different agencies working collaboratively, as a starting point to consider whether it is a single concept or a range of concepts being discussed. The chapter examined the advantages and disadvantages, with a view to ensuring the student is aware that there are costs to working collaboratively, and these costs must be justified by the hoped-for improved outcomes of better co-operation. Identification of obstacles to collaborative working precede a discussion of the dimensions of inter-agency and multidisciplinary working. The ability of agencies to overcome obstacles is the focus of the final section on evaluating collaborative working.

Questions and exercises

1 We have all worked in teams at one point or another in our lives. Consider some of the teams you have worked in. What made those teams work well together? What stopped those teams from working effectively?

2 John (aged nine) is multiply handicapped. He has mobility problems, is hyperactive and has moderate learning difficulties. He has an older brother (aged thirteen) and a younger sister (aged six) and lives with his two parents. His speech is very difficult to understand (which may in part be due to a slight hearing impairment). He is unable to use full sentences in his speech and he tends to use single words to indicate his needs. With intensive support he has been maintained in his local primary school, but parents and professionals are very doubtful about his ability to cope with the requirements of secondary school. Also, his parents find it increasingly difficult to care for him without assistance, and would like to arrange respite care. List as many professionals as you can think of who might need to be involved with John. How can this be co-ordinated so that the parents, and those who will provide future services for John, are not overwhelmed?

Reading

The Green Paper *Every Child Matters* (HM Government, 2003) looks set to change the face of the delivery of children's services. It is well worth reading in full, in order to keep pace with future developments. Payne, *Teamwork in Multiprofessional Care* (2000), looks at the process of teamworking, and provides very useful exercises on how to promote team building.

15
Play in Early Childhood
Branwen Llewelyn Jones

Contents

- What is play?
- The influence of the pioneers
- The influence of the classical theorists
- The contemporary perspective
- The current status of play in early childhood education
- Conclusion

The purpose of this chapter is to give a concise summary of the role of play in early childhood education. It will attempt to define play and to trace its historical significance from the work of the pioneers to the present day. The research of the classical theorists into play will be discussed and the current perspective of the status of play in the education of young children will be explored. The chapter will conclude with the identification of some of the central issues which must be addressed if play is to assume its rightful place in young children's learning.

What is play?

When one observes children at play, certain common characteristics emerge. First, play is fun; children enjoy engaging in it. It may be accompanied by laughter, talk, props or, indeed, none of these things. It may be solitary or involve groups of children; it may also involve adult participation. Although an episode of play may lead to significant learning outcomes, these are not planned at its outset. True play is an impromptu experience and, other than the intention of having fun, its outcomes do not exist in children's minds when they initiate it. In addition, play is spontaneous and children engage in it from choice (Garvey, 1991; Bruce, 1994; Moyles, 1994). Observers of children at play describe them as being actively engaged in their play and giving it their all. This is not a recently observed phenomenon; Caldwell Cook recognised the value of play to both adults and children at the beginning of the twentieth century:

When work and play are separated, the one becomes mere drudgery, the other mere pastime. Neither is then of any value in life. It is the core of my faith that the only work worth doing is really play, for by play I mean the doing anything with one's heart in it.

(1917: 4)

When playing, children demonstrate and develop capacities, skills and ideas which are not in themselves play. Groos (1898) argued that the purpose of play is to create opportunities for children to practise future life skills such as perseverance, compromising, engaging in social discourse, taking the lead and co-operation. What is clear is that observation of children at play informs the adult that children engaged in it are making sense of the world around them. This conclusion is reinforced by the realisation that children's play replicates adults' language, social discourse, attitudes and common interactive situations with a great deal of accuracy and a discomfiting degree of percipience.

Older theories such as Spencer's (1859) propose that play is an essential outlet for the release of excess energy. This is bound up in the theory of evolution, explaining why it is that only the higher forms of life engage in it. Bruner (1960), in his studies of play as part of children's development, devotes a significant amount of attention to the way in which the play of animals can help us to understand the nature and purpose of play – in particular play with tools – of humans. Like Piaget (1965b) and Vygotsky (1978b), he examines the way in which children are able to explore their hopes and anxieties, to try things out safely in pretend play, attributing to it a cathartic function.

It is important to distinguish between what constitutes play and what does not. Caldwell Cook's (1917) definition of play as expressed above is, significantly, not directed at children alone. The mind set of today's adults is very different from that of past generations. They have higher expectations of life and there is a movement towards a more subtle division between work and leisure. A person may demonstrate many of the common characteristics observed in children at play but the activity in which they are engaged cannot be defined as play. For example, painting and ceramics may be engaged in spontaneously and for pleasure. What separates them from the realm of play is the fact that they are processes which culminate in products. Sport is frequently perceived as adults' play, but sports, particularly when organised or competitive, are product-oriented. Perhaps the most intriguing characteristic of play is its inextricable link with such social and cognitive phenomena as creativity, socialisation, problem solving, adaptability and language acquisition.

Although researchers and educators have a shared interest in the effect of play on children's development, their perspectives frequently differ. The lack of a single, precise definition of play has led to the adoption of the widely used term 'free-flow' play (Bruce, 1994). This term is used to describe play which is characterised by common features identified by all the literature on play. What is significant about free-flow play is that it is observed among children of all cultures and can be defined as an essential characteristic of being human. Such are the capacities which arise from it – for example, adaptive intelligence, imagination, creativity and the ability to transfer knowledge from one area to another and apply it another context – that Bruce argues it is essential for adult life: 'The kind of curriculum which encourages learning in context and free-flow play is not a romantic view of education. It is a survival view' (in Moyles, 1994: 198).

Play is a dominant element of the infrastructure of cultures throughout the world and it may be that the question 'What is play?' is best answered by a five-year-old child:

> *Child*: When I play with my friends we have lots of fun … do lots of things … think about
>   stuff … and … well …
> *Adult*: Do you learn anything?
> *Child*: Heaps and heaps – not like about sums and books and things … um … like … like …
>   well … like real things!

(Moyles, 1994: 20)

The influence of the pioneers

In order to understand the centrality of the role of play in early childhood education it is necessary to examine the work of the early educators. These great visionaries laid the foundations for a clear philosophy of early childhood education founded in child-centred experiences contextualised in play. Their core principles have withstood the test of time and continue to stand firm. Indeed, they are as relevant today as they were a century ago, as Bruce (1997) illustrates by placing them in a contemporary context. What the pioneers did was to observe children, reflect, theorise and, with the courage of their convictions, put their theories into practice. A fundamental characteristic of their philosophy was that education must be concerned with the whole child, his or her physical, cognitive, social and spiritual growth, feelings, attitudes, relationships and sense of self.

Froebel and play

In 1816 Friedrich Froebel, one of the most influential of the pioneers, opened his own school in a French village. His philosophy of education was clearly influenced by his own experience of an unhappy childhood. His first book, *The Education of Man*, was published in 1826. It proposed a theory of education which was a masterpiece of far-reaching vision. Its originality had a profound influence on the course of education, which he viewed as a continuous and lifelong process. His ambition was to found an educational centre comprising a nursery school, a school for mothers and a technological school. He was a man ahead of his time whose vision is being realised in Early Excellence Centres more than a century later. He later turned his attention to establishing better places of learning for young children and was the founder of the kindergarten.

Froebel (1826) believed that play, both group and individual, should underpin children's learning at all stages of education. He made a clear distinction between play and work which is a core principle of the pioneers' philosophy. He defined play as a child-centred activity whereas work is the engagement of the child in an activity which is set by the adult, thus denying children the opportunity to be creative and inventive by making them submit to the ideas of the adult. His ideas reached the United Kingdom in the second half of the nineteenth century, where they were put into practice, albeit in infant education only. At last the play activities of children became recognised as part of the educational process when they were put into practice by a few women pioneers in their infant schools.

The McMillan sisters and play

With the establishment of universal elementary education and the inception of secondary education, the twentieth century began full of promise. The restructuring of society in the wake of a world war had a profound effect on the climate of thought in education. Margaret McMillan and her sister Rachael were active social reformers who began campaigning on behalf of poverty-stricken children. They not only asked but published very uncomfortable questions about the education of young children. Margaret McMillan's theory of education was firmly based on play and first-hand experience. The McMillan sisters founded clinics, remedial centres and schools for children.

When planning her nursery school, which opened in 1917, Margaret McMillan rejected the pattern of contemporary schools in favour of models based on the good home of the wealthier family presided over by the mother. She successfully adapted this model to her nursery schools by establishing them near the children's homes and maintaining close contact with their mothers. Her theory placed great emphasis on creating an environment for the child which contained all manner of natural materials: in particular clay, mud, sand, water and wood. She believed that the best opportunities for children's holistic development lay in the domain of their play with materials such as these. Margaret McMillan believed that it is when children are engrossed in their play and oblivious to onlookers that they reveal their innermost selves, the traits and attitudes which are unique and, most important, characterise a particular stage of childhood. She set out to create a world for children in which they could develop those capacities, attitudes and dispositions which would fit them for life. She believed that observation of children at play in such a setting would inform educators about the needs, progress and potential of children far better than anything else: 'Here in the play-world the greatest opportunities for scientific and original research offer themselves to every worker' (McMillan, in Mellor, 1950: 24).

Susan Isaacs and play

Susan Isaacs was a psychologist who went on to become one of the leading founders of child development in Great Britain. She was appointed head of Malting House School, Cambridge, in 1924. It was designed for children between the ages of two-and-a-half and seven years. Teaching at the school was based on direct observation of the children. They were presented with a vast array of props and experiences to promote play and creativity. There was a strong emphasis on learning outdoors, and the children had ample opportunity to engage in adult activities at their own level: for example, planting, watering and tending small plots of land. Isaacs, like her fellow pioneers, subscribed to the belief that the education of the whole child was essential in order to prepare children for life itself (Isaacs, 1968). This common principle of the pioneer educators is best described by Caldwell Cook: 'It would not be wise to send a child innocent into the big world, but it is possible to hold rehearsals, to try our strength in a make-believe world. And that is through play' (1917: 1).

The influence of the classical theorists

Bruce (1997) argues that the core principles of early childhood education established by the pioneers need to be re-examined and applied to the education of young children today, not only because of their enduring relevance, but so that early childhood education can move forward in the way in which it views young children and their needs in order to better meet them.

The writings of the early educationists on play exerted a profound influence on the classical theorists and continue to influence contemporary early years writers who have developed and extended the work of the pioneers. This has enhanced our understanding of the significance of play in the context of contemporary education of the young child and reaffirmed its centrality to children's development. When considering what later early years educationists have written, it is necessary, at the same time, to understand how the context in which they live will have influenced their work. Just as the pioneers were subject to the socio-cultural influences of their times – characterised by such things as poverty, social injustice, increased enfranchisement – so later writers have been influenced by a changed and changing society and the different cultural influences of their times. Bruce (1977: 36) points out that 'it is the mark of great thinkers that they can readjust to changing times without losing the essentials of their work'.

Bruce herself re-examines the ten principles of the pioneers and places them in a modern context, reinforcing their continuing value and relevance. Piaget, Vygotsky and Bruner have made important contributions to our understanding of the significance of play, extending the work of the pioneers. The next section will therefore briefly examine the significance their work for the role of play in early childhood development.

Vygotsky and play

Despite the fact that the role of play forms only a small part of Vygotsky's work, it is of great significance to early childhood education. He stresses the significance of the role of pretend play on children's development in the earliest years of life. In his view, it merited the status of being a leading factor in child development. Vygotsky placed play in the socio-cultural context: that is, a context in which children's play can and should be extended and nurtured by both adults and peers:

> Play creates a zone of proximal development in the child. In play, the child always behaves beyond his average age, above his daily behavior, in play it is as though he were a head taller than himself … play contains all developmental tendencies in a condensed form and is itself a major source of development.

(Vygotsky, 1978b: 102)

Pretend play provides an inimitable context within which children can reach for and attain increasingly higher levels of cognitive development. Vygotsky believed that pretend play is a major means by which young children can extend their cognitive skills. At the same time, children are also learning about the social constructs of their own culture through being encouraged by adults to become active participants in the social world around them. Vygotsky believed that by identifying the main features of play the observer is able to understand how it influences children's development.

One of its major influences, he believed, is to set the stage for the play of middle and later childhood which is characterised by rules and which necessitates management of one's behaviour and the process of socialisation. These fulfil the vital function of enabling the development of reflective thought in children which is necessary for the acquisition of capacities that are essential not merely in education, but for life. These capacities, such as negotiation, co-operative skills and autonomy, can be developed by children through pretend play. This requires, however, the assisted discovery of adults and children's collaboration with peers. The role of the adult in nurturing this transition is illustrated in his model of scaffolding children's learning. Vygotsky's view of play as a zone of proximal development challenged Piaget's assertion that young children discovered make-believe play independently on reaching a certain stage in their development.

Piaget and play

It is widely acknowledged that Piaget was probably the most influential educationist in child development. He was particularly interested in what he called mastery play during which children absorb information from the world around them and shape it to fit in with their own understanding and experience, changing their actions to meet the demands of their personal world. These processes are called assimilation accommodation.

Piaget considered the development of play to be closely linked with the development of intelligence. Like Vygotsky, he believed that by observing a child at play the adult gained much knowledge of the child's stage of development. He identified three stages of the development of intelligence:

1 Sensory – motor.
2 Pre-operational.
3 Operational.

which he believed to correspond to three different types of play:

1 Mastery play.
2 Symbolic or pretend play.
3 Games with rules.

Piaget's developmental model argued that children begin with mastery play during the first two years of life in which they practise and control movements and the world of their senses and how they can affect them, through repetitive movements. For example, discovering that if they shake a cot it causes a mobile to move, they will repeat this action, thus achieving mastery.

During the stage of symbolic play, which takes place between the ages of two and seven years, corresponding with the pre-operational stage, children transform themselves or objects into something else. A child engaged in pretend play about pirates may pick up a cardboard cylinder and use it as a telescope. For the child, it has become a telescope and the transformation is a very real one.

Play with rules corresponds with Piaget's operational stage. As children's thinking becomes more logical, so their play incorporates more rules, moving from those invented by children to following standard rules of particular games.

The Piagetian view which dominated for thirty years was that pretend play emerged spontaneously at a stage well into the pre-school period. It is only relatively recently, since the translation of Vygotsky's work and through the writing of more recent researchers, that this Piagetian view has been challenged and that pretend play is considered to be the product of social collaboration rather than a developmental process.

Bruner and play

Whereas Piaget's developmental theory minimalises the role of the adult in children's development, Bruner, like Vygotsky, considers the role of the adult in fostering children's development through play to be critical. He argues (1972) that children learn from modelled adult behaviour rather than over-directed intervention.

Bruner identifies two major functions of play. First, play situations permit children to test out and modify the consequences of their actions in a context which poses no threat. This provides them with a meaningful situation in which they can learn about things without risk of fear or failure. Second, it gives children an opportunity to engage in behaviours which they would not do so if under adult pressure. Just as Vygotsky believed children learn social constructs through play, Bruner argues that 'Play can serve as the vehicle for teaching the nature of a society's conventions' (1972: 264).

Bruner, like Vygotsky, subscribes to a socio-constructivist theory of play. He emphasises the significance of symbolic or pretend play in enabling children to work through difficulties and fulfil secret desires at a make-believe level whilst, at the same time, helping children to learn how to cope with rules and social conventions.

> With respect to play ... it is first of all an attitude in which the child learns that outcomes of various activities are not as extreme as he had hoped or feared ... In time, the attitude of play is converted into what may best be called a game attitude in which the child gets the sense not only that the consequences are limited but that the limitation comes by virtue of a set of rules that may govern a procedure.
>
> (Bruner, 1966: 134–5)

Bruner's theory of pretend play developing into play with rules can be illustrated by his detailed study of the game 'peep-bo' which is a universal convention of play between adults and children. Through this form of play, children learn that an object continues to exist when out of sight, to track the location of a disappearing face and to respond to what the adult says. It is a significant demonstration of how a young child quickly learns the rules of the game: that is, appearance followed by disappearance. Children will initiate this game at about fifteen months. The conventions which they learn through this form of play develop later into rules which govern the form of play.

Commonalities

In summary, Vygotsky and Bruner subscribe to the socio-constructivist theory of play, namely that it needs to be scaffolded by sensitive and intelligent adult intervention and that there must be social interaction with peers in order for children to progress to higher levels of cognitive functioning. Piaget, however, theorised that play was developmental and that it took place at a particular stage regardless of adult intervention. This viewpoint is in contrast to the socio-constructivist view of play.

Despite their differences, the classical theorists emphasise the vital importance of pretend play to children's development. They agree that it is an intrinsic part of children's development which serves as vital preparation for the later abstract thought. Such abstract thought is highly prized by society, with its value system of tests and examination in which symbols are manipulated and ideas evaluated without reference to real-life situations. This is a critical outcome for children's learning, as 'The human mind does not engage easily in the manipulation of meaningless symbols' (Donaldson, 1978: 77).

This manipulation of symbols can, however, can be learned through pretend play in which, Donaldson (1978) argues, children are placed in a context which makes what she calls 'human sense'. Once learning is placed in such a context, children are enabled to move on to the stage of abstract thinking. In separating meaning and behaviour, make-believe play also helps teach children to make their own choices from a range of alternative courses of action. Young children who have ample time to engage in pretend play enjoy enhanced intellectual development because it presents a much greater cognitive challenge than non-pretend activities such as puzzles and jigsaws, construction and many of the activities commonly seen in early childhood settings. As a result of learning through play children also demonstrate an ability to 'decentre'. Donaldson (1978) identifies this as being critical to young children's development because it enables them to see things from different perspectives at an earlier age. This, in turn, renders them able to understand the feelings and intentions of others and so makes a critical contribution to their social competence.

The contemporary perspective

Contemporary early years educationists, notably Moyles, Bruce and David, reinforce the value of play and their work develops that of the classical theorists by placing it in a contemporary context.

Moyles (1994) believes that it is practitioners who are best placed to observe and channel the value of children's play into powerful contexts for learning. She points out that children will play with or without adult approval. Thus adults should gain a sound understanding of play and encourage it in order that its harsher elements do not manifest themselves later on in such antisocial activities as vandalism. Moyles argues that if young children's learning is founded in play, not only will they be happier in the present but they are far more likely to be well balanced, rounded and fulfilled adults in future society. Play, she argues, is a social construct, which is essential to a balanced society.

Bruce (1994) examines what she calls 'free-flow' play and evaluates its contribution to children's learning. Bruce argues that the flexible intelligence of children who have enjoyed sustained experience of 'free-flow' play will fit them far better for adult life than the highly controlled experiences of a formal early years education. She describes free-flow play as 'part of the infrastructure of any civilization' (1994: 198) and suggests that it is central to humanity. Importantly, Bruce highlights the erroneous belief that such play is confined to middle-class European and North American children. In reality, she points out, it is in these very countries that such play is at risk because of the cultural emphasis on speed and the development of what has become known as the 'hurried' curriculum. Bruce maintains that the diminution of the value of children's play in wealthier industrial cultures is damaging, thus questioning the widely held perception that the children of these societies are privileged.

David (in Nutbrown, 1996), like Bruce, questions whether or not children's inalienable right to play is being denied by the increasing emphasis on formal education in the early years. She quotes Article 31 of the UN Convention on the Rights of the Child, which sets out requirements for children including 'rest and leisure to engage in play and recreational activities appropriate to the age of the child' (Nutbrown, 1996: 90). David questions whether all the things today's children 'do' in a frenzy of after-school clubs, swimming classes, organised football, rugby and tennis clubs and similar activities constitute play. David also highlights the way in which increasing fears for children's safety is understandably causing parents to confine and restrict their children more. Whatever the causes, the effect is that children's experience of play is far more limited than it has been in the past. David (1996: 91) describes this as 'limited access to children's culture'. She points out that in the school setting, the increasing pressure to teach young children as a whole class for long periods of time each day, together with the increased emphasis on literacy and numeracy has resulted in a reductive curriculum in which there is little room for play. David suggests that 'we appear to have paid insufficient attention to the needs of very young children' (1996: 8). She argues that such is the degree of control exerted by policy makers that although early years teachers generally feel that children learn best through play, they find it increasingly difficult not only to ensure it takes place, but also to articulate how children benefit from it.

The contemporary perspective, as illustrated by Moyles, Bruce and David, places a strong consensual emphasis on the benefits of play in preparing children to take their part in a healthy society. It is fearful of the consequences of the reduction of play and the increasing amount of formal learning on children's development and, later, the adults they become.

This chapter has traced the development of ideology, philosophy and theories about the value of play. It has set out what educationists, past and present, have to say about its centrality to child development. Yet students of early childhood education might be forgiven for their frequent reaction following visits to observe play in early childhood settings, namely 'We didn't see any!' This despite the fact that, as Anning (1999: 129) puts it, 'Early Years educators have always set a high value on children's ability to learn through play.'

The current status of play in early childhood education

Research carried out by Bennett et al. (1997) examines the role and status of play in early childhood education whose philosophy, practitioners agree, has play firmly fixed at its core. This philosophy acknowledges not only children's innate need to engage in play, but equally their right to play. Yet despite the prominence of play in all early childhood literature, it is becoming increasingly rare in early years settings. Bennett et al. conclude that, despite practitioners' strongly expressed belief in the centrality of play to the learning of young children, it is not prominent in pre-school and school settings. Bennett et al. suggest that the absence of a single theory of play has made it difficult for practitioners to articulate why it should be included in the curriculum. They, like David (1996), found that practitioners find arguing the case for play problematic. Bennett et al. maintain that until practitioners can articulate these things they will find themselves increasingly frustrated in their attempts to justify their ideas, particularly when child-centred approaches come under attack.

Other studies of play revealed similarly uncomfortable findings. Sylva et al. (1980) found that an alarming number of interactions between adults and children were for purposes entirely outside the realm of children's learning. These included maintaining discipline and day-to-day business such as locating missing objects. Ofsted (1993) found that play is reduced to a recreational activity in more than a third of the schools they surveyed. Most significant perhaps of all the findings was that practitioners used the time when children were at 'play' to catch up with their personal tasks such as updating records and listening to children read. Hutt et al. (1989) found that children's play became elaborated with adult intervention but that adult interactions were brief, subject to constant interruption and mostly to do with controlling behaviour and mundane tasks such as tidying up. Meadows and Cashdan (1988) found, like Sylva et al., that not only were child–adult interactions scarce, but they were not of the kind which promotes learning: 'It seems to be the case that teachers, who are generating a "free play" regime do not interact with their children in stimulating ways, nor do they have sustained conversations' (Meadows and Cashdan, 1988). Meadows and Cashdan propose that there needs to be a clearer definition of the play-based curriculum if play is to make a significant contribution to the learning of young children. They favour a social constructivist model based on practitioners scaffolding children's learning by taking an interactive role.

There is little difference in the status of play in pre-school settings despite their far more favourable adult–child ratio and the absence of a prescribed curriculum. The situation in reception classes is particularly problematic, as expectations at the top end of the school may be thrust ever downwards. Although reception teachers like other early years practitioners widely accept that it is through play that young children learn, it appears that the 'three Rs' dominate and children rarely have free choice. This early formalisation and reduction in learning through play is the cause of considerable disquiet. It is telling that far more concern is currently expressed about the nature and appropriateness of the curriculum of the four-year-old than of the five-year-old child, highlighting the downward spiral of formality. The National Curriculum is not a statutory requirement until year 1, but in practice, preparation of Key Stage 1 begins much earlier, with increased formal learning, whole-class work and direct teaching. This is not a recent phenomenon. Sestini (1987) noted, as did Meadows and Cashdan (1988) and Hutt et al. (1989), that the status of play activities was minimised by the amount of attention given by practitioners to literacy and numeracy in particular. Sestini also found that teachers involved themselves with those children who were engaged in 'work', leaving those who were playing to their own devices, thus reinforcing the distinction between 'work' and 'play'.

One of the major reasons for the increase in more formal learning is that the outcomes of play are difficult to measure. This places practitioners in a vulnerable position in a climate which demands of them constant proof of children's learning and achievement for purposes of accountability. Current developments in assessing such intangible things as children's dispositions are, fortunately, proving successful. Gammage and Kreig (2001) have developed an assessment tool which measures the factors that contribute to the long-term benefits of early childhood provision founded in child-centred, play-focused learning experiences.

The significance of play to children's social development is emphasised by Vygotsky (1978b), Bruner (1972), Moyles (1994), Bruce (1997) and David (1999), who agree that the contribution of play to children's social competence is critical. There is clear and widespread support among current researchers for Vygotsky and Bruner's socio-constructivist theories of play. Sestini (1987), Tizard et al. (1988), Bennett and Kell (1989), Hutt et al. (1989) and Smilansky and Shefataya (1990) stress the necessity for the practitioner to intervene in order to scaffold the children's learning and raise the quality, and, by so doing, the status, of play as a promoter of learning in early childhood education. In order for this to happen, the practitioner must be actively involved in children's play in a meaningful way. The non-interventionist stance of practitioners which is reported in research (Sylva et al., 1980; Meadows and Cashdan, 1988; Hutt et al., 1989) is at odds with the social constructivist theories of Vygotsky and Bruner, which view the practitioner as instrumental in enabling young children to extend and apply their knowledge. Seifert (1993, cited by Bennett et al., 1997) argues that 'If play provides a rich context for learning then surely it must provide a rich context for teaching' (Bennett et al.,1997: 15).

The notion of a curriculum founded in play is not new. *Starting with Quality* (Department of Education and Science, 1990) supported a socio-constructivist approach to play, yet what exists at present is far removed from a curriculum which has, at its core, child-centred play experiences. The lack of clarification not only of how teaching and learning through play take place, but of what play actually is, is unhelpful to those who are trying to promote it. For those of us who have been fortunate enough to witness it, it is perhaps the suspension of disbelief which best defines pure play. It rarely occurs, but when it does, it is breathtaking. Situations which come to mind involve the adult taking an active part in the children's pretend play. Many practitioners will have seen halls full of infant children waiting for Father Christmas cast their eyes upwards when told that he, and his reindeer, of course, are on the roof. Such suspension of disbelief can, and does, take place in more prosaic pretend play situations but it is a rare and precious thing to behold. It is only when practitioners reflect on and articulate their personal ideas and experiences, which are, after all, theories drawn from their own practice, that there will be a clear and unified understanding of what is meant by learning through play and how it can be successfully achieved.

Conclusion

There is an overwhelming subscription among early years practitioners to the principle that children learn best through play. This philosophy is founded in the observation, reflection and practice of the pioneers. The work of the classical theorists reinforced this philosophy with expanded theories based on extensive research. The perspective put forward by contemporary writers reaffirms what both the pioneers and the classical theorists argued and continues to stress its centrality not only to children's learning, but to their holistic development. Yet, despite what practitioners say, the status of play remains low and practitioners are unconfident about either articulating the argument for its inclusion or engaging in the actual practice of teaching and learning through play. This suggests strongly that they are paying lip service to the value of play: 'The view that the education of young children is founded on play has almost attained the status of a commandment, but it is a commandment observed more in the telling than the doing' (Bennett and Kell, 1989: 78).

Every education system reflects the values of its society. Today's education system like today's society, is characterised by speed, pressure and constant accountability. It may not be until we become a less hurried society which is more concerned with the here and now than with future deadlines that play will regain its rightful place in our children's education.

Questions and exercises

1   What is play and why do children engage in it?
2   What was the contribution of the pioneers to the role of play in the education of young children?
3   What are the differences between Piaget, Vygotsky and Bruner's theories in terms of the function of play in child development?
4   What contribution do the contemporary educationists make to the case for an early years curriculum which is founded in play?
5   Give the reasons for the difference between what teachers say about the importance of play in children's learning and the current status of play as evidenced in classroom practice.

Reading

Broadhead, *Early Years Play and Learning* (2004), provides a framework for observing and assessing young children's learning through play. The links between children's cognitive development, the progress of language and emotional growth are considered. The author's concept of a social play continuum as an instrument of observation and a means of monitoring children's social progress is presented in depth. The content reflects a combination of theory and practice to indicate what constitutes quality provision for young children. Craft, *Creativity and Early Years Education* (2002), studies creativity in all its forms in depth, including the close link between play and creativity. The kinds of creative thinking promoted by socio-dramatic play are discussed, as is the connection between play and metacognitive development. The book looks at higher-order play, through which children pose and respond to challenges which they themselves have set and which enables them to have ownership of and to control their own learning. In Fisher, *Starting from the Child* (2002), the centrality of play to young children's learning is explored, together with its role as a motivator and as a vehicle for exploring feelings, ideas and relationships. It is addressed in the context of establishing firm foundations for young children's learning which underpin their subsequent dispositions, values, attitudes and achievements. Macintyre, *Enhancing Learning through Play*, synthesises play (2001), learning and child development for three primary purposes: to explain what most children are able to do at different stages, to enhance learning by using the medium of play in the light of assessments made on the basis of developmental issues and to devise learning activities which match and extend children's learning. The intervention of the adult in children's play in order to support and extend their learning is explored, and the author looks at children who find it difficult to play and considers the reasons.

16
Child Observation
Bob Sanders

Contents

- Setting up and undertaking a child study
- Learning from the child study
- Conclusion

There are a number of reasons for undertaking a child study, and a variety of different models of child observation (Fawcett, 1996). Observation may be of the setting, of an individual child, or of a group of children. The focus in this chapter is on observation of an individual child. The aim of this model of child study is to provide an opportunity to link theory and practice in child development.

Some models of child observation make use of a systematic scoring system that records predefined behaviours (for example, number and targets of verbal communications, patterns of interaction with siblings, frequency of aggressive and prosocial behaviours, etc.). Observers work with a grid that lists the relevant behaviours, and at the end of the observation session the researcher totals the number of different types of behaviours observed. Such models have been developed by researchers looking for data to be analysed.

In the model used by the Tavistock Institute, a well known centre for the study of human relations, observations are followed by extensive and detailed 'process recordings', and the observer is invited to reflect on personal factors within him or herself that contribute to the observation (Bridge and Miles, 1997). This model highlights observation as an active process of selection and interpretation, rather than as a passive process of recording; one in which we learn not only about the child, but about ourselves. In the model we consider the impact of what we observe on ourselves – our identification with the child's anxiety, our anger or sadness when the child is ignored, hurt or treated with a lack of dignity and respect. Such a model may open channels to reflection on one's own childhood experiences and how they relate to what is being observed. One learns about child development through reflecting on one's own childhood, the childhood of the child being observed, and the relationship between the two. Needless to say, such a model requires a relatively small group in which an atmosphere of trust has been created, before people may be comfortable enough to share.

The model set forth in this chapter is an adaptation of the Tavistock model, but with a more academic emphasis. It relies on a similar methodology of detailed post-observation recording, but uses the observation to help us to understand theories of child development. Within this overall aim, there are three main objectives for the observer:

1 To become familiar with theories of child development, and to understand better how children develop, with the emphasis on social, emotional and identity development.
2 To understand the distinctions between observation, evaluation and assessment.
3 To develop an understanding of how contextual factors such as class, gender, race, culture, language and poverty influence child development.

Setting up and undertaking a child study

This child study model requires a minimum of six observations of a child in a pre-school setting – normally arranged with support from a tutor. There is a rationale for requiring a number of observations. During the first observation the observer is confronted with an array of behaviour; a good observer will come away with a rich palette of behaviours the child is capable of producing, but there will be no sense of which behaviours are typical or atypical for that particular child. During the second observation, the observer is again confronted with an array of behaviour, but this time should be able to note which behaviours occurred in only one session, and which occurred in both sessions. In other words the observer is beginning to weave a *pattern* out of the individual units of observed behaviour. But even two is too few: there may be a significance in which behaviour appeared in one or other session; some behaviours may be typical of a particular child but not observed on every occasion; some behaviours may be new, others disappearing. The third observation should begin to give the careful observer a good sense of which behaviours are highly characteristic of this child; which are less frequent, and which are unusual.

It is important that the observer notes behaviours which do *not* occur, as well as those that do. For example, it might be expected, if a child is in the vicinity of another child who is distressed, perhaps because of some slight injury, that the child would engage in some type of prosocial behaviour such as comforting, distracting or bringing the distress to the attention of a carer. A child who is impervious to the distress of other children may thus display 'non-behaviour' which may be just as significant as what he or she actually does. Of course this behaviour may be related to gender differences; boys are often less likely to respond with prosocial behaviour than girls, or may require a higher threshold before responding.

After the third observation, the observer should begin to develop some hypotheses about what the child is like, which types of behaviour might be expected, and which not. The next three sessions enable the observer to test these hypotheses, as well as drawing a richer picture of the child's repertoire by remaining open to new behaviours. By six weeks, the observer should have a good idea of who this child is.

Another reason to aim for a minimum of six sessions is more pragmatic. It usually takes about four weeks to set up and begin the observation, and there are ordinarily only about ten weeks in an academic term, or eleven or twelve weeks in a semester. However, if the study is not limited to a single term or semester, more observations may be undertaken.

Setting up the child study

In this model, the observer is responsible for identifying a target child (aged one to five) for the study. The tutor does not arrange placements; however, the programme can facilitate the process of negotiating access by students. Letters are sent to local providers of day care and nursery schooling *via* the local education authority, social services and voluntary organisations such as the Preschool Playgroups Association (and in Wales Mudiad Ysgolion Meithrin), informing them of the purpose of the child study and the names of the students who will be undertaking it. The regional office of the National Care Standards Commission is also notified. Second, the observer is given a signed letter of introduction to use when negotiating agreement to observe a child. These steps are taken to create confidence for professionals approached by students that the request is *bona fide*. It is unfortunate that those who wish to harm children frequently use professional roles as a means to gain access to children, and Early Childhood Studies programmes must take precautions not to be used in this way.

The target child should *not* be a child in the observer's family or immediate social network, because this can result in uncomfortable complications. For example, students undertaking observations of children frequently become aware that the care provided for children in many settings is less than ideal. The most likely settings to find a child to observe are nursery classes, nursery schools, day nurseries and play-groups, but observations can also be undertaken of children in a family centre, or with a registered childminder. If the opportunity arises, it may be helpful for group learning if some students can observe children of ethnic minority background, with special needs, or whose first language is not English (including Welsh-speaking children).

To find these places, it is usually sufficient to go through word of mouth. Through friends who have young children one can learn where early years facilities are located. Alternatively, if other students are living in the same locality, it may be pos-sible to share collective knowledge of local facilities. If all else fails, try contacting the local authority to request a list of local pre-school facilities; such lists are main-tained for parents seeking day care provision.

Having identified a setting, the observer needs to establish contact and explain the request. Initial contact would be with the playgroup or nursery supervisor. In a school setting, it would be appropriate to go through the school headteacher. Sometimes writing in advance will enable the supervisor or headteacher to think ahead about the proposal, although this may need to be balanced against the need for fairly quick action.

In addition to the agreement of the pre-school supervisor or nursery teacher, observation of the child can be undertaken only with the agreement of the parent or carer, or person with parental responsibility. There should normally be direct contact with the parent or carer at this stage, although in exceptional cases an observation can proceed with the assurance from the programme supervisor that the parents have consented. The supervisor and parent or carer will need to be assured that information obtained in the study is confidential and will be shared with others only for purposes of learning. On any written material produced, the child's initials, or fictitious names, should be used, and identifying information must be avoided. An example might be where a parent has a very specific type of employment that would identify him or her.

The child should be told that he or she is going to be observed. Usually this can be in the form of something like: 'I am here to learn how children play and I would like to watch you at play.' This can be in advance, or at the time of the first observation (in advance is preferable). This is not the same as asking the child for consent, as usually children of such an age would be too young to give informed consent, but if the child indicates that she or he is unhappy with being watched, then one should not coax or persuade, but should think about identifying another child. Mostly children don't mind. Occasionally one learns that a student has not told the child about the observation, and then it is necessary to remind the student that the child will be aware of being watched (no matter how discreet the student may try to be), and that if not given a proper reason which makes sense, they may create fantasies about what is the reason for being watched. This can cause unnecessary worries for the child.

As a student or other observer, you must ensure that the supervisor and parent/carer are aware that the observations are for your own learning about child development. Sometimes people may expect you to provide information about the child, and it is therefore necessary to clarify that you are *not* undertaking an assessment. As observation notes are descriptive rather than evaluative, it should not be a problem if parents want to see them. However, it is for you to decide whether or not to share your notes with the parent or carer.

Before the first observation, try to ascertain the following information:

1 The child – sex, age, date of birth, ethnicity, position in family, physical appearance, personality, relationships with adults and other children, preferred activities.
2 The family – age and occupation of mother and father and other significant relatives in the home (siblings, grandparents, etc.).
3 The group setting – type, size, physical conditions, aims, training and attitudes of supervisor and other staff, how the provision fits into the local and national context.

Undertaking the child study

The aim is to schedule six one-hour observations. If time and circumstances permit, and if parents/carers and school/playgroup are agreeable, one may undertake more. However, observations should not extend beyond an hour; an hour is long enough for sustained concentration and observation. After each session, a full chronological recording should be made of everything observed during the session. This should include what the child does, where the child goes, how long the child spends on different activities, who the child speaks to and interacts with in other ways, etc. Such detailed recording is normally quite time-consuming. Usually, the writing up afterwards will take at least *twice* as long as the time spent observing. It is important to plan for this time; it is no good leaving it for a few days and then expecting the recall of detail still to be there. Do not take contemporaneous notes during the observation sessions, because that can distract from observing what is actually happening. If notes are taken, they should be confined to brief and simple reminder markers.

As indicated, there are different models of child observation. In this one, rather than attend to the whole range of children's development, the observer is particularly asked to tune into three particular aspects: identity, emotional development and social development. Therefore, in addition to the descriptive account of the sequence of events, it will be helpful to incorporate observations concerning the child's expression of self, his or her social interactions (including both verbal and non-verbal communication), and any indications of his or her emotional state. The observer should try to be aware of any selective attachments the child has; to whom is the child attached, and how does he or she cope with their absence? One should try to recall and record what is said by the child to whom, and by others to the child, as an indication of social interaction. In all observations one should be alert to class, language, culture, race and gender influences. After each observation is transcribed, take a moment to reflect on the relevance of theory and research to what has been observed.

Being an observer is a difficult role to undertake, and the observer should make every effort to stay in that role, avoiding interaction as far as possible unless it is necessary for reasons of the child's safety. *You should not be left in a position of being responsible for the child; carers or staff should always be present.* Interactions initiated by the child or other children should be gently discouraged, if necessary by responding in a way that does not invite further interaction but without being brusque, dismissive or unnecessarily abrupt.

If parents, staff or other adults try to interact with the observer during the observation, it may be necessary to remind them of the purpose of the exercise. No matter how much one clarifies the nature of the observation, and attempts to keep one's focus on the child, it frequently happens that those responsible for caring for the child show concern about being watched. They may attempt to engage the observer in conversation about the child; they may ask questions or make statements that show their concern that they themselves are being evaluated! This is understandable, because being watched by somebody with whom one has no interaction can cause us to feel threatened and stimulate fantasies about what the other person thinks. One response is to try to pull the observer out of role by engaging them in social interaction. The observer may find it very difficult to stay in role, and may have to resist social pressures.

There are also internal pressures. Many students, because of their fondness for children, find it very difficult to be in the presence of children without wanting to get down on the floor and interact. Some actually do get down and play with the children, attempting to engage in participant observation, but don't reveal it to the tutor! It is usually only towards the end of the series of observations, as students realise how many things they have observed that were missed by the carers (some of which are very significant for the child's well-being), that they begin to appreciate the benefit of being in a non-interactive role as an observer.

Sometimes students ask whether the presence of the observer alters the dynamics and therefore creates a lack of accuracy in the observation. The answer is of course, yes, the presence of the observer does affect the dynamics. You are watching people who are being watched and who are aware of being watched. There is no attempt to claim objectivity in the observation process. It is not the same, nor is it intended to be the same, as having a video camera installed and watching the child through closed circuit television. Likewise, observation not only affects the person being observed, it also has an impact on the observer. You will often see things that invoke personal memories, or strong attitudes about the way children are or should be treated. This is all part of the process of observation.

Learning from the child study

In the model described here, child observation is combined with a series of lectures on theories of child development and a series of seminars in which students reflect on their observations. In these seminars each student presents at least one of their observations to the rest of the class, who are expected to contribute their own ideas to help understand the behaviour of the child who is being presented. Students have a collective responsibility for their own learning, and in particular for drawing on relevant theory to help understand the child's behaviour. In the Swansea pro-gramme the focus of discussion in the seminars has included the following themes.

Approval seeking

Children can often be seen engaging in behaviour that they know will be approved of by adult care takers. If they don't spontaneously get it, they will sometimes approach the carer to ensure that they have been noticed:

> George [fictitious name], after seeing the teacher congratulate another student on her hard work, brings his drawing up to the teacher to see. 'Well, I worked hard too!' he says.

Attachment

There are at least two ways in which the issue of attachment emerges in the child studies. First, it emerges in the children's attachment to their primary care taker, usually a parent. This may be observed in how children separate from, or are reunited with, their primary carers at the beginning and end of the day. Sometimes students will vary the time of their observation on occasion in order to be able to observe how the child deals with these events. These separations and reunions mirror the three-minute episodes in Ainsworth et al.'s (1978) 'strange situation' procedure designed to measure attachment. An important consideration for those children showing some level of distress at the separation is how long it takes for the child to develop a sense that reunions follow the separations, and a sense that the place where the child is being left is not quite so threatening as might have been imagined on the first day.

The attachment to the primary carer can also be seen in the way children recreate within the setting play, stories, and events which recapture for them the absent parent:

> Gemma was seen to start a flying game. It emerged that her father has his own plane.

A second sense in which attachment emerges is in the way in which children become attached to their temporary carers in the classroom or nursery. In time children build up very strong bonds, which are linked with their initial insecurity and become more apparent whenever anxiety is heightened:

> Alice was noted to be very 'clingy with the teacher'.
> Sharon appears to be very aware of the teacher all the time.
> Alun showed a look of concern when the teacher left the room.

Sometimes it is interesting to speculate on how different patterns of attachment may have developed:

> Charlie is 'more comfortable with male carers, to the extent of being clingy'; he doesn't have a best friend, but he is quite close to the male carer.

Continuity of behaviour

Another important theme arising is continuity in children's behaviour. This arises in two senses: (1) continuity between how the child behaves at home and in the out-of-home setting, and (2) continuity between how the child behaves at different times. This usually will be related to concepts of identity, and consideration of the relationship between psychological and social identity – between an inner sense of self as continuous and a sense of self derived from social context which may be experienced somewhat differently in the various settings where a child may be:

> The observer noted a 'difference between how he is described by his parents (boisterous and outgoing) and how he appears to be in the group (reserved, almost isolated); in this session, he behaved differently; today, he has been quite aggressive ...'

> The observer refers to speculation as to why Sharon might have been so different today; comparison was made with how she had been on previous occasion (quiet).

Dominance

A frequently seen aspect of children's interactions is the devices and stratagems they use to achieve dominance. James (1998) suggests that in children's play there are universal themes relating to children constructing and reconstructing power relations between people. Children adopt devices to get other children to comply with their wishes, and employ means to avoid having to comply with the wishes of others. One strategy is to enforce recognised authority, exemplified by children who try to play the role of helper to those in charge; often such children's interactions with the staff tend to reinforce those roles. In other situations, children may simply try to bully others to comply. In pre-school situations, overt bullying is much less likely to go unnoticed by staff than in school, but there are covert means that children adopt to gain the compliance of others.

> Emma tells girl to wash herself; Emma is in control and in charge; She ... takes over, and counts out the pieces ... 'You can have these.' Emma thumps Rebecca on the arm quite violently and then walks away; Emma hits Rebecca and tells her to play properly.

> Anna shouted across the room to a little girl to get on with her work; bossing the others around ... wagging her finger at the other girls.

Gender

It is inevitable that at some point seminar discussions will focus on gender. There are contentious and complex issues one needs to address. One is the balance between 'nature' and 'nurture' in determining gender characteristics; students sometimes overestimate the effect of heredity and underestimate the influence of environment. Even when the influence of environment is appreciated, one may struggle to see how in relation to the observed child the influence of other children and adults often serves to reinforce stereotypes about the ways in which boys and girls are supposed to behave. Statham (1986) notes how parents who strive to bring their children up with non-sexist values find much of their work is undone when children's social worlds expand with their entry into school – likewise with pre-school:

> Alex was seen as odd because he likes dressing up in girls' clothes when they have the drama session.

The following extract reminds us that this is an age when strong gender associa-tion patterns emerge. In part this may be because of common interests, in part it may be for other reasons:

> Boys go to the lego/popoid play area, and the girls go the stick-and-paste area ...

> Jane gets on with the other girls in the class, but not so much with the other boys; they shout a lot; she is in the playhouse with four other girls.

> Maria and Sharon return to the home area to tidy it.

> Alice: playing in an all-girl group; one of the boys is the doctor ... The other girl is the patient and Alice is a nurse.

Physical behaviour

Children are often much more physical than adults, and one may tune into the things that children do that would be frowned upon if done by an adult. For example:

Emma scratches herself a lot; she has a habit of sticking her hands down the back of her tights.

Megan plays with her hair a lot; scratches herself; during the story she is fidgety, and sticks her fingers in her mouth.

Sarah sitting cross-legged on the floor, playing with her hair … Sometimes during the session she leans on her knees and elbows … Later she sits on a chair with one leg crossed over the other in a way that [observer] considers to appear very grown up.

Observer role

I have already commented on how important it is that the child is aware of being observed and has had the opportunity to say if they are not happy. In some cases students, supported by staff, have thought it better not to inform the child. As often as not the child can work out what is happening; the child enters a distinctive relationship with the observer – the watcher and the watched:

Anna doesn't know she is being observed.

Alun was not told that he in particular would be observed; selected by teacher for the observation 'as an interesting specimen'.

Teacher did not tell Megan that she in particular was being observed, although the class were told; Megan comes over to talk to [observer]; she smiles at Megan.

A girl comes up to Emma and tells her that the observer is watching her; they both look in the direction of observer.

Sometimes children may play a game with you, putting themselves in places where they cannot be seen and then looking to see if you are still watching, as if to say 'You can't see me now … now you can.' As previously noted, there are forces that work to pull you out of the observer role, both from staff and from other children:

Alex looks at observer, which is the first sign he shows of being aware of him; another child comes and stares at [observer] which distracted her to the extent of losing concentration on Alex.

Prosocial behaviour

Examples of children learning concern for others can be frequent even in a short period of observation. It is important to be aware of this, in order to counteract a tendency to emphasise negative and disruptive behaviour rather than behaviour that serves to promote social interaction, facilitation and support.

Emma shows concern about boy crying.

Alexa explains to a new girl about sandplay.

Sarah showed a new child who was just up from the nursery class how to play with trains.

Greg draws the teacher's attention to a little girl who has a runny nose, and the teacher tends to it.

Billy appears concerned when John fell over and hurt himself.

Peer relationships and friendships

Observations of social interactions are an important feature of child study, and sometimes a cause of concern for carers or observers. Sometimes a child's lack of relationships may be of concern; sometimes carers may be concerned about particular associations.

Billy has a very close friend, John; they are together during registration; 'like being attached by a string'; why do the leaders want to separate Billy and John?

Carl's verbal interactions with other children were very low; 95 per cent of the time playing on his own; he doesn't have a best friend, but he is quite close to the male carer; he watches the children playing, but does not get involved; today was the first time Charlie was actually seen interacting with other children; [observer] wondered whether he should be interacting more with the other children.

Alex was quite introverted and did not interact well; he has no mate in class. He is involved with one boy and they are play-wrestling.

Sarah gives a lot of attention to her friend; she has friends but not one particular friend in the class; hasn't sat next to the same girl twice throughout the sessions. She doesn't appear to have a particular friend.

Paul has a relationship with another child (Ellen) which the teachers are trying to discourage; they are trying to keep Paul and Ellen apart.

Socialisation

Evidence usually emerges in observation about how children are socialised to behave 'correctly'. Values of courtesy, tidiness and self-control begin at home and are generally continued within the out-of-home setting. One sees various indicators of the way children are taught 'proper' behaviour. It is sometimes interesting as well to look for children who are 'over-socialised', who have integrated so strongly the messages of self-control that they have sacrificed their spontaneity, individuality and rebelliousness. The 'self' here has become submerged under an idealised notion of 'proper' behaviour. One may find oneself hoping that the child will show some sign of breaking out of the constraints that bind her. These observations can lead to very interesting discussions about different conceptions concerning the 'true' nature of children (for example, innately good, in need of drawing out versus innately savage, in need of controlling). This may also lead to discussion of the application of external controls leading to the internalisation of controls, and the development of fears about what might happen if things get out of control. Several children's books are very relevant to this theme, for instance *Super Dooper Jezebel* by Tony Ross and *Where the Wild Things Are* by Maurice Sendak.

Barry was very concerned about mess – glue.

Pamela tells girl to wash herself; she then bangs two figures on the floor. 'Stop it, you two! Behave!'

Alice was clearly shocked by the new girl's tantrum.

Emily is not naughty or disobedient.

Other themes

These are some of the main themes that have emerged from observations, showing how they can provide students with a strong foundation from which to discuss and learn about issues in child development. Some other issues that have cropped up are: the types of play that children engage in; children being disciplined and how; the exercise of adult authority; how much of what is observed is down to temperament, character or personality. This is not an exhaustive list of the material that might emerge from child observations. The range of themes and issues is as varied and wide-ranging as are children themselves. No doubt in your observations you will find many more.

Conclusion

Despite there being a variety of means of undertaking a child observation, as a method it has been found to be effective as a way of facilitating student learning. In this chapter I have described the value of the approach in relation to integrating the theory of child development that you read about with the behaviour of the child that you see before you. The chapter described how to set up and undertake the observation, and discussed some of the themes that have emerged from observations previously undertaken by students. The developmental focus of this particular approach has been on the social, emotional and identity dimensions of children's growth and development.

Questions and exercises

1 It is suggested in this chapter that very young children cannot give 'informed consent' to being the subject of observation. What do you understand by 'informed consent' in this context? Do you think that children should be asked to agree to being observed? Can you think of difficulties, other than those described here, that might arise if the observation is undertaken without informing and seeking the approval of the child?

2 Many of the comments made in the chapter about the children being observed are *normative* – children are described as showing some behaviour more or less than they 'should'. Do our values and assumptions get in the way of seeing children objectively, or do they help in giving us a focus?

Reading

Clearly there are too many texts and journals that deal with child development to begin to list them here. You are advised to ensure you have access to a good overview child developmental text (for example, Bee, *The Developing Child*, in the latest edition, as it is frequently revised and updated). Crain, *Theories of Development* (1992), is a useful outline of a number of theoretical approaches to understanding how children develop. Barnes, *Personal, Social and Emotional Development of Children* (1995), is one of a series of Open University texts that are a very useful source of information on how children develop, and is especially relevant to the themes developed in this approach to child observation. Beaty, *Observing the Development of the Young Child* (1998), is a very useful book for highlighting the link between what one may observe in young children and theoretical considerations. Durkin, *Developmental Social Psychology* (1996), is also good for its focus on the less tangible aspects of children's development, in particular their social development. You may find it useful as well to look at some of the literature on the process of child observation. Fawcett, *Learning through Child Observation* (1996), provides an overview of the different methods of child observation. Bridge and Miles, *On the Outside Looking in* (1997), give examples of observations undertaken by students using the Tavistock approach.

17
Inclusive Practice in the Early Years
Sharon Airey

Contents

- What is inclusive practice?
- Who is affected by exclusion?
- What are the effects of discrimination?
- The benefits of inclusive practice
- Inclusive language
- Barriers to inclusive practice
- Law and legislation affecting inclusion
- Conclusion

Inclusion is an area that many early years practitioners are wary of. All too often the issue is avoided – not owing to any malicious intent or ignorance but rather to a fear of getting it 'wrong'. People often feel uncomfortable dealing with the terminology, worrying in case they are not 'politically correct', using the right language or that they might offend certain people. Often the issue is avoided or brushed over owing to embarrassment or lack of information, but this does not have to be the case.

It is vital that early years professionals, no matter what their role, consider all children as individual children first and foremost and not just a 'type' of child. All children have individual needs which must be provided for, regardless of their gender, race, ability or background. It is not enough to simply group certain children together owing to an obvious characteristic, such as race, impairment or family situation. It is also important that anyone working with early years children examines their own attitudes and assumptions. Everyone has individual views and experiences that contribute to their attitudes, and it is not expected that all early years professionals already have a comprehensive knowledge of inclusive policy and practice. However, what is essential is that they examine their views and challenge any that might not contribute to an inclusive work practice.

It is not surprising that people might have difficulty addressing their personal values. People's opinions and perceptions evolve from their own experiences, knowledge and exposure to others' attitudes and behaviour. This will be discussed in more depth later in the chapter.

This chapter will not attempt to provide you with the detailed information relating to various groups of children and families' specific needs. It is often thought that, in order to provide a fully inclusive setting, early years practitioners need to have a detailed knowledge of various disabilities, cultures and other factors that might have implications for the child or family. This is not necessarily true. Whilst such knowledge is valuable and can be gained by experience of working with a range of individuals over time, it is more important that staff's values and attitudes are examined and the practice and policy are in place to make a provision as inclusive as possible. Advice and training on specific areas of expertise can be sought from the relevant sources, but working with your own individual children and families will provide you with the most valuable experience. The main aim of this chapter is to examine inclusive practice, to explore the main barriers that prevent it occurring in early years settings and to offer practical means of ensuring you can begin to examine your own values and attitudes as well as the effectiveness of the early years provision that you experience.

What is inclusive practice?

It is perhaps easier to first define what is not inclusive practice. This could be any setting or service where some children and families are not valued or seen as important as the others, or a provision that does not cater for the needs of all its users. Early years practitioners do not usually just work with the child. The family is very much involved and it is vitally important that all members of the family, and the wider community, are also able to access and use the early years provision. It is as important for parents to be able to easily access the provision as the children themselves, as 'parental involvement ... seems to be a more important influence [on children's achievements] than poverty, school environment and the influence of peers' (Ofsted, 2003: 18). An inclusive setting or service should be inclusive for all. Consider these scenarios:

1   It is Emma's first day at nursery and she is a little nervous. She sees a group of boys playing noisily with toy cars, and would very much like to play with them, as they are her favourite toys and she has the same cars at home. However, the nursery nurse guides her away from the group of boys and suggests she plays nicely with the girls in the home corner. Emma does not like to play with dolls very much and gets upset.
2   A new family moves into the area and the mother takes her youngest child to the doctor's surgery. A notice board in the waiting room is covered with valuable information regarding the services available for babies, children and their families. However, as the information is entirely in English and the mother does not read English, she remains unaware of the services and does not access them.
3   A father cannot enter his child's classroom to speak to the class teacher easily, as the room is on the first floor of a Victorian school. The father uses a wheelchair and there is no lift in the old building. He feels uncomfortable having to ask the class teacher to come downstairs each time he wishes to speak to her. Consequently, the father often feels that he has missed out on hearing details of his child's work and behaviour at school.

Figure 17.1   The hierarchy of expertise (*based on an idea presented by Dynamix, Swansea, www.seriousfun.demon.co.uk*)

These situations may not be caused by malice or neglect. All too often people can be excluded unintentionally. The staff at an early years centre may not know about the needs of a new child attending the setting, or they may assume that they know about any special measures the child might need. But it is dangerous to presume. One of the biggest difficulties is knowing what is appropriate. But how do you find out what the individual's needs are in order to meet them?

Initially when attempting to provide appropriate provision, practitioners often turn to the 'experts' to provide them with the information they require in order to set about meeting specific children's needs. But who are the experts, after all? Are they the professionals who perhaps spend their career researching the social and medical requirements of particular groups? Or are they the individuals who live their lives each day and have first-hand experience of their needs, abilities and requirements? Usually it is the individual themselves, or the people closest to them, such as parents, carers and their family, who are the experts. (See Figure 17.1.). Obviously, very young children or those with particular communication impairments might not be able to specify their needs explicitly. But those who care for them on a daily basis will have the relevant knowledge about that particular child's requirements. Whilst legislation is imperative for enforcing and advising of the requirements and targets for implication, policy and the subsequent practice should originally stem from the needs of the individual children and families.

So, what is inclusive practice? Successful inclusive practice would result in an early years setting or service that values all children and families the same. All children and families using the provision would feel equally welcome using it, would have be able to access the provision with ease, would not be, or feel, 'left out' in any way. It is important to consider the feelings of the child and family. Whilst you may think you are providing a service that includes all, there may still be certain individuals who do not feel included. Equal opportunities do not mean that all individuals need, or indeed want, to be treated the same. Treatment should be appropriate to the needs of the individual. The word 'individual' is vital here. To consider the needs of a group of people is often not effective; not everyone in a group has the same needs. To assume all visually impaired children, for example, all require the same treatment as the one child you have previously dealt with is not enough. Careful planning, good communication and addressing the known, and anticipated, needs of all users are vital for success.

Who is affected by exclusion?

Inclusion often refers to steps taken to include, and adequately provide for, children with special educational needs or disabilities. However, inclusive practice must ensure that *all* children are provided with appropriate early years provision, regardless of their individual or family circumstances. Children and families that might otherwise be excluded include, but are by no means limited to, the following (Ofsted, 2000: 4):

1   Girls and boys.
2   Minority ethnic and faith groups, Travellers, asylum seekers and refugees.
3   Pupils who need support to learn English as an additional language (EAL).
4   Pupils with special educational needs.
5   Gifted and talented pupils.
6   Children 'looked after' by the local authority.
7   Other children, such as sick children; young carers; children from families under stress; pregnant schoolgirls and teenage mothers.
8   Any pupils who are at risk of disaffection and exclusion.

It must be recognised that a simple list will never even begin to cover all children and families that an early years professional may deal with; indeed, to try and reduce these children and families could be seen as dangerous and narrow-minded. A child or family may not fit into any of the above groups, or indeed may fall into two or more categories at the same or at different times. However, for the purposes of this chapter it is important to acknowledge the types of people potentially affected by inclusive practice. Even attempting to discuss individuals adversely affected by exclusion or discrimination is to run the risk that some groups or individuals may be omitted or offended. However, care has been taken to limit any offence or omissions.

Bizarre as it may seem to think that children could be discriminated against simply because they are children, especially in early years settings where children are the main focus, it can and does happen. Children's views and needs are often overlooked by the adults who think they know best. Children are often told to 'be quiet' or that it is 'nothing to do with you', yet often children are the experts on what they need and want. Article 12 of the UN Convention on the Rights of the Child states that 'children have the right to express their views freely in all matters affecting the child … the views of the child being given due weight in accordance with the age and maturity of the child'. Whilst the appropriate age and maturity of a child may be entirely subjective, even very young children can express likes and dislikes, needs and desires which may be valuable when deciding what is best for the children in your care.

What are the effects of discrimination?

People's attitudes and values alone may not be harmful, but when this is translated into discriminatory behaviour there is a real danger that others could be treated unfairly. Discrimination is the action resulting from people's attitudes, prejudices and ingrained stereotypes. 'The risk of experiencing negative outcomes is concentrated in children with certain characteristics and experiences … including: low parental income and parental unemployment; homelessness; poor parenting; and community factors, such as living in a disadvantaged neighbourhood' (DfES, 2002). It must be considered whether it is simply the nature of certain children and families with particular characteristics or backgrounds that results in negative outcomes, or if it is due to the less favourable treatment and lack of opportunities that they are exposed to in life. Often it can be a vicious circle, where individuals who are treated less favourably or are offered limited choices develop low self-esteem and expect to fail and have limited opportunities and therefore become accustomed to expecting and accepting less than they are entitled to.

Tassoni (1998) examined the long-term effects of discrimination resulting from lack of inclusion in the early years and concluded that:

1 The effects are lifelong.
2 Children may not reach their full potential.
3 Low self-esteem may have a negative impact on the child's ability to form relationships.
4 Children may have lack of confidence to experiment.
5 Children may feel ashamed of their race or culture.
6 Children may internalise negative views and feel they deserve poor treatment.

It is vitally important then, that all children and families are empowered and feel they are capable of achieving anything and that their options in life are not limited by their individual circumstances. All babies are born equal and it is only society and their environment that limits their opportunities. 'If those who work with young children are able to undermine children's self-esteem (however unintentionally this might be) through negative beliefs about children's ability due to their gender, religion, socio-economic status, language or ethnicity, then we have to evaluate these actions very carefully' (Siraj-Blatchford, 2001: 28).

Achievement at school is often a major factor that is studied to reflect on the long-term effects of discriminatory practice in society and educational settings. Research has consistently shown that certain groups underachieve. These groups may include: children with disabilities, ethnic minorities, Traveller children and boys. In the early 1970s girls were shown to be underachieving in certain academic areas, such as science and mathematics. However, strategies were successfully put into place to narrow the gap between the genders. Since the 1990s the under-achievers have been shown to be boys, across most areas of the curriculum, but particularly in literacy and creative subjects. Following the success of raising girls' achievement, this is an area under investigation to discover good practice and meth-ods to prevent boys from falling behind (Ofsted, 2003). Therefore it follows that any identified group that is at risk of underachieving may only be doing so owing to the lack of good practice and appropriate measures.

It is imperative not to over-generalise when referring to groups of children. For example, ethnic minority children are often grouped together for studies or provi-sion; however, on closer inspection there are wide and varying needs within the group. For example, a study looking at achievement later in ethnic minority children's school lives found that 'Students from Chinese and Indian backgrounds achieve significantly above average GCSE results; black pupils and those from Pakistani and Bangladeshi backgrounds achieve poorer GCSE results' (HM Government, 2003: 16).

Certain groups of children might not have the opportunity to attend any form of pre-school provision. One such group are Gypsy Traveller children, who often move seasonally and are therefore likely to miss out on regular attendance at an early years setting as well as the usual baseline assessments. Procedures are in place to ensure such children are identified and that suitable provision is made for them, for exam-ple through the Traveller Education Support Services (DfES, 2003).

By the time children reach secondary school age, patterns of failure and success are already ingrained and the effects reach far further than purely academic achieve-ment. Long-term effects of lack of inclusion and acceptance in the early years extend beyond the individual and family, and can impact on the local community and society years later. Therefore, it is vital that in the early years learning experiences, both formal and informal, are as inclusive as possible, giving all children adequate opportunities to achieve their full potential. Teaching methods and learning experi-ences must evolve to ensure appropriate and effective measures are in place to ensure all children are taught, formally and informally, in ways that do not limit their potential.

The benefits of inclusive practice

Inclusive practice can have long-lasting and far-reaching effects, not only for the child and his or her future, but also for society in general. The users of the setting will experience the benefits of inclusive practice in the short and the long term. If all children and families can easily access and make use of the provision, they will be able to take advantage of all that it has to offer, regardless of whether the provi-sion is related to health, education, welfare or a combination of all. If an early years setting or service meets the needs of all children, they will benefit in a variety of ways. If the child feels included and valued by the staff and other children, he or she will have the opportunity to reach their full potential and have the confidence and self-esteem to tackle challenges and develop with confidence. If the child sees that his or her culture or identity is not limiting or something to be ashamed of, they will hopefully grow up proud and have a strong sense of identity.

The benefits often reach further, though, with all users of the setting learning to be accepting of others and valuing diversity in the society around them. This applies equally to the children and their families, and of course the staff as well. As we know, children construct views and opinions based on their early experiences. Children exposed to inclusive settings, where everyone is accepted equally, where differences are celebrated and respected, and where negative stereotypes are challenged, will be able to form personal attitudes based on understanding and open-mindedness. The wider society will benefit if the youngest members grow up with inclusive attitudes and barriers to achievement can be eliminated. If children and families are able to access a fully inclusive early years setting, it will go some way to eliminating the negative effects of discrimination and allowing all children to reach their full potential.

Inclusive language

One of the problems that many people encounter when trying to establish an inclusive practice is knowing what language to use. The words used when we speak or write are often a reflection of our own personal values and attitudes. People rarely want to be intentionally offensive, but inappropriate language can exclude or offend certain individuals or groups. Practitioners may feel they should be 'politically correct' and not use the wrong words, but people often note that this political correctness can go too far. For example, is it appropriate to sing, 'Baa baa, black sheep' in a nursery, or should it be changed to 'Baa baa, black and white sheep'? And if so, which colour should come first? It is possible to take this too far, but practitioners should be aware of language that is deemed acceptable. This can be a very difficult area to address as acceptable language changes over time. Words such as 'handicapped', 'spastic', 'coloured' and 'gypsy' were previously widely used but are now seen as offensive among certain groups. It is important that effort is taken by staff at early years settings and services to use sensitive language that avoids discriminating against children and families on the basis of their race, gender, sexuality, religion, disability or ethnic background.

Often the most effective way to ascertain the most acceptable term to refer to a group is to ask individuals from that group itself. However, you must consider whether it is actually appropriate to group individuals together in the first place, purely on the basis of perceived characteristics. There are many resources, from various organisations, that can used to learn about the appropriate language to use (see 'Websites' for suggestions). It is vital not only that any literature produced by an early years provision uses appropriate language, but also that all staff are trained about acceptable and appropriate language.

Practitioners must demonstrate caution when attempting to assign a label to a child or family. All too often a label infers unwanted restrictions. However, a label is often sought, for example by a family attempting to access special provision for

Table 17.1   Integration and inclusion compared

Integration	Inclusion
Child physically included in setting, and has to adapt	Setting adapted to suit child's needs
Barriers often remain	Barriers removed as far as possible
Child still labelled	Child no longer labelled
Child included in some but not all activities	Increased participation in all activities

their child's needs, which can only be reached once a label, perhaps an educational statement of needs, has been decided upon by the relevant professionals.

To add to the confusion, definitions of certain groups vary according to the context or setting. Early years professionals regularly work closely with professionals from other disciplines or services who may have different definitions and criteria. Definitions and language can potentially conflict. Acceptable language changes over time as different approaches are implemented. In the early 1990s the shift moved from the ethos of 'integration' to 'inclusion' with particular regard to children with special educational needs (Table 17.1).

Inclusion, therefore, addresses the needs of the individual and requires appropriate changes to be made by services and settings, rather than the compromises being made by the child or family. For a setting to be fully inclusive, the child must not simply be placed alongside other children and receive inferior or different treatment. Every child must be included and valued and provided with the same opportunities as everyone else.

Barriers to inclusive practice

So what causes, or contributes to, exclusion? The main reasons vary widely and differ from place to place, person to person. These issues can be addressed as 'barriers', and ways of combating exclusion can be looked upon as the removal, or tackling, of these barriers. Barriers to inclusion are widespread, and are not all visible to the eye.

Attitudes

Barriers are not only physical, but can also be created by attitudes and omission. In fact, negative or unchallenged attitudes can be the most dangerous and limiting barriers to inclusion. If early years practitioners have prejudices and attitudes that might restrict the quality of service they provide to the children and families in their care, then inclusive practice will not happen. Prejudice literally means to pre-judge someone, often with no real knowledge of the individual, and prejudiced attitudes can be very damaging in all situations, not least early years settings. But where do we get our attitudes?

As children we are exposed to a wide range of influences about a wide range of issues, resulting in a huge array of possible combinations about views and issues for any one person, adult or child, to make sense of. Children are not born with attitudes; they form them as a result of exposure to their family, parents, experiences, local/wider society, media, peers, teachers and carers. Values and beliefs are very personal and can be extremely emotive, as a challenge to them is almost a challenge to one's own identity and experience. Attitudes can be harmful when translated into behaviour. It may not actually be negative or even intended discrimination, but it can still be damaging. It is important to understand the history of stereotypes and beliefs, for each of us to recognise our family's and society's attitudes in order to challenge and tackle them.

Attitudes often differ according to person and subject – as children, we are exposed to a confusing array of others' personal opinions – all of which have been formed based on other people's wide and varied experiences and influences. It is very difficult for a growing child to make sense of mixed messages and it is difficult for practitioners to even start to address their own attitudes, let alone decide what is appropriate to teach children in their care. However, 'teachers' attitudes towards including pupils with special educational needs in regular classes and their personal sense of efficacy in working with them are crucial factors in inclusion success' (Hasazi et al., 1994).

Valuing the diversity of our society is addressed later on in children's school life through the National Curriculum. 'The statutory programme of Citizenship ensures that all pupils will be taught about the origins and implications of the diverse national, regional, religious and ethnic groups in the United Kingdom and the need for mutual respect and understanding' (HM Government, 2003). This education to encourage respect for differences should begin in the very early years to enable children to grow into adults with attitudes that do not encroach upon and limit others.

Iram Siraj-Blatchford (2001) suggests that differences can be celebrated if we all recognised and valued our individuality. 'It would be even better if staff worked with all children to make them aware they all have an ethnic/racial identity and that they all have a linguistic, gendered, cultural and diverse identity. Surely this is the way forward.'

Inclusive practice is not a static process and must be ever changing as society changes. The presence of ethnic minorities is growing and has changed radically within the last few generations. Gender roles have also changed drastically in the last few decades. Integration of special needs pupils away from special schools and into the mainstream is a very recent move, since the Education Act 1981. Family structures have become more diverse in recent years, with same-sex parents and lone parents increasing. This can mean that attitudes are not in keeping with the rapid changes in society or perhaps they are indeed caused by the fast change.

What about children's own attitudes and behaviour? One of the key roles of an early years practitioner is tackling children's behaviour if it is discriminatory. This is difficult, as you may conflict with the messages the child is receiving at home or from his peers. But it is important to challenge any negative attitudes that children may have. If discriminatory behaviour is witnessed it is important to challenge it, otherwise it may be seen as acceptable. The children involved should be gently corrected, explanations as to why the behaviour is not acceptable should be given, perhaps ask them how the other child(ren) might feel as a result of their actions. The best way to teach children to be accepting and non-discriminatory is to lead by example. Children do notice differences and often comment on them, much to any parents' embarrassment! But unlike adults, children do not often make judgements based on their observations. Prejudiced attitudes come later, and are usually learned from adults. We too can notice differences, but must not judge or assume about the individual because of them. Inclusion is not about ignoring differences. Far from it. It is about acknowledging them, and valuing them.

Physical barriers

When people consider physical barriers to inclusion, the typical image is often of a flight of stairs causing obstruction to a person in a wheelchair. Whilst this is an all too common scenario, it is by no means the only example of a physical barrier. For a setting to be inclusive, everyone needs not only to be able to reach and enter the building, but also to be able to move easily around the building and access all facilities. Consider the following situation.

A child with a hearing aid is placed in a nursery that is very noisy. The child has difficulty hearing the nursery teachers and assistants through the background noise. The child may be missing instructions, new vocabulary from teachers and peers and could find the strain of actively listening very tiring. The environment is 'handicapping' the child. With improvements in the nursery environment – lowering the background noise levels, increasing sound-absorbing materials and learning methods to help the child hear and, more vitally, understand, the practitioners can reduce the barriers this child encounters daily so they are not unintentionally causing the child difficulties in gaining as much as the other children from the setting.

Other physical barriers might include:

1 Lighting that is inadequate for people with visual impairments.
2 Inadequate toilet facilities for people who use a wheelchairs.
3 Signage in one language that is ineffective for people who have difficulty seeing, reading or understanding the language used.
4 Badly marked changes in level, e.g. steps.
5 Lack of lifts or ramps for people unable to use stairs or steps.
6 Temperatures that could be uncomfortable for certain people, such as those confined to a seat or wheelchair for long periods of time.

These barriers do not just limit people with disabilities or impairments. Often the parents of early years children will appreciate improved access if they are have a child or children in a pram or pushchair. In fact, physical improvements for one specific user will usually be an improvement for all.

A major issue when considering accessibility around an early years facility is the cost of making changes to the structure or interior. In a new building, care should be taken to ensure accessibility for all at the design stage, and the required features must be viewed as essentials, not luxuries. When making changes to an existing building, cost and space may limit the options. Early years managers could be faced with difficult choices and the decisions need to be made based on detailed consideration of the individuals, the legal requirements and any other issues.

By October 2004 early years service providers may have to make 'reasonable adjustments' in relation to physical features of their premises in order to overcome physical barriers to access in order to meet the requirements of the Disability Discrimination Act, Part III. The actual physical location of a provision can occasionally be a barrier to some children and families. Can the child and family actually get to the setting to access the provision? Can they afford transport, public or private? Certain families living in rural locations have very limited public transport to enable them to access services that may be taken for granted by people living in towns or cities. Whilst peripatetic provision is widespread, consideration should be given to any families that may not be able to physically access the setting or service, whether owing to locality or lack of suitable transport.

Other barriers

There are many other barriers to inclusion, not least the all too familiar lack of money and time. Lack of funding is one of the many reasons used for the lack of inclusive practice. Whilst training, resources and possible building alterations can cost money, challenging previously held beliefs, stereotypes, negative behaviour and attitudes does not have to. Nor should lack of time be used as a reason not to address inclusion. Inclusive practice does not have to be a separate activity, removed from the day-to-day running of a centre and addressed only at certain meetings. On the contrary, inclusion should be viewed as a fundamental, ongoing process. Initially, extra time may be spent formulating inclusion policies and deciding on changes in practice, but this time may well be saved later trying to deal with unwanted situations that arise from exclusive behaviour.

Law and legislation affecting inclusion

There are many pieces of legislation that impact upon different types of early years settings and services, and these change regularly, so it is important for the practitioner to be aware of any relevant updates. As the legislation changes so frequently, a detailed account of present laws will not be covered here. Instead, the main legislative areas will be identified and you are encouraged to identify the relevant areas and keep up to date with any changes.

The Disability Discrimination Act 1995 (DDA) is being implemented over several years, owing to the nature of the physical changes to buildings that are required for compliance. This Act requires service providers to make 'reasonable adjustments' to any policies, practices and procedures that discriminate against disabled people and to 'provide auxiliary aids and services to enable or make it easier for disabled people to use the service'. It also requires that settings 'make their services available by reasonable alternative methods where a physical feature is a barrier'. The service providers covered by this Act include indoor and outdoor adventure playgrounds, leisure centres, play areas in public parks, playgrounds and some private nurseries. The DDA duties are anticipatory, so the setting or service must consider not only the needs of its existing users, but also how disabled people may use it in the future. 'Reasonable adjustment' is a subjective term, and open to debate. However, the DDA does not mean that settings and services should incur unreasonable expense, ignore general health and safety considerations or actually alter the core purpose of the provision. The Special Educational Needs and Disability Act 2001 is an extension of the DDA which relates to educational settings and states that to have been discriminated against an individual will have received 'less favourable treatment and/or there has been a failure to make a reasonable adjustment which puts the person at a substantial disadvantage'.

The UN Convention on the Rights of the Child is relevant to any early years setting and certain articles relate directly to valuing diversity. Article 2 states:

> That each child should enjoy the rights set out in the convention without discrimination of any kind, irrespective of the child's parent's or guardian's race, colour, sex, language, religion, political or other opinion, national, ethnic or social origin, property, disability, birth or status.

Article 23 relates specifically to children with disabilities:

> A disabled child has the right to special care, education and training to help him or her enjoy a full and decent life in dignity and achieve the greatest degree of self-reliance and social integration possible.

Article 31 relates to the child's right to play and to be provided with:

> the provision of appropriate and equal opportunities for cultural, artistic, recreational, and leisure activity.

The Race Relations (Amendment) Act 2000 (RRAA) was introduced in response to the Stephen Lawrence inquiry, and gives all educational settings a statutory duty to promote race equality. The general duties for schools, which are also relevant to all early years settings, include:

1   Eliminate unlawful racial discrimination.
2   Promote equality of opportunity.
3   Promote good relations between people of different racial groups.

It also sets out specific duties for schools which include preparing a race equality policy, assessing its impact on children, parents and staff, and continuing to monitor the impact, particularly the attainment levels of pupils by ethnicity and race (CRE, 2002).

There are numerous other international, national and local pieces of legislation that relate to inclusive practice, including the Children Act 1989 and the Sex Discrimination Act 1975. However, whilst legislation is present and progressing to attempt to meet the needs of all members of society, it is only when the practice is put into place on all levels that true inclusion can begin. It is useful, but not adequate, to have laws that organisations and individuals must adhere to: inclusive practice can truly begin only once attitudes are changed and ignorance is replaced by acceptance.

Conclusion

Inclusive practice is not a mystery that can be solved only by individuals with expertise in specific areas of disabilities, cultures, gender differences and society. It can be achieved by all early years practitioners who are prepared to address and challenge their own attitudes and practice. It is essential that all children and families have easy access to, and are valued by, the relevant early years providers. Simple steps can be taken to ensure that everyone receives the appropriate and equal consideration when reviewing the provision. Every child and family should be able to see something of themselves in their early years setting. It is not sufficient, for example, to simply consider a variety of cultures at times of different festivals. Can any child look around the setting and see pictures, books, toys, images and artefacts that are representative of 'their' world? These resources should aim to go beyond the children's and adults' own experiences so their perceptions are not limited by the images and objects they encounter.

Early years practitioners should consider what role models the children and families are being presented with. Are all the staff white able-bodied females around a certain age? If new people come to work or volunteer at the setting, are they assigned tasks on the basis of their characteristics? For example, are male staff assigned tasks such as sports or woodwork, does the Indian mother always take small groups for ethnic cookery? It is important for children to see that any person can fill any role and it is not necessarily dependant on gender, ability or ethnicity.

An inclusion plan or policy is essential for every early years setting, and should address the needs of the children, families, communities and staff. Each setting's policy will probably differ from others' and will change over time as the individuals' requirements change. However, when devising an inclusion policy for your setting, it is important to talk to other professionals and agencies, and to learn from good practice. It is also wise to learn from your own and others' bad experiences! Be aware of current legislation and language, but do not be limited by or scared of it. You and your colleagues will be the experts on the individuals you encounter on a daily basis – or at least you will have access to the first-hand experts, the children and families themselves. Devising a policy for inclusion can be achieved by a combination of 'top down' advice, consulting legislation and experts, as well as 'bottom up' contributions from the individuals involved; the children, parents and staff. Even very young children can have valuable contributions as to how everyone can be included if listened to appropriately. Policy and practice must be continuously monitored, evaluated and reviewed to ensure the needs of all users are being adequate addressed. As the effects of discrimination can be far-reaching and long-lasting, so too can the positive effects of inclusive practice.

Questions and exercises

1   What are you? Consider your age, sex, race, class, ability/disability, size, appearance, upbringing, colour. What implications do each of these 'labels' have for you, or for others? How do they make you different from others? If someone knew just one or two of these facts about you, would they be able to provide for all your needs and requirements?

2   Watch the television adverts at peak child viewing time. What messages are the adverts sending to children about gender roles, sex-stereotyped play, diversity of society, etc.?

3   Consider where you learnt your personal beliefs and values. Was it from your own personal experience or were they learnt from your family and peers? Have your attitudes changed over the years with experience?

4   As you move around your work or college building consider the barriers that you encounter on your way and the effect they may have on certain users of the facility.

5   Consider a variety of books aimed at early years children in your setting. Are the characters representative of wider society, are there any stereotypes or any negative/positive examples of groups?

6   In a primary school, a lift installation to allow a child who uses a wheelchair access to the library upstairs requires funding previously allocated to new books, and means taking the space used previously for learning support. How would you decide what the priorities are?

7   What measures could be taken in an early years setting, such as a nursery school, in order that every child sees 'something of themselves' in their environment?

8   What are the most important factors to consider when devising an inclusive practice policy for an early years provision?

Reading

Booth and Ainscow, with Black-Hawkins, *Index for Inclusion* (2000), is a set of materials, devised by a multidisciplinary team of professionals, parents and disabled people, that guides schools (and other settings) through stages to develop an inclusive environment for all. Campbell, *Developing Inclusive Schooling* (2002), offers an insight into recent developments relating to all aspects of inclusive schooling. Gillbourn and Mirza, *Educational Inequality* (2000), is a report which examines the research concerning inequalities in opportunities and achievements in the education system, but is a useful insight for all professions. Millam, *Anti-discriminatory Practice* (2002), is a useful guide to anti-discriminatory practice for all early years professionals, and includes practical advice as well as theoretical and legal issues. Siraj-Blatchford and Clarke, *Supporting Identity, Diversity and Language in the Early Years* (2000), provides practical guidance to ensure that early years children and families of all cultures are successfully included by practitioners.

Websites

Commission for Racial Equality   www.cre.gov.uk
Department for Education and Skills   www.dfes.gov.uk
Alliance for Inclusive Education   www.allfie.org.uk
Centre for Accessible Environments   www.cae.org.uk
Children's Play Council   www.ncb.org.uk/cpc
Children's Rights Office   319 City Road, London (phone: 020 7278 8222)

Glossary

Accommodation According to Piaget's theory, the process by which children adjust their knowledge structures in response to new information.

Animism The tendency of pre-operational children to attribute lifelike qualities and intentions to non-living things.

Assimilation According to Piaget's theory, the process by which children integrate new information into their existing knowledge structures.

Centration The tendency of pre-operational children to focus attention on a single aspect of a problem at a time.

Chronosystem According to Bronfenbrenner's theory, the influences on children's development that pertain to a particular historical period.

Class inclusion The ability of concrete-operational children to reason about problems to do with hierarchical relations.

Concrete operational stage The third of Piaget's stages of cognitive development, during which children are capable of using various mental operations to deal logically with problems involving concrete objects and events.

Conservation The ability of concrete-operational children to understand that the amount of a substance does not change when its appearance is altered in some superficial way.

Constructivist An approach to cognitive development that assumes children actively construct knowledge in reaction to their experiences.

Core domains Aspects of knowledge that are presumed to be in place at birth, for example, in the form of intuitive and rudimentary understanding of physics, biology and psychology.

Cultural tools Language, other symbol systems, artefacts, skills and values that are important to a particular culture.

Dialetical theory A theory that emphasises the development of cognition under social influence.

Discourse Ways of speaking, writing, thinking or behaving that are unquestioningly accepted within a particular group.

Egocentricism The tendency of pre-operational children to focus on their own point of view rather than another person's view.

Epigenesis The idea that later stages of cognitive development build on earlier achievements.

Equilibration According to Piaget's theory, the child's attempts to balance assimilation and accommodation to create stable understanding.

Exosystem According to Bronfenbrenner's theory, the influences on a child's development coming from the extended social network of the family and the media.

External speech According to Vygotsky's theory, external speech represents thinking that comes from a source external to the child.

Formal operational stage The fourth of Piaget's stages of cognitive development, during which children are able to consider abstract situations and to formulate and test hypotheses in a systematic manner.

Gender-typed The extent to which a person conforms to what is considered 'appropriate' behaviour for a particular gender. This term is also applied to toys, activities and language.

Gender identity Gender identity refers to an individual's concept of herself or himself as female or male. Not all children develop a gender identity that is consistent with their biological sex. Some children may feel strongly that they want to be, or simply are, the other sex. These children are generally termed as having a gender identity disorder.

Gender roles When we talk about gender roles we refer to the behaviour or activities associated with – and expected from – males and females within a particular culture or society.

Guided participation The process by which adults assist children to achieve higher levels of functioning than they would be capable of attaining on their own.

Hegemonic Hegemony is a concept derived from the work of Antonio Gramsci which is used to describe the control of a dominant group that is so successful that it is seen as the ways things should be. Hegemonic masculinity is thus a concept of masculinity that sees the dominance of males over females as something normal and obvious.

Information-processing framework A framework that attempts to understand cognitive development in terms of age-related changes in processing mechanisms, memory capacity and knowledge.

Internal speech According to Vygotsky's theory, the stage of development at which children have succeeded in internalising their thought processes.

Intersubjectivity A characteristic of social interactions representing joint attention to the same topic and sensitivity to the other person's point of view.

Macrosystem According to Bronfenbrenner's theory, the macrosystem comprises cultural influences on a child's development that are characteristic of their socio-economic or ethnic background.

Mental operations According to Piaget's theory, mental operations are particular modes of thinking that support logic.

Microsystem According to Bronfenbrenner's theory, the microsystem comprises the influences on a child's development from the social settings in which he or she directly participates, for example, home, school and neighbourhood.

Preoperational stage The second of Piaget's stages of cognitive development, during which children rehearse the newly acquired symbolic function through language and make-believe play.

Private speech According to Vygotsky's theory, the stage of development at which children talk to themselves to direct their own thinking.

Representational redescription The process by which the mind spontaneously converts existing knowledge into new, superior forms of knowledge.

Scripts Mental representations of the usual sequence of activities for commonly experienced routines.

Sensorimotor stage The first of Piaget's stages of cognitive development, during which infants rely on sensorimotor schemas to develop their notions of time, space and causality.

Seriation According to Piaget's theory, the ability to understand spatial and temporal sequences.

Social scaffolding The process by which adults provide a temporary framework to support a child's thinking at a higher level than they can yet reach on their own.

Symbolic function According to Piaget's theory, the symbolic function is the ability to represent experiences mentally, using imagery and language.

Theory theories Theories that assume that children refine and extend their core-domain knowledge by testing naive theories in these domains.

Transitive inferences According to Piaget's theory, transitive inferences allow children to mentally rearrange a set of objects along a quantifiable dimension.

Zone of proximal development According to Vygotsky, the zone of proximal development is the area of functioning just beyond the child's current level to which they are capable of progressing given appropriate assistance.

References

Abbott, L. and Nutbrown, C. (eds) (2001) *Experiencing Reggio Emilia: Implications for Pre-school Provision*. Buckingham and Philadelphia: Open University Press.

Abbott, L. and Pugh, G. (1990) *Training to Work in the Early Years: Developing the Climbing Frame*. Buckingham: Open University Press.

Abbott, L. and Pugh, G. (eds) (1998) *Training to Work in the Early Years – Developing the Climbing Frame*. Buckingham: Open University Press.

Aber, J.L. and Allen, J.P. (1987) 'Effects of maltreatment on young children's socioemotional development: an attachment theory perspective', *Developmental Psychology,* 23: 406–14.

Abrams, Rebecca (1996) *Woman in a Man's World*. London: Methuen.

ACCAC (1996) *Desirable Outcomes for Children's Learning before Compulsory School Age*. Cardiff: ACCAC.

Archard, D. (1993) *Children: Rights and Childhood*. London: Routledge.

Acheson, D. (1998) *Independent Inquiry into Inequalities in Health*. London: Department of Health.

Ainsworth, M. (1967) *Infancy in Uganda: Infant Care and the Growth of Love*. Baltimore, MD: Johns Hopkins University Press.

Ainsworth, M., Blehar, M., Waters, E. and Wall, S. (1978) *Patterns of Attachment: a Psychological Study of the Strange Situation*. Hillsdale, NJ: Erlbaum.

Aitchison, J. (1998) *The Articulate Mammal* (4th edn). London: Unwin Hyman.

Allen, N. (1998) *Making Sense of the Children Act: a Guide for the Social and Welfare Services* (3rd edn). Chichester: Wiley.

Anderson, A.M. (1996) 'Factors influencing the father-infant relationship', *Journal of Family Nursing*, 2 (3): 306–24.

Anning, A. (1999) 'The Influence of Socio-cultural Context on Young Children's Meaning Making'. Paper presented at the British Educational Research Association conference, Sussex University, September.

Applebaum, B. (1996) 'Moral paralysis and the ethnocentric fallacy', *Journal of Moral Education*, 25 (2): 185–99.

Ariès, P. (1962) *Centuries of Childhood*. London: Jonathan Cape.

Arnold, J.C. (2000) *Endangered: Your Child in a Hostile World*. Robertsbridge: Plough.

Ashdown, R. (2003) 'Policies to support inclusion in the early years' in C. Tilstone and R. Rose (eds) *Strategies to Promote Inclusive Practice*. London: Routledge Falmer.

Athey, C. (1990) *Extending Thought in Young Children: a Parent–Teacher Partnership*. London: Paul Chapman.

Atkinson, M., Wilkin, A., Stott, A., Doherty, P. and Kinder, K. (2002) *Multi-agency Working: a Detailed Study*. Slough: NFER.

Audit Commission (1994) *Seen but not Heard: Co-ordinating Community Child Health and Social Services for Children in Need*. London: HMSO.

Baggott, R. (2000) *Public Health: Policy and Politics*. Basingstoke: Macmillan.

Bainham, A. (1998) *Children: the Modern Law* (2nd edn). Bristol: Family Law.

Baker, C. (2000) *A Parents' and Teachers' Guide to Bilingualism and Bilingual Education* (2nd edn). Clovedon: Multilingual Matters.

Barker, D. (1992) *Fetal and Infant Origins of Adult Disease*. London: British Medical Journal Publishing.

Barnes, P. (1995) *Personal, Social and Emotional Development of Children*. Oxford: Blackwell/Open University.

Barrett, J. (1998) 'New knowledge and research in child development', *Child and Family Social Work*, 3 (4): 267–76.

Barrett, S. (1996) *Anthropology: a Students' Guide to Theory and Method*. Toronto: University of Toronto Press.

Bartley, M., Blane, D. and Davey Smith, G. (1998) *The Sociology of Health Inequalities*. Oxford: Blackwell.

Barton, C. and Douglas, G. (1995) *Law and Parenthood*. London: Butterworth.

Beal, C.R. (1994) *Boys and Girls: the Development of Gender Roles*. New York: McGraw Hill.

Bean, P. and Melville, J. (1990) *Lost Children of the Empire: the Untold Story of Britain's Migrants*. London: Unwin Hyman.

Beaty, J. (1998) *Observing Development of the Young Child* (4th edn). London: Prentice Hall.

Beckman Murray, R. and Proctor Zentner, J. (1985) *Nursing Assessment and Health Promotion through the Lifespan*. Englewood Cliffs NJ: Prentice Hall.

Bee, H. (1997) *The Developing Child* (8th edn). New York: Harper Collins.

Bell, M.A. and Fox, N.A. (1994) 'Brain development over the first year of life: relations between electroencephalogram frequency and coherence and cognitive and affective behaviours' in G. Dawson and K.W. Fischer (eds) *Human Behaviour and the Developing Brain*. London: Guilford Press.

Belsky, J. (1996) 'Parent, infant and social-contextual antecedents of father–son attachment security', *Developmental Psychology*, 32 (5): 905–13

Belsky, J. (2001) 'Developmental risks (still) associated with early child care' (Emanuel Miller Lecture), *Journal of Child Psychology and Psychiatry*, 42 (7): 845–59.

Belsky, J., Campbell, S.B., Cohn, J.F. and Moore, G. (1996) 'Instability of infant–parent attachment security', *Developmental Psychology*, 32: 921–4.

Bem, S.L. (1989) 'Genital knowledge and gender constancy in preschool children', *Child Development*, 60: 649–62.

Bennett, N. and Kell, J. (1989) *A Good Start: Four-year-olds in Infant Schools*. Oxford: Blackwell.

Bennett, N., Wood, E. and Rogers, S. (1997) *Teaching through Play: Teachers' Thinking and Classroom Practice*. Buckingham: Open University Press.

Bentham, C. (1984) 'Mortality rates in the more rural areas of England and Wales', *Area*, 16: 219–26.

Benzeval, M., Judge, K. and Whitehead, M. (1995) *Tackling Inequalities in Health: an Agenda for Action*. London: King's Fund.

Berk, L.E. (1992) 'Children's private speech: an overview of theory and the status of research', in R.M. Diaz and L.E. Berk (eds) *Private Speech: from Social Interaction to Self-regulation*. Hillsdale NJ: Erlbaum.

Berk, L.E. (2003) *Child Development* (6th edn) Boston, MA: Allyn & Bacon.

Berko, J. (1958) 'The child's learning of English morphology', in *Word*, 14: 150–77.

Berney, L., Blane, D. and Davey Smith, G. (2000) 'Socioeconomic measures in early old age as indicators of previous lifetime exposure to environmental hazards to health', *Sociology of Health and Illness*, 22: 415–30.

Bjorklund, D.F. (2000) *Children's Thinking: Developmental Function and Individual Differences* (3rd edn). Belmont, CA: Wadsworth.

Bjorklund, D.F., Miller, P.H., Coyle, T.R., and Slawinsky, J.L. (1997) 'Instructing children to use memory strategies: evidence of utilization deficiencies in memory training studies', *Developmental Review*, 17: 411–42.

Blaxter, M. (1990) *Health and Lifestyles*. London: Tavistock/Routledge.

Blenkin, G. and Kelly, V. (1994) 'The death of infancy' in *Early Education 3–13*. Harlow: Longman.

Blenkin, G. and Kelly, V. (1998) *Principles into Practice*. London: Paul Chapman.

Blenkin, G. and Kelly, V. (2000) 'The concept of infancy: a case for reconstruction', *Early Years*, 20 (2): 31–8.

Bloom, L. (1970) *Language Development: Form and Function in Emerging Grammars*. Cambridge, MA: MIT Press.

Boland, A.M., Haden, C.A., and Ornstein, P.A. (2003) 'Boosting children's memory by training mothers in the use of an elaborative conversational style as an event unfolds', *Journal of Cognition and Development*, 4: 39–65.

Booth, T. and Ainscow, M., with Black-Hawkins, K. (2002) *Index for Inclusion: Developing Learning and Participation in Schools*, ed. M. Vaughan and L. Shaw. Bristol: Centre for Studies on Inclusive Education.

Bornstein, M.H. and Bruner, J.S. (eds) (1989) *Interaction in Human Development*. Hillsdale, NJ: Erlbaum.

Bossard, J. and Boll, E. (1966) *The Sociology of Child Development*. New York: Harper & Row.

Boushel, M., Fawcett, M. and Selwyn, J. (eds) (2000) *Focus on Early Childhood: Principles and Realities*. Oxford: Blackwell.

Bowlby, J. (1951) *Maternal Care and Mental Health*. Report to the World Health Organisation. Geneva: World Health Organisation.

Bowlby, J. (1953, 1965) *Child Care and the Growth of Love*. Harmondsworth: Penguin.

Bowlby, J. (1969) *Attachment and Loss* I, *Attachment*. New York: Basic Books.

Bowlby, J. (1973) *Attachment and Loss* II, *Separation*. New York: Basic Books.

Bowlby, J. (1980) *Attachment and Loss* III, *Loss*. New York: Basic Books.

Bowlby, J. (1988) 'Developmental psychiatry comes of age', *American Journal of Psychiatry*, 145: 1–10.

Boyd Webb, N. (1984) *Preschool Children with Working Parents: an Analysis of Attachment*. New York: University Press of America.

Brandon, M., Schofield, G. and Trinder, L. (1998) *Social Work with Children*. London: Macmillan.

Brannen, J. and Moss, P. (2003) *Rethinking Children's Care*. Buckingham: Open University Press.

Brannen, J., Heptinstall, E. and Bhopal, K. (2001) *Connecting Children: Care and Family Life*, London: Routledge Falmer.

Brannon, L. (2002) *Gender: Psychological Perspectives*, (3rd edn). Boston, MA: Allyn & Bacon.

Braungart-Rieker, Garwood, M.M., Powers, B.P. and Wang, X. (2001) 'Parental sensitivity, infant affect, and affect regulation: predictors of later attachment', *Child Development*, 72 (1): 252–70.

Brazelton, T.B. and Greenspan, S.I. (2000) *The Irreducible Needs of Children*. New York: Perseus Publishing.

Bredekamp, S. (ed.) (1987) *Developmentally Appropriate Practice in Early Childhood Programs Serving Children from Birth through Age 8*. Washington DC: National Association for the Education of Young Children.

Bredekamp, S. and Rosegrant, T. (eds) (1992) *Reaching Potentials: Appropriate Curriculum and Assessment for Young Children*. Washington, DC: National Association for the Education of Young Children.

Bretherton, I., McNew, S. and Beegley-Smith, M. (1981) 'Early person knowledge as expressed in gestural and verbal communication: when do infants acquire a "theory of mind?"' in M.E. Lamb and L.R. Sherrod (eds) *Infant Social Cognition*. Hillsdale, NJ: Erlbaum.

Breton, M. (2001) 'Neighbourhood resiliency', *Journal of Community Practice*, 9 (12): 21–36.

Bridge, C. and Swindells, H. (2003) *Adoption: the Modern Law*, Bristol: Family Law.

Bridge, G. and Miles, G. (1997) *On the Outside looking in: Collected Essays on Young Child Observation in Social Work Training.* London: CCETSW.

Broadhead, P. (2004) *Early Years Play and Learning.* London: Routledge Falmer.

Bronfenbrenner, U. (1979) *The Ecology of Human Development.* Cambridge, MA: Harvard University Press.

Bronfenbrenner, U. (1986) 'Ecology of the family as a context for human development: research perspectives', *Developmental Psychology*, 22: 723–42.

Bronfenbrenner, U., and Morris, P.A. (1998) 'The ecology of developmental processes' in R.M. Lerner (ed.), *Handbook of Child Psychology, Theoretical Models of Human Development* (5th edn). New York: Wiley.

Brown, A.L. (1997) 'Transforming schools into communities of thinking and learning about serious matters', *American Psychologist*, 52: 300–413.

Bruce, T. (1991) *Time to Play in Early Childhood Education.* London: Hodder & Stoughton.

Bruce, T. (1994) 'Play, the universe and everything!' in J. Moyles (ed.) *The Excellence of Play.* Buckingham: Open University Press.

Bruce, T. (1997) *Early Childhood Education.* London: Hodder & Stoughton.

Bruner, J. (1960) *The Process of Education.* Cambridge, MA: Harvard University Press.

Bruner, J. (1966) *Towards a Theory of Instruction.* Cambridge, MA: Harvard University Press.

Bruner, J. (1972) 'Functions of play' in J. Bruner, A. Jolly and K. Sylva (eds) *Play and its Role in Evolution and Development.* Harmondsworth: Penguin Books.

Bruner, J. (1983) *Child's Talk: Learning to Use Language.* Oxford: Oxford University Press.

Bruner, J. (1986) *Actual Minds, Possible Words.* Cambridge, MA: Harvard University Press.

Bruner, J. (1990) *Acts of Meaning.* Cambridge MA: Harvard University Press.

Bruner, J., Jolly, A. and Sylva, K. (1976) *Play: its Role in Evolution and Development.* Harmondsworth: Penguin Books.

Bryant, B., Harris, Miriam, and Newton, Di (1980) *Children and Minders.* Oxford: Oxford Pre-school Research Project.

Burnett, J. (1982) *Destiny Obscure: Autobiographies of Childhood, Education and Family from the 1890s to the 1920s.* London: Routledge.

Bussey, K. and Bandura, A. (1999) 'Social cognitive theory of gender development and differentiation', *Psychological Review*, 106: 676–713.

Butler, I. and Roberts, G. (2003) *Social Work with Children and Families* (2nd edn). London: Jessica Kingsley.

Caldwell Cook, H. (1917) *The Play Way.* London: Heinemann.

Campbell, C. (ed.) (2002) *Developing Inclusive Schooling: Perspectives, Policies and Practices.* London: Institute of Education.

Carey, S. and Spelke, E.S. (1994) 'Domain-specific knowledge and conceptual change' in L.S. Hirschfeld and S.A. Gelman (eds) *Mapping the Mind: Domain Specificity in Cognition and Culture.* Cambridge: Cambridge University Press.

Carr, M. and May, H. (1992) *National Early Childhood Curriculum Guidelines in New Zealand* (the Meade report). Hamilton: Waikato University.

Carr, M. and May, H. (2000) 'Te Whariki: curriculum voices' in H. Penn (ed.) *Early Childhood Services: Theory, Policy and Practice.* Buckingham: Open University Press.

Case, A. (2000) 'The *Economic Journal*' in K. McKeown and J. Sweeney (eds) *Family Well-being and Family Policy: a Review of Research on Benefits and Costs.* Dublin: Kieran McKeown.

Case, R. (1985) *Intellectual Development: Birth to Adulthood.* New York: Academic Press.

Catherwood, D. (1999) 'New views on the young brain: offerings from developmental psychology to early childhood education', *Contemporary Issues in Early Childhood*, 1 (1): 23–35.

Cazden, C. (1972) *Child Language and Education*. New York: Holt Rinehart & Winston.

Central Advisory Council for Education (1967) *Children and their Primary Schools*. London: HMSO.

Central Statistical Office (1995) *Social Trends* (1995 edn). London: HMSO.

Channel 4 Television (1992) *Childhood* (television series). London: Channel 4.

Chenoweth, L. and Stehlik, D. (2001) 'Building resilient communities: social work practice and rural Queensland', *Australian Social Work*, 54 (2): 47–54.

Chi, M.T.H. (1978) 'Knowledge structure and memory development' in R. Siegler (ed.), *Children's Thinking: What Develops?* Hillsdale, NJ: Erlbaum.

Children and Young People's Unit (2000) *Tomorrow's Future: Building a Strategy for Children and Young People*. London: CYPU.

Chomsky, N. (1959) Review of Skinner's *Verbal Behavior*, *Language*, 35: 26–58.

Chorodow, N. (1978) *The Reproduction of Mothering: Psychoanalysis and the Sociology of Gender*. Berkeley, CA: University of California.

Clarke, A. (2001) 'Early adversity and adoptive solutions', *Adoption and Fostering*, 25 (1): 24–32.

Cleave, S. and Brown, S. (1991) *Early to School*. Slough: NFER/Nelson.

Cohen, R. (1992) *Hardship Britain: Being Poor in the 1990s.* London: Child Poverty Action Group.

Cohen, B., Moss, P., Petrie, P. and Wallace, J. (2004) *A New Deal for Children? Re-forming Education and Care in England, Scotland and Sweden*. Bristol: Policy Press.

Colton, M., Drury, C. and Williams, M. (1995) *Children in Need*. Aldershot: Avebury.

Colton, M., Sanders, R. and Williams, M. (2001) *An Introduction to Working with Children: a Guide for Social Workers*. Basingstoke: Palgrave.

Commission for Racial Equality (2002) *Statutory Code of Practice on the Duty to Promote Race Equality: A Guide for Schools*. London: CRE.

Commission on Social Justice (1994) *Social Justice: Strategies for Social Renewal*. London: Verso Books.

Congdon, P., Shouls, S. and Curtis, S. (1997) 'A multi-level perspective on small area health and mortality: a case study of England and Wales', *International Journal of Population Geography*, (3): 243–63.

Connell, R.M. (1995) *Masculinities*. Cambridge: Polity Press.

Connell, R.W. (1987) *Gender and Power*. Cambridge: Polity Press.

Cooper, P.J. and Murray, L. (1998) Fortnightly review: postnatal depression, *British Medical Journal*, 316 (7148): 1884–6.

Coppock, V. (1996) 'Mad, bad, or misunderstood? A critical analysis of state responses to children and young people whose behaviour is defined as "disturbed" or "disturbing"', *Youth and Policy*, 53: 53–65.

Corlyon, J. (1999) 'The impact of divorce and separation on children's mental health: a review of three recent reports', *Family Mediation*, 9 (3): 3–8.

Corsaro, W. (1997) *The Sociology of Childhood*. London and Pine Forge CA: Sage.

Craft, A. (2002) *Creativity and Early Years Education*. London: Continuum.

Crain, W. (1992) *Theories of Development: Concepts and Applications* (3rd edn). Englwood Cliffs, NJ: Prentice Hall.

Curtis, H. and Sanderson, M. (2004) *The Unsung Sixties: Memoirs of Social Innovation*. London: Whiting & Birch.

Curtis report (1946) *Report of the Care of Children Committee*. London: HMSO.

Curtis, S. and Rees Jones, I. (1998) 'Is there a place for geography in the analysis of health inequality?' in M. Bartley, D. Blane and G. Davey Smith (eds) *The Sociology of Health Inequalities*. Oxford: Blackwell.

Dahlberg, G. (2000) 'Everything is a beginning and everything is dangerous: some reflections on the Reggio Emila experience' in H. Penn (ed.) *Early Childhood Services: Theory, Policy and Practice*. Buckingham: Open University Press.

Dahlberg, G., Moss, P. and Pence, A. (1999) *Beyond Quality in Early Childhood Education and Care*. London: Routledge Falmer.

Daniel, P. and Ivatts, J. (1998) *Children and Social Policy*. Basingstoke: Macmillan.

David, T. (1990*) Under Five, Under-educated*? Milton Keynes: Open University Press.

David, T. (1996) 'Their right to play' in C. Nutbrown (ed.) *Respectful Educators – Capable Learners: Children's Rights and Early Education*. London: Paul Chapman.

David, T. (1998) *Researching Early Childhood Education: European Perspectives*. London: Paul Chapman.

David, T. (ed.) (1999) *Teaching Young Children*. London: Paul Chapman.

David, T., Gooch, K., Powell, S. and Abbott, L. (2003) *Birth to Three Matters: a Review of the Literature*. London: DfES.

David, T. (2001) 'Curriculum in the early years' in G. Pugh (ed.) *Contemporary Issues in the Early Years: Working Collaboratively for Children*. London: Paul Chapman.

David, T. (2002) 'Managing "quality" in early childhood services in England', *Education 3–13*, 30 (2): 4–8.

Davies, B. (1989) *Frogs and Snails and Feminist Tails*, Sydney: Allen & Unwin.

Davies, D. (1999) *Child Development: A Practitioner's Guide*. New York: Guilford Press.

Davies, E. (1994) *'They All Speak English Anyway': Yr Iaith Gymraeg ac Ymarfer Gwrth–Orthrymol/The Welsh Language and Anti-oppressive Practice*. Cardiff: Central Council for Education and Training in Social Work.

Davies, J. (ed.) (1993) *The Family: is it just another Lifestyle Choice?* London: IEA Health and Welfare Unit.

Daycare Trust (2004) *Childcare Facts*. info@daycaretrust.org.uk.

de Gaay Fortman, B. (2003) 'Poverty as global failure', *Development Issues*, 5 (1): 16–17.

DeMause, L. (1974) *The History of Childhood*. London: Souvenir Press.

Dempster, F.N. (1993) 'Resistance to interference: developmental changes in a basic processing mechanism' in M.L. Howe and R. Pasnak (eds) *Emerging Themes in Cognitive Development* I, *Foundations*. New York: Springer.

Department for Education and Employment (1994) *Code of Practice on the Identification and Assessment of Special Educational Needs*. London: HMSO.

Department for Education and Skills (2001a) *Special Educational Needs Code of Practice*. London: HMSO.

Department for Education and Skills (2001b) *Inclusive Schooling: Children with Special Educational Needs*. London: HMSO.

Department for Education and Skills (2001c) *Supporting Pupils with Medical Needs*. London: HMSO.

Department for Education and Skills (2001d) *Promoting Children's Mental Health within Early Years and School Settings*. London: HMSO.

Department for Education and Skills (2002) *Participation in Education and Training by 16 and 17 Year Olds in Each Local Area in England 1998–2000* (internet only). www.dfes.gov.uk/rsgateway/DB/SBU/b000369/index.shtml (as accessed 01/05/04).

Department for Education and Skills (2003) *Aiming High: Raising the Achievement of Gypsy Traveller Pupils*. Nottingham: DfES Publications.

Department of Education and Science (1978) *The Report of the Committee of Enquiry into the Education of Handicapped Children and Young People* (the Warnock report). London: HMSO.

Department of Education and Science (1990) *Starting with Quality*. London: HMSO.

Department of Health (1989) *A Study of Enquiry Reports, 1980–1989*. London: HMSO.

Department of Health (1991a) *The Children Act 1989: Guidance and Regulations* II, *Family Support, Day Care and Education Provision for Young Children.* London: HMSO.

Department of Health (1991b) *The Health of The Nation: a Consultative Document* (Cmnd 1523). London: HMSO.

Department of Health (1993) *Children Act Report 1992.* London: HMSO.

Department of Health (1995a) *Looking after Children: Trial Pack of Planning and Review Forms and Assessment and Action Records* (revised edn). London: HMSO.

Department of Health (1995b) *Child Protection: Messages from Research.* London: HMSO.

Department of Health (1998) *Supporting Families: a Consultation Document.* London: HMSO.

Department of Health and Ministry of Agriculture, Fisheries and Food (1995) *National Diet and Nutrition Survey: Children Aged One-and-a-half to Four-and-a-half.* London: HMSO.

Department of Health and Social Security (1974) *Report of the Committee of Inquiry into the Care and Supervision Provided in Relation to Maria Colwell.* London: HMSO.

Department of Health and Social Security (1988) *Working Together: a Guide to Arrangements for Inter-agency Co-operation for the Protection of Children from Abuse.* London: HMSO.

Department of Health, Home Office and Department for Education and Employment (1999) *Working Together to Safeguard and Promote the Welfare of Children: a Guide to Inter-agency Working to Safeguard and Promote the Welfare of Children.* London: Stationery Office.

Department of Health, Department for Education and Employment and Home Office (2000) *Framework for the Assessment of Children in Need and their Families.* London: Stationery Office.

Department of Social Security (1998) *New Ambitions for Our Country: A New Contract for Welfare* (Cm3805). London: Department of Social Security.

Deven, Fred and Moss, Peter (2002) 'Leave arrangements for parents: overview and future outlook', *Community, Work and Family*, 5: 237–55.

Dingwall, R. and McIntosh, J. (1978) 'Teamwork in theory and practice' in R. Dingwall and J. McIntosh (eds) *Readings in the Sociology of Nursing.* Edinburgh: Churchill Livingstone.

Disability Rights Commission (2003) 'Know your Rights: SENDA 2001 and Education (DSPER) (Scotland) Act 2002' at http://www.drc-gb.org/rights/newsdetails.asp?id=51& section=1 (accessed 27 September 2003).

Donaldson, M. (1978) *Children's Minds.* London: Fontana.

Dorling, D. (1995) *A New Social Atlas of Britain.* Chichester: Wiley.

Dowler, E. and Calvert, C. (1995) *Nutrition and Diet in Lone-parent Families in London.* London: Family Policy Studies Centre.

Dowling, M. (2003) 'All about resilience', *Nursery World*, 103 (3891): 15–22.

Downie, R., Fyfe, C. and Tannahill, A. (1991) *Health Promotion Models and Values.* Oxford: Oxford University Press.

Doyle, B. (1997) 'Transdisciplinary approaches to working with families' in B. Carpenter (ed.) *Families in Context: Emerging Trends in Family Support and Early Intervention.* London: David Fulton.

Draper, L. and Duffy, B. (2001) 'Working with parents', in G. Pugh (ed.) *Contemporary Issues in the Early Years.* London: Paul Chapman Publishers.

Duncan, G.J., and Brooks-Gunn, J. (2000) 'Family poverty, welfare reform, and child development', *Child Development*, 71: 188–96.

Dunn, J. (1984) S*isters and Brothers.* London: Fontana.

Dunn, J. (1993) *Young Children's Close Relationships: Beyond Attachment.* Newbury Park CA: Sage.

Dunn, J. (1999) 'Mind reading and social relationships' in M. Bennett (ed.) *Developmental Psychology.* London: Taylor & Francis.

Durkin, K. (1996) *Developmental Social Psychology*. Oxford: Blackwell.

Dyhouse, C. (1989) *Feminism and the Family in England, 1880–1939*. Oxford: Blackwell.

Elfer, P., Goldschmied, E. and Selleck, D. (2002) *Key Persons in Nurseries: Building Relationships for Quality Provision*. London: NEYN.

Elkin, F. (1960) *The Child and Society: the Process of Socialisation*. New York: Random House.

Elkind, D. (1987) *Miseducation: Pre-schoolers at Risk*. NewYork: Knopf.

Elman, J.L., Bates, E.A., Johnson, M.H., Karmiloff-Smith, A., Parisi, D. and Plunkett, K. (1996) *Rethinking Innateness: a Connectionist Perspective on Development*. Cambridge, MA: MIT Press.

Englander, D. and O'Day, R. (1995) *Retrieved Riches: Social Investigation in Britain, 1840–1914*. Aldershot: Scolar Press for the Open University.

Equal Opportunities Commission (1992) *An Equal Start: Guidelines on Equal Treatment for the Under Eights*. Manchester: EOC.

Everiss, E. (2003) 'Family day care in New Zealand: training, quality and professional status', in A. Mooney and J. Statham (eds) *Family Day Care: International Perpectives on Policy, Practice and Quality*. London: Jessica Kingsley.

Fagin, L. (1981) *The Forsaken Families: the Effects of Unemployment on Family Life*. Harmondsworth: Penguin Books.

Fagot, B.I. and Hagan, R. (1991) 'Observations of parent reactions to sex-stereotyped behaviours', *Child Development*, 62: 617–28.

Fausto-Sterling, A. (1992) *Myths of Gender: Biological Theories about Women and Men*. London: Basic Books.

Fawcett, M. (1996) *Learning through Child Observation*. London: Jessica Kingsley.

Feldman, C. (1992) 'The theory of theory of mind', *Human Development*, 35: 107–17.

Ferri, E. (1991) *Combined Nursery Centres*. London: National Children's Bureau.

Fisher, J. (2002) *Starting from the Child* (2nd edn). Buckingham: Open University Press.

Fivush, R., Kuebli, J., and Clubb, P.A. (1992) 'The structure of events and event representations: a developmental analysis', *Child Development*, 63: 188–201.

Flavell, J. (1996) 'Piaget's legacy', *Psychological Science*, 7: 200–03.

Flekkoy, M. and Kaufman, N. (1997) *The Participation Rights of the Child: Rights and Responsibilities in Family and Society*. London: Jessica Kingsley.

Foley, P., Roche, J. and Tucker, S. (eds) (2001) *Children in Society: Contemporary Theory, Policy and Practice*. Basingstoke: Palgrave.

Forrest, G. (ed.) (1997) *Bonding and Attachment: Current Issues in Research and Practice*. Occasional Paper 14, London: Association of Child Psychology and Psychiatry.

Fortin, J. (1998) *Children's Rights and the Developing Law*. London: Butterworth.

Fox, N.A., Kimmerley, N.L. and Schafer, W.D. (1991) 'Attachment to mother/attachment to father: a meta-analysis', *Child Development*, 62: 210–25.

Froebel, F. (1826) *The Education of Man*. New York: Appleton.

Fromberg, D.P., and Bergen, D. (1998) *Play from Birth to Twelve and Beyond: Contexts, Perspectives and Meanings*. New York: Garland.

Fromkin, V., Rodman, R. and Hyams, N. (2003) *An Introduction to Language* (7th edn). New York: Harcourt Brace.

Gammage, P. (1999) 'The once and future child', *European Early Childhood Education Research Journal*, 7 (2): 103–17.

Gammage, P. (2002) 'Early childhood education and care *vade mecum* for 2002', *Early Years: An International Journal of Research and Development*, 22 (2): 185–8.

Gammage, P. (2003) Keynote speech at PACE conference, Swansea, March.

Gammage, P. and Kreig, W. (2001) *Reflect and Evaluate for Learning: an Early Childhood Tool*. Adelaide: University of South Australia.

Gardiner, M.F., Fox, A., Knowles, F. and Jeffrey, D. (1996) 'Learning improved by arts training', *Nature*, 381: 284.

Gardner, K. and Lewis, D. (1996) *Anthropology, Development and the Postmodern Challenge*. London: Pluto Press.

Garvey, C. (1977) *Play*. London: Fontana.

Garvey, C. (1991) *Play*. London: Fontana.

Gauvain, M. (2001) *The Social Context of Cognitive Development*. New York: Guilford Press.

Geary, D.C., and Bjorklund, D.F. (2000) 'Evolutionary developmental psychology', *Child Development*, 71: 57–65.

Gibbons, J., Conroy, S. and Bell, C. (1995) *Operating the Child Protection System: a Study of Child Protection Practices in English Local Authorities*. London: HMSO.

Giddens, A. (1976) *The New Rules of Sociological Method*. London: Hutchinson.

Giddens, A. (1993) *Sociology*. Cambridge: Polity Press.

Gilgun, J.F. (1996) 'Human development and adversity in ecological perspective', I: 'A conceptual framework', *Families and Society*, 77 (7): 395–402.

Gill, O. (1992) *Parenting under Pressure*. Cardiff: Barnardo's.

Gillbourn, D. and Mirza, H.S. (2000) *Educational Inequality: Mapping Race, Class and Gender: a Synthesis of Research Evidence*. London: Office for Standards in Education.

Gilligan, C. (1982) *In a Different Voice: Psychological Theory and Women's Development*. Cambridge, MA: Harvard University Press.

Goldschmied, E. and Jackson, S. (1994, 2004) *People under Three: Young Children in Day Care*. London: Routledge.

Goleman, D. (1996) *Emotional Intelligence: Why it can Matter more than IQ*. London: Bloomsbury.

Golombok, S. and Fivush, R. (1994) *Gender Development*. Cambridge: Cambridge University Press.

Gopnik, A., Melzoff, A. and Kuhl, P. (1999) *How Babies Think: the Science of Childhood*. London: Weidenfeld & Nicolson.

Graham, H. (ed.) (2000) *Understanding Health Inequalities*. Buckingham: Open University Press.

Groos, K. (1898) *The Play Animal*. New York: Appleton.

The Guardian (2001) 'UK "most racist" in Europe on refugees', 3 April.

Hagekull, B., Stenberg, G. and Bohlin, G. (1993) 'Infant–mother social referencing interactions: description and antecedents in maternal sensitivity and infant irritability', *Early Development and Parenting*, 2 (3): 183–91.

Hall, D. and Elliman, D. (2003) *Health for all Children* (4th edn). Oxford: Oxford University Press.

Hall, S. (1992) *Modernity and its Futures*. Cambridge: Polity Press.

Hallden, Gunilla (1991) 'The child as project and the child as being: parents' ideas as frames of reference', *Children and Society*, 5 (4): 334–46.

Hallett, C. and Birchall, E. (1992) *Coordination and Child Protection: a Review of the Literature*. London: HMSO.

Halliday, M.A.K. (1975) *Learning How to Mean*. London: Edward Arnold.

Halpern, D. (2000) *Sex Differences in Cognitive Abilities* (3rd edn). Mahwah, NJ: Erlbaum.

Hardman, C. (1973) 'Can there be an anthropology of children?' *Journal of the Anthropological Society of Oxford*, 4: 85–99.

Harkness, S. and Super, C.M. (1994) 'The developmental niche: a theoretical framework for analyzing the household production of health', *Social Science and Medicine*, 38 (2): 217–26.

Harris, F., Law, J. and Kermani, S. (2003) *The Second Implementation of the Sure Start Language Measure*. London: City University. (www.surestart.gov.uk)

Harris, P. (1989) *Children and Emotion: the Development of Psychological Understanding*. Oxford: Blackwell.

Harwood, R., Miller, J. and Lucca Irizarry, N. (1995) *Culture and Attachment: Perceptions of the Child in Context*. New York: Guilford Press.

Hasazi, S.B., Johnston, A.P., Liggett, A.M. and Schattman, R.A. (1994) 'A qualitative policy study of the least restrictive environment provision of the Individuals with Disabilities Education Act', *Exceptional Children*, 60: 491–507.

Hatano, G., and Inagaki, K. (1996) 'Cognitive and cultural factors in the acquisition of intuitive biology' in D.R. Olson and N. Torrance (eds) *Handbook of Education and Human Development: New Models of Learning, Teaching and Schooling.* Cambridge: Blackwell.

Haynes, R., Bentham, G., Lovett, A. and Einemann, J. (1997) 'Effect of labour market conditions on reporting of limiting long-term illness and permanent sickness in England and Wales', *Journal of Epidemiology and Community Health*, 51 (3): 282–8.

Health Visitors' Association and General Medical Services Committee (1989) *Homeless Families and their Health.* London: HVA/GMSC.

Hearnshaw, L.S. (1979) *Cyril Burt, Psychologist.* London: Hodder & Stoughton.

Hendrick, H. (1994) *Child Welfare: England, 1872–1989.* London: Routledge.

Herbert, E. (1994) 'Becoming a special family' in T. David (ed.) *Working Together for Young Children.* London: Routledge.

Herbert, E. and Carpenter, B. (1994) 'Fathers – the secondary partners: professional perceptions and a father's reflections', *Children and Society*, 8 (1): 31–41.

Hershman, D. and McFarlane, A. (2002) *Children Act Handbook.* Bristol: Family Law.

Hertz, N. (2003) 'An ever-widening chasm between social justice and the global economy', *Developmental Issues*, 5 (1): 14–15.

Heward, C. (1988) *Making a Man of Him: Parents and their Sons' Education at an English Public School, 1929–1950.* London: Routledge.

Heywood, C. (2001) *A History of Childhood: Chidren and Childhood in the West from Medieval to Modern Times.* Cambridge: Polity Press.

Hill, M. (ed.) (1999) *Effective Ways of Working with Children and their Families.* London: Jessica Kingsley.

Hill, M. and Aldgate, J. (eds) (1996) *Child Welfare Services.* London: Jessica Kingsley.

Hill, M. and Tisdall, K. (1997) *Children and Society.* Harlow: Longman.

Hirst, P.Q. and Thompson, G. (1996) *Globalization in Question: the International Economy and the Possibilities of Governance.* Cambridge: Polity Press.

HM Government (2003) *Every Child Matters* (Cmnd 5860). London: Stationery Office.

Hodgkin, R. (1994) 'Cultural relativism and the UN Convention on the Rights of the Child', *Children and Society*, 8 (4): 296–9.

Holterman, S. (1994) *Becoming a Breadwinner*, London: Daycare Trust.

Home Office, Department of Health, Department of Education and Science, and Welsh Office (1991) *Working Together under the Children Act 1989: a Guide to Inter-agency Co-operation for the Protection of Children from Abuse.* London: HMSO.

Hopkins, E. (1994) *Childhood Transformed: Working Class Children in Nineteenth Century England.* Manchester: Manchester University Press.

Horn, P. (1994) *Children's Work and Welfare, 1780–1890.* Cambridge: Cambridge University Press.

Howes, C. (1987) 'Peer interaction of young children', *Monographs of the Society for Research in Child Development*, No. 217, 53: 1.

Howes, C., Hamilton, C.E. and Matheson, C.C. (1994) 'Maternal, teacher and child care history correlates of children's relationships with peers', *Child Development*, 65 (1): 264–73.

Hull, D. and Johnston, D. (1987) *Essential Paediatrics.* Edinburgh: Churchill Livingstone.

Hutchins, T. and Sims, M. (1999) *Program Planning for Infants and Toddlers: an Ecological Approach.* London: Prentice Hall.

Hutt, J., Christopherson, H., Tyler, S. and Hutt, C. (1989) *Play, Exploration and Learning: a Natural History of the Pre-school.* London: Routledge.

Inhelder, B. and Piaget, J. (1958) *The Growth of Logical Thinking from Childhood to Adolescence: an Essay on the Construction of Formal Operational Structures.* New York: Basic Books.

Isaacs, S. (1926) *The Nursery Years.* London: Routledge and Kegan Paul.

Isaacs, S. (1968) *The Nursery Years.* London: Routledge.

Jackson, Brian and Jackson, Sonia (1979) *Childminder: a Study in Action Research.* London: Routledge.

Jackson, Sonia (1993) 'Under-fives: thirty years of no progress?' in G. Pugh (ed.) *Thirty Years of Change for Children.* London: National Children's Bureau.

Jagger, G. and Wright, C. (eds) (1999) *Changing Family Values.* London: Routledge.

James, A. (1998) 'Play in childhood: an anthropological perspective', *Child and Adolescent Mental Health*, 3 (3): 104–9.

James, A. and Prout, A. (eds) (1990, 1997) *Constructing and Reconstructing Childhood: Contemporary Issues in the Sociological Study of Childhood.* London: Falmer Press.

James, A., Jenks, C. and Prout, A. (1998) *Theorizing Childhood.* Cambridge: Polity Press.

Jenks, C. (1996) *Childhood.* London: Routledge.

John, M. (ed.) (1996a) *Children in Charge: The Child's Right to a Fair Hearing.* London: Jessica Kingsley.

John, M. (ed.) (1996b) *Children in Our Charge: The Child's Right to Resources.* London: Jessica Kingsley.

John, M. (ed.) (1997) *A Charge Against Society: The Child's Right to Protection.* London: Jessica Kingsley.

Kağitçibaşi, Çiğdem (1996) *Family and Human Development across Cultures.* Mahwah, NJ: Erlbaum.

Kail, R. (1997) 'Processing time, imagery, and spatial memory', *Journal of Experimental Child Psychology*, 64: 67–78.

Karlsson, Marlene (2003) 'The everyday life of children in family day care as seen by their carers' in A. Mooney and J. Statham (eds) *Family Day Care: International Perspectives on Policy, Practice and Quality.* London: Jessica Kingsley.

Karmiloff-Smith, A. (1992) *Beyond Modularity: a Developmental Perspective on Cognitive Science.* Cambridge, MA: MIT Press.

Karmiloff-Smith, A. (1994) *Baby It's You.* London: Ebury Press.

Keats, D.M. (1997) *Culture and the Child.* Chichester: Wiley.

Kempson, E. (1996) *Life on a Low Income.* York: Joseph Rowntree Foundation.

Kenway, J. and Willis, S. (1997) *Answering Back: Girls, Boys and Feminism in Schools.* Sydney: Allen and Unwin.

Kimura, D. (1992) 'Sex differences in the brain', *Scientific American*, September: 119–125.

Kincheloe, J. and Steinberg, S. (1997) *Changing Multiculturalism.* Buckingham: Open University Press.

Knight, T. and Caveney, S. (1998) 'Assessment and action records: will they promote good parenting?' *British Journal of Social Work*, 28 (1): 29–43.

Kohlberg, L. (1966) 'A cognitive-developmental analysis of children's sex-role concepts and attitudes' in E.E. Maccobby (ed.) *The Development of Sex Differences.* Stanford, CA: Stanford University Press.

Konner, M. (1991) *Childhood: a Multicultural View.* London: Ebury Press.

Korbin, J. (ed.) (1981) *Child Abuse and Neglect: Cross-cultural Perspectives.* Los Angeles: University of California Press.

Kottak, C.P. (1994) *Anthropology: the Exploration of Human Diversity* (6th edn). New York: McGraw Hill.

Kumar, R.C. (1997) '"Anybody's child": severe disorders of mother-to-infant bonding', *British Journal of Psychiatry*, 171: 175–81.

Labour Party (1996) *Early Excellence: a Head Start for Every Child.* London: Labour Party.

Lamb, Michael (1997) *The Role of the Father in Child Development.* New York: Wiley.

Laming, Lord (2003) *The Victoria Climbié Inquiry Report.* London: Stationery Office.

Leathard, A. (1990) 'Backing a united front', *Health Services Journal*, 100 (29 November): 1776.

Leathard, A. (1994) *Going Inter-professional: Working together for Health and Welfare.* London: Routledge.

Lerner, R.M. (1998) 'Theories of human development: contemporary perspectives' in R.M. Lerner (ed.) *Handbook of Child Psychology* I, *Theoretical Models of Human Development* (5th edn). New York: Wiley.

LeVine, R.A. and Miller, P.M. (1990) 'Commentary', *Human Development*, 33: 73–80.

Lewis, M.D. (2000) 'The promise of dynamic systems approaches for an integrated account of human development', *Child Development*, 71: 36–43.

Lloyd, B. and Duveen, G. (1992) *Gender Identities and Education: the Impact of Starting School.* New York: Harvester Wheatsheaf.

Lloyd, C. (1997) 'Inclusive education for children with special educational needs in the early years' in S. Wolfendale (ed.) *Meeting Special Needs in the Early Years: Directions in Policy and Practice.* London: David Fulton.

Lowe, N. (2002) *White, Carr and Lowe: The Children Act In Practice.* London: Butterworth Tolley.

Lubeck, S. (1986) *Sandbox Society.* London: Falmer Press.

Lynn, A., Karoly, M., Kilburn, R., Bigelow, J., Caulkins, J. and Cannon, J. (2002) 'Assessing costs and benefits of early childhood intervention programs: overview and application to the *Starting Early Starting Smart* program', www.rand.org/publications/MR/MR1336.

Lynn, D. (1974) *The Father: his Role in Child Development*, Monterey, CA: Brooks Cole.

Lyons-Ruth, K. and Zeanah, C. (1993) 'The family context of infant mental health' I, 'Affective development in the primary caregiving relationship' in C.H. Zeanah Jr (ed.) *Handbook of Infant Mental Health.* New York: Guilford Press.

Lytton, H. and Romney, D.M. (1991) 'Parents' different socialisation of boys and girls: a meta-analysis', *Psychological Bulletin*, 109: 267–96.

Mac an Ghaill, M. (1994) *The Making of Men.* Milton Keynes: Open University Press.

Maccoby, E.E. and Jacklin, C.N. (1974) *The Psychology of Sex Differences.* Stanford, CA: Stanford University Press.

Macdonald, J. (1998) *Primary Health Care.* London: Earthscan.

MacIntyre, C. (2001) *Enhancing Learning through Play: a Developmental Perspective for Early Years Settings.* London: David Fulton.

MacNaughton, G. (2000) *Rethinking Gender in Early Childhood Education.* London: Paul Chapman.

Mallory, B. and New, R. (eds) (1994) *Diversity and Developmentally Appropriate Practices: Challenges for Early Childhood Education.* New York: Teachers College Press.

Mandell, N. (1991) 'Children's negotiation of meaning' in F.C. Waksler (ed.) *Studying the Social Worlds of Children: Sociological Readings.* London: Falmer Press.

Mandler, J.M. (1992) 'How to build a baby' II, 'Conceptual primitives', *Psychological Review*, 99: 587–604.

Marsh, J. and Millard, E. (2000) *Literacy and Popular Culture: Using Children's Culture in the Classroom.* London: Paul Chapman Publishing.

Martin, C.L. and Little, J.K. (1990) 'The relation of children's understanding to children's sex-typed preferences and gender stereotypes', *Child Development*, 61: 1427–39.

Masson, J. and Morris, M. (1992) *Children Act Manual.* London: Sweet & Maxwell.

Masten, A.S. and Coatsworth, J.D. (1998) 'The development of competence in favourable and unfavourable environments: lessons from research on successful children', *American Psychologist*, 53 (2): 205–20.

Mayall, B. (ed.) (1994) *Children's Childhoods: Observed and Experienced.* London: Falmer Press.

Mayall, B. (1996) *Children, Health and the Social Order.* Buckingham: Open University Press.

Mayall, B. and Petrie, P. (1977) *Minder, Mother and Child.* London: Institute of Education.

Maynard, T. (2002) *Boys and Literacy: Exploring the Issues.* London: Routledge Falmer.

McGuire, J. (1991) 'Social interactions of young, withdrawn children in day nurseries', *Journal of Reproductive and Infant Psychology,* 9: 169–79.

McIntyre, S. (1997) 'The Black Report and beyond: what are the issues?' *Social Science and Medicine,* 44: 723–45.

McKeown, K. and Sweeney, J. (2001) *Family Well-being and Family Policy: a Review of Research on Benefits and Costs.* Dublin: Kieran McKeown.

McShane, J. (1991) *Cognitive Development: an Information Processing Approach.* Oxford: Blackwell.

Meadows, S. and Cashdan, A. (1988) *Helping Children Learn.* London: David Fulton.

Melhuish, E. and Moss, P. (eds) (1991) *Day Care for Young Children: International Perpectives.* London: Routledge.

Mellor, E. (1950) *Education through Experience in the Infant School Years.* Oxford: Blackwell.

Menzies Lyth, I. (1995) 'The development of the self in children in institutions' in J. Trowell and M. Bower (eds) *The Emotional Needs of Young Children and their Families: Using Psychoanalytic Ideas in the Community.* London: Routledge.

Millam, R. (2002) *Anti-discriminatory Practice.* London: Continuum.

Miller, P.H. (2002) *Theories of Developmental Psychology* (4th edn). New York: Freeman.

Mittler, P. (1990) 'Prospects for disabled children and their families: an international perspective', *Disability, Handicap and Society,* 5 (1): 53–64.

Mooney, A. (2003) 'Mother, teacher, nurse? How childminders define their role' in J. Brannen and P. Moss (eds) *Rethinking Children's Care.* Buckingham: Open University Press.

Morgan, P. (1995) *Farewell to the Family.* London: IEA Health and Welfare Unit.

Morrow, V. (1994) 'Responsible children? Aspects of children's work and employment outside school in contemporary UK', in B. Mayall (ed.) *Children's Childhoods: Observed and Experienced.* London: Falmer Press.

Morrow, V. (1998) *Understanding Families: Children's Perspectives.* London: National Children's Bureau.

Mortimer, H. (2001) *Special Needs and Early Years Provision.* London: Continuum.

Moses, L.J., Baldwin, D.A., Rosicky, J.G. and Tidball, G. (2001) 'Evidence for referential understanding in the emotions domain at twelve and eighteen months', *Child Development,* 72 (3): 718–35.

Moss, P. (2001) 'Britain in Europe: fringe or heart?' in G. Pugh (ed.) *Contemporary Issues in the Early Years: Working Collaboratively for Children.* London: Paul Chapman Publishing.

Moss, P. and Pence, A. (eds) (1994) *Valuing Quality in Early Childhood Services.* London: Paul Chapman.

Moss, P. and Penn, H. (1996) *Transforming Nursery Education.* London: Paul Chapman.

Moss, P. and Petrie, P. (2002) *From Children's Services to Children's Spaces.* London: Routledge Falmer.

Moyles, J. (1989) *Just Playing?* Buckingham: Open University Press.

Moyles, J. (1994) *The Excellence of Play.* Buckingham: Open University Press.

Murray, L. and Andrews, L. (2000) *The Social Baby: Understanding Babies' Communication from Birth.* Richmond: Children's Project.

Murray, L. and Trevarthen, C. (1985) 'Emotional regulation of interactions between two-month-olds and their mothers' in T.M. Field and N.A. Fox (eds) *Social Perception in Infants.* Norwood, NJ: Ablex.

Najman, J., Behrens, B., Anderen, M., Bor, W., O'Callaghan, M. and Williams, G. (1997) 'Impact of family type and family quality on child behaviour problems: a longitudinal study', *Journal of the American Academy of Child and Adolescent Psychiatry,* 36 (10): 1357–65.

Nash, M. (1997) 'Fertile minds', *Time Magazine*, 149 (5): 1–8.

National Assembly for Wales (2000a) *Framework for the Assessment of Children in Need and their Families*. Cardiff: Stationery Office.

National Assembly for Wales (2000b) *Working Together to Safeguard Children: a Guide to Inter-agency Working to Safeguard and Promote the Welfare of Children*. Cardiff: Stationery Office.

National Research Council and Institute of Medicine (2000) *From Neurons to Neighborhoods: the Science of Early Child Development*. Washington, DC: National Academy Press.

National Assembly for Wales (2002) *Special Educational Needs Code of Practice for Wales*. Cardiff: Stationery Office.

National Evaluation for Sure Start (2003) www.ness.bbk.ac.uk

NCH Action for Children (1991) *NCH Poverty and Nutrition Survey*. London: NCH Action for Children.

Neath and Port Talbot Borough Council (2002) *Draft Cymorth Plan: Neath EYDCP*. Neath and Port Talbot Borough Council.

New Zealand Ministry of Education (1996) *Te Whariki*. Wellington: Learning Media.

Newton, M. (2002) *Savage Girls and Wild Boys: a History of Feral Children*. London: Faber.

NICHD Early Child Care Research Network (2002) 'Child-care structure–process–outcome: direct and indirect effects of child-care quality on young children's development', *Psychological Science*, 13: 199–206.

Nutbrown, C. (1996) *Respectful Educators, Capable Learners: Children's Rights and Early Education*. London: Paul Chapman.

Oakley, A. (1992) *Social Support and Motherhood: the Natural History of a Research Project*. Oxford: Blackwell.

Ochsner, M.B. (2000) 'Gendered Make-up', *Contemporary Issues in Early Childhood*, 1 (2): 209–13.

Odofsky, J.D. (ed.) (1987) *Handbook of Infant Development*. New York: Wiley.

Ofsted (1993) *The Standards and Quality of Education in Reception Classes*. London: HMSO.

Ofsted (2000) *Evaluating Educational Inclusion: Guidance for Inspectors and Schools*. London: Office for Standards in Education.

Ofsted (2003) *Boys' Achievement in Secondary Schools*. London: Office for Standards in Education.

Oliver, M. (1990) *The Politics of Disablement*. Basingstoke: Macmillan.

Oppenheim, G. and Harker, L. (1996) *Poverty: The Facts*. London: Child Poverty Action Group.

Organization for Economic Co-operation and Development (2001) *Starting Strong: Early Childhood Education and Care*. Paris: Organization for Economic Co-operation and Development.

Øvretveit, J. (1990) *Cooperation in Primary Health Care*. Uxbridge: Brunel Institute of Organisation and Social Studies.

Øvretveit, J., Mathias, P. and Thompson, T. (1997) *Interprofessional Working for Health and Social Care*. London: Macmillan.

Owen, S. (2003) 'The development of childminding networks in Britain: sharing the caring', in A. Mooney and J. Statham (eds) *Family Day Care: International Perpectives on Policy, Practice and Quality*. London: Jessica Kingsley.

Paechter, C. (1998) *Educating the Other: Gender, Power, and Schooling*. London: Falmer Press.

Pahl, J. and Vaile, M. (1986) *Health and Health Care among Travellers*. Canterbury: University of Kent Health Service Research Unit.

Paley, V.G. (1984) *Boys and Girls: Superheroes in the Doll Corner.* Chicago: University of Chicago Press.

Palincsar, A.S. and Herrenkohl, L.R. (1999) 'Designing collaborative contexts: lessons from three research programs' in A.M. O'Donnell and A. King (eds) *Cognitive Perspectives on Peer Learning.* Rutgers Invitational Symposium on Education series, Mahwah, NJ: Erlbaum.

Parent, S., Normandeau, S. and Larivee, S. (2000) 'A quest for the Holy Grail in the new millennium: in search of a unified theory of cognitive development', *Child Development,* 71: 860–1.

Parton, N. (1997) *Child Protection and Family Support: Tensions, Contradictions and Possibilities.* London: Routledge.

Pascal, C., Bertram, A., Ramsden, F., Georgeson, J., Saunders, M. and Mould, C. (1995) *Effective Early Learning Research Project.* Worcester: Worcester College of Higher Education/Amber Publishing.

Pascall, G. (1986) *Social Policy: a Feminist Analysis.* London: Tavistock.

Payne, M. (2000) *Teamwork in Multiprofessional Care.* London: Macmillan.

Pedro-Carroll, J. (2001) 'The promotion of wellness in children and families: challenges and opportunities', *American Psychologist,* 56 (11): 993–1004.

Phillimore, P. and Morris, D. (1991) 'Discrepant legacies: perinatal mortality in two industrial towns', *Social Science and Medicine,* 33 (2): 139–52.

Phillimore, P. and Reading, P. (1992) 'A rural advantage? Urban–rural health differences in northern England', *Journal of Public Health Medicine,* 14: 290–9.

Piaget, J. (1952) *The Origins of Intelligence in Children.* New York: Norton.

Piaget, J. (1965a) *The Child's Conception of Number.* New York: Norton.

Piaget, J. (1965b) *Play, Dreams and Imitation in Childhood.* London: Routledge.

Piaget, J. (1969) *The Child's Conception of the World.* Totowa, NJ: Littlefield & Adams.

Piaget, J. and Inhelder, B. (1969) *The Psychology of the Child.* New York: Basic Books.

Pilcher, J. and Wagg, S. (eds) (1996) *Thatcher's Children? Politics, Childhood and Society in the 1980s and 1990s.* London: Falmer Press.

Pinker, S. (1994) *The Language Instinct.* London: Penguin Books.

Pollard, A. (ed.) (1987) *Children and their Primary Schools: a New Perspective.* Lewes: Falmer Press.

Pollard, A. with Filer, A. (1996) *The Social World of Children's Learning.* London: Cassell.

Power, C. (1995) 'Health-related behaviour' in B. Botting (ed.) *The Health of our Children.* (OPCS Decennial Supplement), London: HMSO.

Prout, A. and James, A. (1990) 'A new paradigm for the sociology of childhood? Provenance, promise and problems' in A. James and A. Prout (eds) *Constructing and Reconstructing Childhood: Contemporary Issues in the Sociological Study of Childhood.* London: Falmer Press.

Pugh, Gillian (ed.) (2001) *Contemporary Issues in the Early Years: Working Collaboratively for Children.* London: Paul Chapman.

Pugh, R. and Gould, N. (1999) 'Globalisation, Social Welfare and Social Work', unpublished.

Putnam, R. (2000) *Bowling Alone: The Collapse and Revival of American Community.* New York: Simon and Schuster.

Qualifications and Curriculum Authority (2000) *Curriculum Guidance for the Foundation Stage.* London: QCA.

Qualifications and Curriculum Authority/Department for Education and Employment (1999) *Desirable Outcomes for Children's Learning on Entry to Compulsory Schooling.* London: DfEE.

Qvortrup, J., Bardy, M., Sgritta, G. and Wintersberger, H. (eds) (1994) *Childhood Matters: Social Theory, Practice and Politics.* Aldershot: Avebury.

Raleigh, V. and Balarajan, R. (1995) 'The health of infants and children among ethnic minorities' in B. Botting (ed.) *The Health of our Children*. OPCS Decennial Supplement. London: HMSO.

Rawson, D. (1994) 'Models of inter-professional work: likely theories and possibilities' in A. Leathard (ed.) *Going Inter-professional: Working together for Health and Welfare*. London: Routledge.

Richardson, K. (1998) *Models of Cognitive Development*. Hove: Psychology Press.

Rinaldi, C. (1998) 'Projected curriculum constructed through documentation – Progettazione: An interview with Lella Gandini' in C. Edwards, L. Gandini and G. Forman (eds) *The Hundred Languages of Children: The Reggio Emilia Approach – Advanced Reflections* (2nd edn). Greenwich, CT: Ablex.

Roberts, H. and MacDonald, G. (1999) 'Working with families in the early years' in M. Hill (ed.) *Effective Ways of Working with Children and their Families*. London: Jessica Kingsley.

Roberts, R. (2002) *Developing Self-esteem in Young Children*. London: Paul Chapman/Sage.

Robertson, J. and Roberston, J. (1989) *Separation and the Very Young*. London: Free Association Press.

Rogoff, B. (1989) 'The joint socialization of development by young children and adults', reprinted in P. Light, S. Sheldon and M. Woodhead (1991) *Learning to Think*. Child Development in Social Context 2, London: Routledge.

Rogoff, B. (1990) *Apprenticeship in Thinking: Cognitive Development in Social Context*. New York: Oxford University Press.

Rogoff, B. and Morelli, G. (1993) 'Perspectives on children's development from cultural psychology' in M. Gauvain and M. Cole (eds) *Readings on the Development of Children*. New York: Scientific American Books.

Rosser, R. (1994) *Cognitive Development: Psychological and Biological Perspectives*. Needham Heights, MA: Allyn & Bacon.

Russell, P. (1992) *Respite Care*. NCB Highlight No. 108, London: National Children's Bureau.

Rutter, M. (1995) 'Clinical implications of attachment concepts: retrospect and prospect', *Child Psychology and Psychiatry*, 36 (4): 549–71.

Ryan, M. (1999) *The Children Act 1989: Putting it into Practice* (2nd edn). Aldershot: Ashgate.

Sameroff, A.J., Seifer, R., Baldwin, A. and Baldwin, C. (1993) 'Stability of intelligence from preschool to adolescence: the influence of social risk factors', *Child Development*, 64: 80–97.

Sanders, R. (1999) *The Management of Child Protection Services: Context and Change*. Aldershot: Arena.

Sanders, R., Colton, M. and Roberts, S. (1999) 'Child abuse fatalities and cases of extreme concern: lessons from reviews', *Child Abuse and Neglect*, 23 (3): 257–68.

Sanders, R., Jackson, S. and Thomas, N. (1996) 'The police role in the management of child protection services', *Policing and Society*, 6: 87–100.

Sanders, R., Jackson, S. and Thomas, N. (1997) 'Degrees of involvement: the interaction of focus and commitment in area child protection committees', *British Journal of Social Work*, 27: 871–92.

Sandow, S. (ed.) (1994) *Whose Special Need? Some Perceptions of Special Educational Needs*. London: Paul Chapman.

Schaffer, H.R. (2004) *Introducing Child Psychology*. Oxford: Blackwell.

Schneider, W. and Pressley, M. (1997) *Memory Development between Two and Twenty* (2nd edn). Mahwah, NJ: Erlbaum.

Schön, D. (1983) *The Reflective Practitioner*. London: Basic Books.

Schultz, J. (1995) The Knowledge of Childhood in the German Middle Ages, 1100–1350. Philadelphia, PA: University of Pennsylvania Press.

Schultz, E. and Lavenda, R. (1990) *Cultural Anthropology: a Perspective on the Human Condition* (2nd edn). St Paul, MN: West Publishing.

Seebohm Committee (1968) *Report of the Committee on Local Authority and Allied Services* (Cmnd 3703). London: HMSO.

Seedhouse, D. (1990) *Health: the Foundation for Achievement.* Chichester: Wiley.

Selleck, D. and Griffin, S. (1996) 'Quality for the under-threes' in G. Pugh (ed.) *Contemporary Issues in the Early Years* (2nd edn). London: Paul Chapman/Sage.

Selwyn, J. (2000) 'Fetal development' in M. Boushel, M. Fawcett and J. Selwyn (eds) *Focus on Early Childhood: Principles and Realities.* Oxford: Blackwell.

Senior, M. (1998) 'Area variations in self-perceived limiting long-term illness in Britain, 1991: Is the Welsh experience exceptional?' *Regional Studies*, 32 (3): 265–80.

Sestini, E. (1987) 'The quality of the learning experience of four-year-olds in nursery and infant classes' in NFER/SCDC, *Four-year-olds in School.* Windsor: NFER.

Seymour-Smith, C. (1986) *Macmillan Dictionary of Anthropology.* London: Macmillan.

Shahar, S. (1990) *Childhood in the Middle Ages.* London: Routledge and Kegan Paul.

Sheldon, A. (1990) 'Pickle fights: gendered talk in preschool disputes', *Discourse Processes*, 13: 5–31.

Siegel, D. (1999) *The Developing Mind.* New York: Guilford Press.

Siegler, R.S. (1976) 'Three aspects of cognitive development', *Cognitive Psychology*, 8: 481–520.

Siegler, R.S. (2000) 'The rebirth of children's learning', *Child Development*, 71: 26–35.

Siegler, R.S., DeLoache, J. and Eisenberg, N. (2003) *How Children Develop.* New York: Worth.

Siraj-Blatchford, I. (2001) 'Diversity and learning in the early years' in G. Pugh (ed.) *Contemporary Issues in the Early Years* (3rd edn). London: Paul Chapman.

Siraj-Blatchford, I. and Clarke, P. (2000) *Supporting Identity, Diversity and Language in the Early Years.* Milton Keynes: Open University Press.

Skinner, B.F. (1957) *Verbal Behavior.* New York: Appleton Century Croft.

Slee, P.T., and Shute, R.H. (2003) *Child Development: Thinking about Theories.* London: Arnold Publishers.

Smilansky, S. and Shefataya, L. (1990) *Facilitating Play: a Medium for Promoting Cognitive, Socio-emotional and Academic Development in Young Children.* Gaithersburg, MD: Psychosocial and Educational Publications.

Smith, P., Cowie, H. and Blades, M. (2003) *Understanding Children's Development* (4th edn). Oxford: Blackwell.

Smith, P. and Sharp, S. (eds) (1994) *School Bullying: Insights and Perspectives.* London: Routledge.

Snow, C. (1977) 'The development of conversation between mothers and babies', *Journal of Child Language*, 4: 1–22.

Social Services Inspectorate (1995) *Inspection of Local Authority Fostering, 1994–1995.* London: Department of Health.

Social Services Inspectorate (1996) *Children in Need: Report of an SSI National Inspection of SSD Family Support Services, 1993/1995.* Wetherby: Department of Health.

Solomon, G.E.A. and Johnson, S.C. (2000) 'Conceptual change in the classroom: teaching young children to understand biological inheritance', *British Journal of Developmental Psychology*, 18: 81–96.

Speier, M. (1976) 'The adult ideological viewpoint in studies of childhood' in A. Skolnick (ed.) *Rethinking Childhood: Perspectives on Development and Society.* Boston, MA: Little Brown.

Spelke, E.S. (1994) 'Initial knowledge: six suggestions', *Cognition*, 50: 431–55.

Spencer, H. (1859) *Education.* London: Williams & Norgate.

Springer, K. and Keil, F.C. (1991) 'Early differentiation of causal mechanisms appropriate to biological and non-biological kinds', *Child Development*, 62: 767–81.

Sprott, J.E. (1994) 'One person's "spoiling" is another's freedom to become: overcoming ethnocentric views about parental control', *Social Science and Medicine*, 38 (8): 1111–24.

Stainton-Rogers, W. and Roche, J. (1994) *Children's Welfare and Children's Rights: a Practical Guide to the Law*. London: Hodder & Stoughton.

Stainton-Rogers, W. and Stainton-Rogers, R. (2001) *The Psychology of Sex and Gender*. Buckingham: Open University Press.

Statham, J. (1986) *Daughters and Sons: Experiences of Non-sexist Childraising*. Oxford: Blackwell.

Statham, J. (2003) 'Provider and parent perspectives on family day care for "children in need": a third party in-between' in A. Mooney and J. Statham *Family Day Care: International Perspectives on Policy, Practice and Quality*. London: Jessica Kingsley.

Steele, M., Steele, H. and Fonagy, P. (1995) 'Associations among attachment classifications of mothers, fathers and infants', *Child Development*, 67: 541–55.

Stephens, W.B. (1998) *Education in Britain, 1750–1914*. Basingstoke: Macmillan.

Stern, D.N. (1985) *The Interpersonal World of the Infant*. New York: Basic Books.

Stevenson, O. (ed.) (1999) *Child Welfare in the UK*. Oxford: Blackwell.

Strachan, D. (1997) 'Respiratory and allergic diseases' in D. Kuh and Y. Ben Shlomo (eds) *A Lifecourse Approach to Chronic Disease Epidemiology*. Oxford: Oxford University Press.

Striano, T. and Rochat, P. (1999) 'Developmental link between dyadic and triadic social competence in infancy', *British Journal of Developmental Psychology*, 17: 551–62.

Sylva, K. (2000) 'Early childhood education to ensure a "fair start" for all' in T. Cox (ed.) *Combating Educational Disadvantage: Meeting the Needs of Vulnerable Children*. London: Falmer Press.

Sylva, K., Melhuish, E., Sammons, P., Siraj-Blatchford, I., Taggart, B. and Elliot, K. (2003) *The Effective Provision of Pre-School Education (EPPE) Project: Findings from the Pre-School Period*. London: Institute of Education.

Sylva, K., Roy, C. and Painter, M. (1980) *Childwatching at Playgroup and Nursery School*. London: Grant McIntyre.

Tassoni, P. (1998) *Child Care and Education*. Oxford: Heinemann.

Thelen, E. and Smith, L.B. (1994) *A Dynamic Systems Approach to the Development of Cognition and Action*. Cambridge, MA: Bradford/MIT Press.

Thomas, G., Walker, D. and Webb, J. (1998) *The Making of the Inclusive School*. London: Routledge Falmer.

Thomas, N. (2002) *Children, Family and the State: Decision-making and Child Participation*. Bristol: Policy Press.

Thompson, N. (2002) *Building the Future: Social Work with Children, Young People and their Families*. Lyme Regis: Russell House.

Thorne, B. (1993) *Gender Play: Boys and Girls in School*. Buckingham: Open University Press.

Tizard, B. and Hughes, M. (1984) *Young Children Learning*. London: Fontana.

Tizard, B., Blatchford, P., Burke, J., Farquhar, C. and Plewis, I. (1988) *Young Children at School in the Inner City*. London: Erlbaum.

Tomlinson, J. (1999) *Globalization and Culture*. Cambridge: Polity Press.

Townsend, P. and Davidson, N. (1982) *Inequalities in Health* (the Black report). Harmondsworth: Penguin Books.

Trawick-Smith, J. (1997) *Early Childhood Development: a Multicultural Perspective*. Englewood Cliffs, NJ: Merrill/Prentice Hall.

Trevarthen, C. (1979) 'Communication and co-operation in early infancy: a description of primary intersubjectivity' in M. Bullowa (ed.) *Before Speech.* Cambridge: Cambridge University Press.

Trevarthen, C. and Aitken, K.J. (2001) 'Infant intersubjectivity: research, theory, and clinical applications' *Journal of Child Psychology and Psychiatry and Allied Disciplines,* 42 (1): 3–48.

Trevarthen, C., Aitken, K., Papoudi, D. and Robarts, J. (1998) *Children with Autism: Diagnosis and Interventions to Meet their Needs.* London: Jessica Kingsley.

Turner, E.S. (1976) *Boys will be Boys: the Story of Sweeney Todd, Deadwood Dick, Sexton Blake, Billy Bunter, Dick Barton et al.* Harmondsworth: Penguin Books.

Tylor, E. (1871, 1958) *Primitive Culture.* New York: Harper Torchbooks.

Tymms, P. (1997) *Young Children in Reception Classes,* London: SCAA.

Tzuriel, D. (1999) 'Parent–child mediated learning interactions as determinants of cognitive modifiability: recent research and future directions', *Genetic, Social and General Psychology Monographs,* 125: 109–56.

UNESCO (1994) *The Salamanca Statement and Framework for Action on Special Needs Education.* Paris: UNESCO.

Utting, D. (1995) *Family and Parenthood.* York: Joseph Rowntree Foundation.

Valsiner, J. (2000) *Culture and Human Development.* London: Sage.

Volling, B.L. and Belsky, J. (1992) 'Infant, father and marital antecedents of infant–father attachment security in dual-earner and single-earner families', *International Journal of Behavioural Development,* 15: 83–100.

Vygotsky, L.S. (1978a) *The Mind in Society: the Development of Higher Psychological Processes.* Cambridge, MA: Harvard University Press.

Vygotsky, L.S. (1978b) 'The role of play in development' in M. Cole, V. John-Steiner, S. Scribner and G. Souberman (eds) *Mind in Society.* Cambridge, MA: Harvard University Press.

Vygotsky, L.S. (1981) 'The genesis of higher mental functions' in J.V. Wertsch (ed.) *The Concept of Activity in Soviet Psychology.* Armonk, NY: Sharpe.

Vygotsky, L.S. (1986) *Thought and Language.* Cambridge, MA: MIT Press.

Waksler, F.C. (ed.) (1991) *Studying the Social Worlds of Children: Sociological Readings.* London: Falmer Press.

Waksler, F.C. (1996) *The Little Trials of Childhood and Children's Strategies for Dealing with Them.* London: Falmer Press.

Walkerdine, V. (1989) *Counting Girls Out.* London: Virago.

Wall, K. (2003) *Special Needs and Early Years: A Practitioner's Guide.* London: Sage.

Walvin, J. (1982) *A Child's World: a Social History of English Childhood, 1800–1914.* Harmondsworth: Penguin Books.

Watson, R.J. (1994) 'Affective tone in a toddler measured during transitions between multiple caregivers', *Early Child Development and Care,* 97: 135–44.

Weikart, D.P. (1972) 'Relationship of curriculum, teaching and learning in pre-school education' in J.C. Stanley (ed.) *Pre-school Programs for the Disadvantaged.* London: Johns Hopkins University Press.

Weinraub, M., Clemens, L.P., Sockloff, A., Ethridge, T., Gracely, E. and Myers, B. (1984) 'The development of sex role steroetypes in the third year: relationships to gender labeling, gender identity, sex-typed toy preference and family characteristics', *Child Development,* 55: 1493–503.

Wellman, H.M. and Gelman, S.A. (1998) 'Knowledge acquisition in foundational domains' in D. Kuhn and R.S. Siegler (eds) *Cognition, Language, and Perceptual Development,* vol. II in W. Damon (gen. ed.) *Handbook of Child Psychology.* New York: Wiley.

Wells, G. (1986) *The Meaning Makers: Children Learning Language and Using Language to Learn*. London: Hodder & Stoughton.

Welsh Assembly Government (2003) *The Learning Country: Foundation Phase 3–7 Years*. Cardiff: Welsh Assembly Government.

Werner, E.E. (1996) 'Vulnerable but invincible: high-risk children from birth to adulthood', *European Child and Adolescent Psychiatry*, 5 (suppl. 1): 47–51.

Weston, C., Robinson, C. and Minkes, J. (1995) 'Promoting the Children Act (1989) in day services to disabled children: findings from an action research project', *Children and Society*, 9 (1): 54–66.

Whalley, Margy and the Pen Green Team (2000) *Involving Parents in their Children's Learning*. London: Paul Chapman.

White, L.A. (1959) *The Evolution of Culture: the Development of Civilization to the Fall of Rome*. New York: McGraw Hill.

Whitehead, M. (1992) 'The health divide' in P. Townsend and N. Davidson (eds) *Inequalities in Health* (the Black report). Harmondsworth: Penguin Books.

Whitehead, M. (1997) *Language and Literacy in the Early Years: an Approach for Education Students* (2nd edn). London: Paul Chapman.

Whitehurst, G.J., Falco, F., Lonigan, C.J., Fischal, J.E., DeBaryshe, B.D., Valdez-Manchaca, M.C. and Caufield, M. (1988) 'Accelerating language development through picture-book reading', *Developmental Psychology*, 24: 552–9.

Wilkinson, R. (1996) *Unhealthy Societies: the Afflictions of Inequality*. London: Routledge.

Williams, F. (1989) *Social Policy: a Critical Introduction*. Cambridge: Polity Press.

Wolger, J. (2003) 'The tide has turned: a case study of one inner city LEA moving towards inclusion' in C. Tilstone and R. Rose (eds) *Strategies to Promote Inclusive Practices*. London: Routledge Falmer.

Wood, D. (1998) *How Children Think and Learn: the Social Contexts of Cognitive Development* (2nd edn). Malden, MA: Blackwell.

Wood, D., Bruner, J.S. and Ross, G. (1976) 'The role of tutoring in problem-solving', *Journal of Child Psychology and Psychiatry*, 17: 89–100.

Woodhead, M. (1996) *In Search of the Rainbow: Pathways to Quality in Large-scale Programmes for Young Disadvantaged Children*. The Hague: Bernard van Leer Foundation.

Woodhead, M. (1999) 'Reconstructing developmental psychology: some first steps', *Children and Society*, 13 (1): 3–19.

Woodroffe, C., Glickman, M., Barker, M. and Power, C. (1993) *Children, Teenagers and Health*. Buckingham: Open University Press.

Wooldridge, A. (1994) *Measuring the Mind: Education and Psychology in England, 1860–1990*, Cambridge: Cambridge University Press.

World Health Organization (1948) *Constitution of the World Health Organization*. Geneva: World Health Organization.

World Health Organization (1984) *Summary Report of the Working Group on Concepts and Principles of Health Promotion*. Copenhagen: World Health Organization.

Index